THE UNEXPECTED WAY

THE UNEXPECTED WAY

On Converting from Buddhism to Catholicism

PAUL WILLIAMS

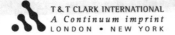
T & T CLARK INTERNATIONAL
A Continuum imprint
LONDON • NEW YORK

T&T CLARK LTD

A Continuum imprint

59 George Street
Edinburgh EH2 2LQ
Scotland

www.tandtclark.co.uk

15 East 26th Street
New York 10010
USA

www.continuumbooks.com

First published 2002

ISBN 0 567 08830 8

British Library Cataloguing-in-Publication Data
A catalogue record for this book is available from the British Library

Typeset by Fakenham Photosetting Ltd, Fakenham, Norfolk
Printed and bound in Great Britain by MPG Books, Bodmin

For
Denys Turner
and
Gavin D'Costa

'Like me,' [Helena] said to them, 'you were late in coming. The shepherds were here long before; even the cattle. They had joined the chorus of angels before you were on your way. For the primordial discipline of the heavens was relaxed and a new defiant light blazed amid the disconcerted stars.

'How laboriously you came, taking sights and calculating, while the shepherds had run barefoot! How odd you looked on the road, attended by what outlandish liveries, laden with such preposterous gifts!

'You came at length to the final stage of your pilgrimage and the great star stood still above you. What did you do? You stopped to call on King Herod. Deadly exchange of compliments in which began that unended war of mobs and magistrates against the innocent!

'Yet you came, and were not turned away. You too found room before the manger. Your gifts were not needed, but they were accepted and put carefully by, for they were brought with love. In that new order of charity that had just come to life, there was room for you, too. You were not lower in the eyes of the holy family than the ox or the ass.

'You are my especial patrons,' said Helena, 'and patrons of all late-comers, of all who have a tedious journey to make to the truth, of all who are confused through knowledge and speculation, of all who through politeness make themselves partners in guilt, of all who stand in danger by reason of their talents.

'Dear cousins, pray for me,' said Helena ...

'For His sake who did not reject your curious gifts, pray always for the learned, the oblique, the delicate. Let them not be quite forgotten at the Throne of God when the simple come into their kingdom.'

(Evelyn Waugh, Helena (1981), pp. 144–5)

Sooner or later, the professional philosopher and the professional theologian will be forced to realise what it is that people expect of them. This expectation far surpasses the external trappings of scholarship. People expect answers to the great questions of life: deep down, what does it mean to be a human being?

Theology can only be missionary when it really goes beyond all traditions, and becomes an appeal to reason itself, in complete openness to truth.

(Cardinal Joseph Ratzinger)

CONTENTS

PREFACE

I would be unlikely to buy, let alone read, a book that began by proclaiming itself 'an essay in radical postmodern theology'. Yet, looking back on it now, two years after its original publication, I suppose that is what this book is. Lest I deter readers straight away, let me explain what I mean.

There is a view – it is often called 'modernist', and springs perhaps from the eighteenth century Enlightenment – that when university academic scholars write and teach about religion or even theology they should be careful to eschew any mention of their own personal religious development, position, and beliefs. The study of religion, including theology in the university, is an academic subject that has no place for subjectivity, one's own religious story. Indeed, supposing you read further you will see that I am myself extremely cautious about bringing in subjectivity when we come to speaking of religious *truth*. Yet this 'modernist' perspective is nowadays coming under more and more critical pressure from a position (or perhaps a family of positions) labelled 'postmodernist'. The modernist approach bases itself on the idea that we can make a clear and rigid distinction between facts (usually thought of as being purely objective and coming under what we call 'science'), and other data (frequently classed as mere sensations or emotions, under which we place 'values', including personal religious positions as well as moral claims), with effectively just the facts deserving to be the topic of hardheaded university teaching and research. But postmodernist perspectives hold in common a decidedly sceptical attitude to this rigorous and rigid separation of 'facts' from 'values', highlighting the inevitable presence of the subject in all our activities, including university scholarship and (dare we say it) science. For it is subjects who frame theories, subjects who choose data with which to examine those theories, subjects who interpret results, and of course subjects who decide what is to count as valid approaches and indeed what perspectives are to be discounted as not worthy of a university setting.

To repeat: In general I am myself extremely cautious of this turn to subjectivity labelled 'postmodernism', particularly when

– becoming a form of relativism regarding truth, or values – the postmodernist perspective rejects any truth or rightness apart from 'true-for-me', 'true-for-a-particular-social-group', or 'good-for-me', and so on. Nothing could be further from the actual, factual, objective truth, goodness and beauty that I want to claim in this book I have found in Christianity and indeed in the Roman Catholic Church. Nevertheless I can see some compensatory benefits in postmodernism in the academic setting if it helps to undermine the fear, the terror, of introducing the religious story of oneself and others into the world of academia, if it helps to make the study of theology and religions in universities more *relevant* because it is (or should be) *life transforming*.

There are many today who think that university academics should spend their time writing research monographs (with, I have to say, a very restricted readership and little deep let alone transformative impact), not telling their own story. But what is to count as 'research'? Who decides? Is it research in theology for a university academic to write a book intentionally involving what Gandhi called his or her own 'experiments with truth'? I think it is – research demanding deep thought, prayer, and indeed perhaps risky self-criticism and examination. Who is to say that these are not among the means – perhaps the most important means – by which to carry out research in theology? Theology, it has sometimes been said, should be done on one's knees. Or, at least, it surely *can* be done on one's knees. And perhaps for a believer that is how it should be done. Otherwise maybe our believer has got his or her priorities confused.

It seems to me a postmodernist perspective justifies avoiding the denial of the subject, the author him- or herself, in the conduct of theological research. So perhaps this book can be called my 'monograph in postmodern theology'. Yet there is a way of reversing all this. It is also possible to do one's religion – one's praying, or one's meditation – through means often thought of as more academic, through writing, even perhaps writing of an argumentative, rational sort. As a Buddhist I was sometimes asked, 'When meditating what exactly do you meditate *on*?'. In my case what I really meditate on more often than not is paper.

This book is a record of my meditations during the first few months after finally deciding, following some twenty years as a

Buddhist, to convert to Roman Catholicism. It was written mainly during the earlier part of my instruction in the Catholic faith. It can perhaps best be approached as a form of what Buddhists call 'analytic meditation', investigating carefully a topic in order to discover the truth about it. As such this is an intensely personal document, written with all the enthusiasms and ignorance of one new to an immensely sophisticated spiritual path. In it I speak first and foremost to myself. It is not apologetics. I am not seeking to defend Christianity against its detractors. Rather, it is an *apologia* and a *confession*. As an *apologia* I am defending myself. But to whom? To myself, to friends, and to others (in that order). As a confession it is a confession of confusion, and a confession of faith.

I started writing all this down for the purpose of systematically explaining to myself what I had decided to do – to become a Roman Catholic. Many of the central arguments expressed here I had thought in some form or another during the years I had meditated on Buddhism and the Christian claims. I had not written them down. But I have long been convinced of something the French philosopher Maurice Merleau-Ponty noticed: that we do not really know what we think until we tell ourselves either by speaking out loud or by writing it down. Writing down these arguments has brought to them – for better or for worse – a clarity and systematic structure that had not been realised and articulated by me in this way previously.

I also wanted to write down these arguments in order to prepare in advance a defence for my apostasy from Buddhism. I much admire Buddhist thought, and I have some very articulate and philosophically sophisticated Buddhist friends who would be sure – in the nicest possible way – to demand that I account for what they will consider an eccentric if not completely crazy decision to become a Catholic. This is not a fully thought-out philosophical defence of my Catholicism. It is just a sketch, notes, my meditations. But in writing them down I have found myself immensely helped in understanding what I have chosen and, I have to say, I have found in that clarity much greater assurance of, and confidence in, the path I have now adopted.

So what I have written is for myself, but what is for myself is for others too. It is offered here in this rather public form because some people may find it interesting, either as a record of the thoughts of one particular convert or because my reader shares with me some of my background, experiences, approach and interests. I am very concerned lest my Buddhist friends should read some of the things I say here as an attack on Buddhism. They are not intended to be. Please believe me when I say that I am really trying to go over and clarify my own problems with Buddhism and the attractions of Christianity, particularly Catholicism. The arguments I use are those *I* find helpful. This is a record of arguments that, for better or worse, persuaded *me*. I am sure others may well find them naïve or confused. There are some very clever people out there. But one has to take a stand sometime. Arguments can go backwards and forwards for ever.

I suppose inevitably, though, that in making my thoughts public I shall also be saying things that might be problematic or hurtful for some. I am sorry. I have no wish to offend, to cause unhelpful doubt, let alone to destroy anyone else's faith. Still, the Buddha is said to have encouraged critical thought about what he taught, so to that extent even those who do not agree with me may find my comments of use (as Māra's advocate) in their own analytic meditations.

In what follows I have included some material of a personal nature. Reading back over what I have written I feel a certain embarrassment at talking so much about myself. It is not very English. It is perhaps not so common for university professors to go round exposing themselves. And I do feel I have exposed myself to an uncomfortable degree. I have nevertheless chosen to incorporate this material because I am trying to explain what brought me to move to Christianity after twenty years of being a Buddhist. I should not hide from others, and certainly not from myself, that there may be psychological or sociological factors in my background and upbringing which predisposed me to make the choices I have done. Apart from anything else, not to draw attention to these would be unfair to my Buddhist friends. I should not pretend that my conversion was simply the result of putting forward a series of compelling philosophical arguments, where failure to appreciate my arguments might be seen as simple intellectual confusion.

Nevertheless, whatever the psychological origins of my abandonment of Buddhism and return to Christianity, it is simply fallacious to think that they have anything to do with the *truth* of Christianity as such (if it is true), or the *falsity* of Buddhism (if it is false). This fallacy even has a name. It is called the 'genetic fallacy'. We should support an assertion of the truth (or falsity) of a statement if need be by an argument, that is, by giving reasons which rationally entail the truth (or falsity) of that statement. The genetic fallacy occurs when we think we have explained a statement's truth or falsity not by an argument but by an account of why the person put forward that statement (such as his or her psychological, or economic, or religious, state at the time). Thus it is simply fallacious (even if true) to argue that Christianity is false, or my becoming a Christian is baseless, because Christians want Christianity to be true (as a form of wish-fulfilment, perhaps). Or I am subconsciously seeking a return to the securities of childhood, or to avoid the punishment of a vengeful God.

I hope I have become a reasonably orthodox Catholic. I hope too that my Buddhist friends will take what I say in good faith. There are those who think that really Jesus was a Buddhist, or that He was a member of a Jewish sect that accepted reincarnation, or that He travelled to India. I do not think any of these things, nor are they the views of any mainstream Christian denomination or reputable critical scholar of early Christianity as far as I know. I do not take them seriously, and I shall not consider them here. Buddhist friends should also note that in this book, after the initial sections in which I establish for myself theism in general and the Christian version of theism in particular, I often write *theologically*. That is, I write from within the Christian tradition, presupposing such things as, for example, a good God and probing what follows from that. Not all the book is about Christianity in its relationship to Buddhism.

Christian friends, on the other hand, should note that in my case conversion to Christianity springs from my conviction that Christianity – indeed Catholicism – is actually, factually, cognitively, *true*. In other words my interest in Christianity, and my conversion, is bound up with issues of how things are, expressed in philosophical and theological *doctrines*, dogmas. The point is worth making because I have found already that failing to appreciate this point can lead to deep misunderstanding.

Christians with an interest in Buddhism are often fascinated primarily by Buddhist *meditation*. They are attracted by the richness and depth of Buddhist meditation practices and keen to learn from Buddhists and find a meeting point in meditation and mystical experience. Sometimes one finds impatience with doctrinal differences, those very things that keep Christians and Buddhists apart. Thus there can be a tendency to portray doctrinal differences as inessential. The religions finally meet on the level of meditative – mystical – experience, and it is mystical experience that tells us how things really are. Mystical experience, however, by its very nature is held to be beyond language and nonconceptual, and (it is claimed) it is in the stammering attempts to express such experiences that differences between Buddhism and Christianity occur. Indeed there is sometimes a feeling that inasmuch as the very expression of mystical experience occurs within the conceptual categories most familiar to the meditator, it is those conceptual categories and thus accidental differences of time and place that force misunderstanding and difference. Moreover the conceptual categories – dogmas – of Christianity are policed by the Church and its hierarchy and theologians. Thus (it might be argued) a quite misleading – indeed false – impression of difference is given by a Church that is perversely wedded to dualistic theological distinctions and divisions.

For all I know this scenario may be true. But I do not myself hold any of it. Thus the convert from Buddhism to Catholicism can find himself distinctly out of sympathy with a lifelong Catholic with a profound interest in Buddhism, who was perhaps expecting to find a soul-mate with a similarity of interests and perspective. Indeed, converts from Christianity to Buddhism often have a deep interest in Buddhist meditation and little interest as such in the very real differences of Buddhist and Christian theology and philosophy, and their importance. If my experience is anything to go by, converts from Buddhism to Christianity have a deep interest in Christian philosophy and theology, and little interest *as such* in purported similarities of Buddhist and Christian meditation and their associated experiences. For philosophical and theological niceties are essential to any articulate understanding of how things really are, i.e. truth, and one thing on which Buddhists and Christians agree is that understanding how things really are is essential to our salvation. Experiences that are said to be nonconceptual and unutterable can be viewed with distinct suspicion – suspicion of their coherence and also of their relevance.

It is my conviction of the truth of Christianity, precisely expressed in its dogmas, that has converted me from Buddhism to Catholicism. All this should be borne in mind in reading what follows by Christian friends with a deep and active interest in Buddhism.

There may be those out there who either are Buddhists or are thinking of becoming Buddhists but who, deep down, if they stop to focus on what they really feel, would truly like to be able to be Christians. It is just that Christianity seems so *bizarre*, so incredible. They are not the first to think like this. In the very earliest days of the Church we learn from St Paul that the Gentiles – by which he really meant the Greeks, the sophisticated thinkers who really counted in this sort of thing – considered the Christian message to be out and out *foolishness*.

I have tried in this book to suggest what is for me a plausible case to show that while, for all I know, Christianity might be false, Christians are not quite as stupid or as gullible as some people might think. It saddens me to find those (even Christians) who think Christianity spiritually and doctrinally naïve, impoverished, when compared with Buddhism. That is simply not true either on the level of doctrine or on the level of spiritual practice.

While writing this work I have found myself returning again and again to three short pieces of contemplative music which particularly move me. No doubt it could have been other music, but it happens to have been these. Each I find exquisite, totally sublime. I hesitated about this, but I think I want to dedicate one piece to each of my three sections. The first two are by the contemporary English composer John Tavener, a convert to Eastern Orthodoxy who draws on Byzantine chant for his compositions. Perhaps I can dedicate his setting of William Blake's 'The Lamb' to my first section. The second is Tavener's *Funeral Ikos*. I know them both (with Tavener's *Ikon of Light*) on the Gimell CD (454 905–2), where Tavener himself conducts 'The Lamb'. The third section, then, can be accompanied by the wonderful setting of 'Ave Maris Stella' – 'Hail,

Star of the Sea', to the Blessed Virgin Mary – by the medieval French composer Guillaume Du Fay. I know it in the version sung by 'Pomerium' on their *A Medieval Book of Hours* CD (Deutsche Grammophon Archiv 457 586–2). I originally wanted to call this book *Out of My Head*, but the publishers thought the title was a bit 'too hippy'. So it was not to be. But when we go quite out of our heads where do we find ourselves? In the heart, perhaps.

Paul Williams
Bristol
October 2004

* * * *

Unless otherwise noted, all quotations from the Bible have been taken from *The New Jerusalem Bible*, Reader's Edition, Darton, Longman & Todd, 1990.

All royalties from the sale of this book will be split equally between the Catholic Fund for Overseas Development (CAFOD) and the Walsingham House Residential Drug Treatment Centre, Broadmead, Bristol, UK.

ACKNOWLEDGEMENTS

At the University of Bristol I have been fortunate to work in a department with, at different times, several of the most distinguished British Catholic philosophers and theologians. I am thinking of Herbert McCabe, Denys Turner, Brian Davies and Gavin D'Costa. I always took in very carefully what they said, and how they said it. It stayed with me. They have had an enormous effect on the respect I developed for the intellectual seriousness of Catholicism. Denys Turner's influence is referred to a number of times in what follows. I should also mention Kieran Flanagan of the Department of Sociology. A devout Catholic very active at Clifton Cathedral, Kieran's joy and support at my conversion, and the joy and support of my other Catholic friends including my university colleagues, Fernando Cervantes, Brendan Smith and Mervyn Davies, and my brother Gerald, have been moving. I am grateful also for the support and encouragement of Stratford Caldecott, at T&T Clark Publishers.

For the last ten years or so I have taught residential weekends for teenagers called 'A Taste of Buddhism' at the Ammerdown Centre, near Bath Spa. This Centre is an ecumenical Christian retreat and conference centre run largely by Catholic nuns. Again, I have been so very, very impressed by the friendliness, openness and tolerance of those nuns – members of an Order originally established to convert the Jews to Christianity. Over the years I found that during my weekends at Ammerdown I would be buying and reading works on Christianity while the guests were enjoying my Buddhism. I suppose it was during those ten years that I gradually discovered what I really was, and developed the courage to say so.

When I made a firm decision to become a Catholic I sent a letter to my colleagues and closest friends. A number of those friends are enthusiastic and experienced Buddhists. Nevertheless almost everyone I wrote to has been sympathetic and wished me well, even where they were clearly shocked and found my move incomprehensible. I am grateful. I should particularly mention in this context my good friend and colleague John Peacock, a former Buddhist monk, who has not wavered in his friendship and good humour. If he thinks me insane he has not said so to me personally. Thank you also to Ken Robinson, Gavin D'Costa and the anonymous reader for T&T Clark, who all read earlier versions of this book and made some comments which stimulated welcome further reflection and writing.

Many, many thanks to all those who took part in the Rite of Christian Initiation of Adults (RCIA) meetings at Clifton Cathedral, Bristol, including Ken and Sue, Jo, Tim and Teresa who were received into the faith at the same time I was. You have become such a dear Christian family to me. In particular I should like to thank the now retired Bishop of Clifton, the Rt Revd Mervyn Alexander, the regular clergy of the Cathedral – Monsignor Mitchell, Father Christopher, Father Tim and Father Gordon – and Caroline Price who led the RCIA classes and Tina Quinn who was my sponsor.

I should also express my thanks for the warm, if amused, support of my family, my brother Peter and our stepmother Heather. Some of their questions and objections stimulated the reflections found later in this book. My wife Sharon, our sons Myrddin and Tiernan and our daughter Tārā are all mentioned at the appropriate points. None was at the time of writing a Christian, although Sharon was brought up under Welsh Baptist influence and Myrddin is now an Anglican. Tārā was brought up a Buddhist. All our children are grown-up.

I want to dedicate this book to my old friends and colleagues Denys Turner and Gavin D'Costa. Very devout Catholics, they never spoke disparagingly of my Buddhism, but showed always respect, interest and tolerance. They were astonished yet delighted at my becoming a Catholic. We do not really know what influences we have on others. Their firm faith and wonderful examples of goodness, humanity, sensitivity and fun have been important to me, and I am very grateful to them. They were and are the very best sort of friends and evangelists.

I am so very happy to be able to sign myself at last 'their (belated) brother in Christ'.

INTRODUCTION

'A little philosophy inclineth man's mind to atheism, but depth in philosophy bringeth him about to religion again.'

(Francis Bacon)

When asked about his views on religion my youngest brother Pete always said to his friends that he did not bother himself with those sorts of questions. His big brother Paul dealt with things like that. Paul would find out the answers and let him know. Pete is very disappointed. His eldest brother has now become a Catholic, following Gerald. Gerald is our other brother, who converted to Catholicism many years ago.

I wonder why my becoming a Catholic should be so disappointing? Is it that it seems as if I have given up the struggle? Returned to the womb of naïve childhood faith? Is it that Pete did not expect me to end up – but late – at broadly the same views as Gerald? Or is it that perhaps we cannot believe that truth can be found so close to home?

('What is truth?', I hear Pilate say with an educated smile. He condemns Christ to death. It's nothing to do with *him*.)

Maybe we cannot imagine that truth should be contained in something so apparently absurd, so repressive and so historically contaminated as the Roman Catholic Church. Truth seems much more likely in the mountains of Tibet, or in the uncharted expanses of the inner world met in meditation. Anyway, it is not in the art galleries and pretentious ritual of the Vatican.

Had I thought, I should have said to Pete that if ever I discovered the truth it would as likely as not be found in the most unexpected place. Well, apart from a certain residual romanticism, there is no particular reason why it should be in India or Tibet. But perhaps truth could be difficult to recognise. Our initial response might be to discard it as not worthy of closer examination.

It is the convert, I think, who has a story to tell concerning why they found their religion so attractive. At least, so has been my experience with becoming a Roman Catholic. Those who were born into the religion, while delighted, often seem secretly astonished that anyone could actually be convinced enough of its attractions to convert. They know of no process that slowly (or suddenly) convinced them of the truth, from being non-believers. The cradle-believers are inclined to see their faith as an act of primordial grace, a blessing intrinsic to their very being, and the faith of the convert as something akin to a miracle. Yet one reason why I think my Buddhism was always deep down a sham is that I never really had much of a story to tell about why I became a Buddhist. If asked, I responded with some embarrassment that I had spent so many years studying Buddhism that I had come to see the world as a Buddhist does. It just happened. (I wonder if people who spend many years studying slugs come to see the world as a slug?) Actually, there was no process of conversion at all, and even though in 1978 I finally went through the ceremony of 'Taking Refuge' in a Tibetan Buddhist context, I now think no real conversion took place.

So I wasn't always a Buddhist. As far as I recall our immediate family was not particularly religious, although on our father's side there were practising Anglicans and relatives had been Anglican clergy. On our mother's side I do not remember any especial interest in religion. I heard once that our maternal grandmother had said she would be a Buddhist if she were anything at all. I discovered fairly recently that in fact our maternal grandfather's family had been Roman Catholic, although he had abandoned the faith.

One of my earliest memories was of my mother complaining bitterly to my father that I was always arguing with her, always answering back, always asking 'Why?'.

I am not sure now why, but for some reason when I was really quite young I joined the local Anglican church choir. I loved singing church music. I still remember the village church, which dated back to Saxon times. My brother Gerald and I took our religion terribly seriously. We would sit up in bed having theological discussions, our heads respectfully nodding like Pelham puppets every time we mentioned the name of Jesus. I sometimes wondered (with no doubt some

2

form of hero-worship) whether I might not become eventually a Church of England vicar. As far as I recall the only society I joined at my secondary school was the Christian Union. I remember even then feeling myself to be different from others in taking Christianity so seriously. Oh, but I was different! For I had walked and spoken with Jesus in the Garden. I remember distinctly dreaming at about this time that I walked and talked with Jesus. Jesus was, of course, in white. The Garden was, of course, green. I do not remember what we said. I like to think He was sending me on my path through life, away from the Garden into adolescence and adulthood – never really to leave Him, and to return in His own good time. When I have forgotten so much about my childhood, that remains vividly with me still. Was the philosopher Hobbes right when he said that the man who thinks that God spoke to him in a dream merely dreamt that God spoke to him?

Our mother died when I was twelve or thirteen – I forget which exactly. On our mother's death we eventually moved to another part of southern England, and after accompanying our father in a brief flirtation with Christian Science I rejoined the local Anglican church choir. I sometimes sang solo and in addition took part in a folk singing group outside the church context. My two brothers were also in the choir and in time I became Head Chorister. Unfortunately my voice broke rather early and, since I was thought to be too young to be a bass, as far as I recall I spent my entire time as Head Chorister miming. This perhaps gave me an early taste of the bluff necessary for an academic career.

At the appropriate age early in the 1960s I was confirmed in the Anglican Church by the Bishop of Dover. I became a server at Holy Communion. One day Gerald brought home a book on yoga from the local library. Thus started my interest in Indian thought. As the 60s wore on I became involved in the teenage lifestyle and all the normal things that teenage boys get up to. As public examinations loomed larger, I left the choir, ceased to be a server and lost contact with the Church. I grew long hair, and dressed strangely. Still, I remember taking Holy Communion at Canterbury Cathedral when I must have been about eighteen. Even then I was concerned, as I recall, by some

3

of my companions who I was sure had not been confirmed, but who also went up to take Communion.

I continued – and do continue – to love village churches, cathedrals, ruined abbeys and monasteries, medieval philosophy and church music. I have nothing but affection for my early days, the Anglican Church, my schools and all my teachers.

I went to the University of Sussex to read Philosophy. By that time, in common with many in the late 1960s, I had developed an interest in meditation and things Indian. I channelled this interest particularly into Indian philosophy. I wanted to look more closely at philosophical theories that developed largely uninfluenced by Graeco-Semitic ideas. I switched to Philosophy and Religion in the School of African and Asian Studies at the University of Sussex, since that way, as a philosophy student, I could also study Indian philosophy for my degree. I became very involved with Maharishi Mahesh Yogi's Transcendental Meditation, which was popular at that time, but eventually I became bored and frustrated with what seemed to me to be its superficiality and distortion of Indian tradition and ideas.

By the time I had finished my undergraduate degree Sharon and I were married and Myrddin had been born.

I subsequently took my doctorate (DPhil.) in Madhyamaka Buddhist philosophy at the University of Oxford, although initially I had considered working in Hindu epistemology (Nyāya). One reason for opting for Buddhism was that it meant I would not be restricted entirely to Indian thought if ever I decided to move over to, say, Tibetan or Chinese philosophy. In fact much of my recent work, as it turned out, has been in Tibetan. During my early days at Oxford I recall drinking gin and tonics one New Year's Eve with R. C. Zaehner, himself a Catholic convert and the Spalding Professor of Eastern Religions and Ethics. An eccentric character who managed to set fire to his rooms at All Souls College with a cigarette, Zaehner died long before the 1970s had finished. I still remember on that New Year's Eve his Aristotelian (or maybe Augustinian) toast: 'May you become what you always were.'

By about 1973 I was already beginning to think of myself as a Buddhist. I finally 'Took Refuge', formally becoming a Buddhist, in the dGe lugs pa (pronounced: Gelukpa) Tibetan tradition. That was after a weekend on the Buddhist philosopher Nāgārjuna's *Suhṛllekha* ('A Letter to a Friend') given by Ven. Geshe Damchö Yönten, Spiritual Director of the Lam Rim Buddhist Centre, which is on the borders of Wales. It was, I think, 1978. I had just finished my doctorate. Our father had died, still quite young, the previous year. When I found myself teaching at the nearby University of Bristol in the early 1980s, I re-established contact with the Lam Rim Centre, setting up with others a group in Bristol that also now has its own Dharma (Buddhist) Centre. I became involved in occasional teaching within the context of practising Buddhism at both Buddhist Centres, and I was invited to be a trustee of the Lam Rim Centre. As well as my academic work in Buddhist philosophy I wrote and spoke as a Tibetan Buddhist on television, on radio and at conferences. I took part in public and private dialogue with Christians, including Hans Küng and Raimundo Panikkar. My dialogues with both of these have been published. Perhaps one day I shall debate with Küng again, this time from a very different position.

One's past, especially one's early conceptual outlook, cannot be easily avoided. I remember feeling very uncomfortable when, in the context of Tibetan Buddhism, one of my fellow Buddhists teased me with having broken my religious vows made to the Bishop of Dover at my confirmation. It was true. I had broken my vows. I had made promises. Now I had problems with the notion of a creator God, particularly in the light of evil. But I also knew that many intelligent people were nevertheless able to be Christians, including some people I much admired. Was I certain that I could not be a Christian, that my rejection of Christianity was well founded? Could I stake my (eternal) life on it? Or had I simply drifted away from Christianity, and into Buddhism, because I had a professional interest in the subject and to be a Buddhist was fashionable and my knowledge of the subject flattered me?

That wasn't all. When chanting Tibetan I sometimes felt distinctly unhappy when using the prefix *rjes su*, pronounced *jesu*, as if I was in some sense committing blasphemy in that environment, recalling choices previously made, commitments gone back on, and perhaps decisions yet to come. It sounds silly, I know. But that is how I sometimes felt. I once attended a series of workshops on Jung's psychology and Tibetan Buddhism. We were given various guided visualisations, and I found that whenever I was asked to visualise a peaceful scene I always tended to see the classic English countryside with a medieval church. I still loved visiting cathedrals and country churches. I remember a strong feeling, when turning up at a church on a Sunday afternoon, that I was looking in at the scene of a party after all the guests had departed. Deep down I wanted to be part of it, yet I could only bring myself to view the setting. I was invited, yet I always arrived too late. Once when I was in Dharamsala, the north Indian hill station where the Dalai Lama lives, I remember telling a young woman that she didn't need to come all the way to India to find spirituality. She could find it back home in Europe. Had she tried Christian meditation? She seemed surprised and, I think, very relieved. But it was not what she had expected me to say. For all I know perhaps she is now a Catholic nun. Either way I hope she is happy.

I always liked Catholics. When I was at Oxford a friend, Michael Barnes, was training to be a Jesuit priest and my wife Sharon and I were invited to his final ordination. I used to say that any tradition that produced St Thomas Aquinas must have something to be said for it. I remember trying to read works on Aquinas in the cloisters of Canterbury Cathedral while still at school. And since Vatican II the Catholics had seemed to me (rightly or wrongly) to be by far the most open and under-standing of the Christian traditions I was familiar with, while still preserving a fair degree of doctrinal and moral clarity. A combination of openness, tolerance and the rich Catholic intel-lectual and spiritual tradition was very tempting. Pity about the problem with God though.

One time in the early 1980s I happened to mention to the eminent Catholic theologian and philosopher Herbert McCabe that I had received an initiation into a high Tantric meditation practice. As far as I recall we were not told until *afterwards* about the strict commitments to which someone who has taken these initiations is expected to adhere. I defended taking an initiation knowing that it would involve some commitments, while not knowing until afterwards what those commitments might be. McCabe said quite simply that he thought it was 'wicked'. And I doubt he meant 'wicked' with the sense of approval.

I was interviewed by the well-known psychiatrist Anthony Clare for a television programme on Buddhism in Britain. He asked me, quite reasonably, whether, since I worked in the study of religions, I had considered carefully the claims of each religion before finally choosing Buddhism. I was momentarily thrown, although I said that any theistic religion was out of consideration because of the problem of God and evil. But he had touched a sensitive point. Had I really considered carefully the claims even of Christianity, the religion I was baptised and confirmed into? Had I really considered what the Christian responses to the problem of evil might be?

G. K. Chesterton has commented somewhere that usually when a Westerner converts to a non-Christian religion they never really convert to that religion at all. All they really convert to is Christianity minus the parts of Christianity they find unpalatable. He was over-stating his case, of course, and writing at a very different time when the direct influence of Christianity on European culture was so much stronger than it is now. Nevertheless, again and again it has seemed to me that what he said is broadly correct. If we look at Western Buddhists, and so-called Western Buddhism, we regularly find that it is a form of Christianity stripped of the parts that post-Christian Christians find so difficult to accept.

I remember being absolutely appalled many years ago when the leader of the Friends of the Western Buddhist Order (FWBO, with which I was not myself involved), Sthavira Sangharakshita, suggested that many Western Buddhists were deep down still Christians. They should break the hold of Christianity upon them. This they could do by 'therapeutic blasphemy'. I always have found that a very, very unhealthy and distasteful suggestion. But I think Sangharakshita was right in one respect. I strongly suspect that many Western Buddhists are deep down still Christians. I was. I was a lapsed Christian perhaps, but still a Christian.

Buddhism the way it is presented by so many Western practitioners ('Western Buddhism') is, of course, pre-eminently a religion of kindness and compassion to others. Western Buddhists are keen to emphasise that Buddhism is not world negating, but implies one way or another direct action in the world to benefit all *sentient* beings. There is a tendency in Western Buddhism to push the laity and the option of social engagement to the ideological forefront. This care is to be for all sentient beings, not just human beings. It includes wiggly worms as much as humans. And Western Buddhism as a religion also has a major advantage over Christianity. It is liberated from the idea of a Creator God. It downplays the role of faith (which, as it is employed by Christians Buddhists always seem to think of as 'blind faith') and stresses direct personal experience.

For what this Buddhism is all about is in its widest sense *positive experiences*. 'We all want to be happy and avoid suffering', the Dalai Lama regularly begins his talks. Buddhism is the supreme way to do this. Buddhism (as thus popularly understood by its Western enthusiasts) leads to happiness in day-to-day life, feelings of harmony, feelings of love and compassion, insight into reality, and *mystical experiences* through meditation. All this is without requiring, unlike Christianity, an extensive (and apparently bizarre) belief system and regular attendance at communal ritual. Even a belief in rebirth is often said to be unessential. We can be confident also that Buddhism is in conformity with the latest discoveries of science. In fact Western Buddhism is a religion of self-development, 'self-empowerment'. Any moral code tends to be explained as 'rules of training', to be adopted for its *usefulness* in one's day-to-day life and spiritual training, not because it is imposed by an external authority (particularly a patriarchal authority like God). Western Buddhism involves pre-eminently meditation, which has direct psychological benefits. Meditation is not like prayer, or a church service. It need not involve being with others, or God as an Other. And it is to be judged through its benefits, the pleasant sensations of calm, relaxation, loving feelings, and so on that it engenders.[1]

I was interested in philosophy, but I was also interested in meditation and the exotic East. Many of us found Buddhism attractive originally because among other things it seemed so much more *rational* than the alternatives, as well as promising direct, practical, tangible benefits. In particular Buddhism seemed much more sensible (and much, much more exotic) than a theistic religion like Christianity. When we stood back and tried to be as objective as possible God looked less and less *likely*. In Buddhism one has an immensely sophisticated system of appropriate recommended behaviour, spirituality and philosophy which does not require God at all. At a stroke difficulties involved in accepting the existence of God were bypassed. Instead, in becoming a Buddhist one could centre a whole religion on practical experiences deriving from meditation, on direct and obvious personal *returns*.

Often part of the problem, it now seems to me, is that the knowledge of Christian thought and experience of Christian practice possessed by many Westerners is quite childish and elementary. It is what we learnt at school. It is no more sophisticated than that of an eleven year old. Very few people are sufficiently interested in Christianity to study Christian theology and philosophy in any depth during their teens. The situation is perhaps even worse in the United States, where religious education is not a compulsory part of the school curriculum. In a Gallup poll taken in the mid-1980s, 70 per cent or more of Americans polled affirmed that Jesus was a historical figure, and was God and not just another religious leader like the Buddha or Mohammed, and that belief in Him was 'very important' or 'fairly important' to them. Yet only 42 per cent of those polled knew that Jesus preached the Sermon on the Mount, only 46 per cent could name the first four books of the New Testament, and only 70 per cent knew that He was born in Bethlehem.[2] When we come to Buddhism as adults we immediately start studying Buddhism at a level that traditionally would have been the preserve of an elite of highly talented and advanced practitioners, usually monks and nuns. We read the advanced stuff (even if we cannot practise it). This knowledge of really quite advanced Buddhist thought gained from the many books now available in the West, plus deference to a dominant culture and the level of Western education, is one reason why Tibetans tend to think Westerners are so very clever (if lacking in self-discipline and application). Thus when we come to compare Christianity and Buddhism it is not surprising that Buddhism often seems so much more doctrinally and spiritually sophisticated. The Christian thought outside the New Testament that many people are familiar with is commonly the

9

Christian 'mystics'. These are often presented in rather watered-down versions by people more interested in similarities between religions than detailed textual study of the sources in their cultural context. All too often we end up with Christian mystics who are thought to be saying, in a rather naïve and misleading fashion, what was expressed so much more penetratingly by the Buddhists. We are simply not comparing like with like. If we really want to compare Christianity and Buddhism we have to include the thought of sophisticated Christian philosophers such as St Anselm, St Thomas Aquinas, or, in contemporary philosophy, Alvin Plantinga or Peter van Inwagen. And that requires time.

We (I speak, of course, only for myself) became Buddhists not (deep down) because of any clear idea of the positive attractions of Buddhism as it has been practised in traditional Buddhist cultures, or any sense of profound conversion. Rather, we became Buddhists partly because Buddhism impressed with its philosophy, and partly because Buddhism is a religious tradition that can be portrayed in terms attractive to the contemporary Western world and postmodern individualism. It is a world with an interest in the exotic, good returns for investment, pleasant sensations, a craving for the 'feel-good factor' as well as deep experiences, the moulding of an elite superiority not just in wealth or luxury but also in wisdom, all bundled together as 'spirituality'. The New Age has become a way of fending off old age. Perhaps also we are impressed by the Dalai Lama, or by other Buddhists we meet. Everyone likes Tibetans. However, I am not sure if all this is a basis for real conversion. To become a Buddhist because it lacks the perceived problems of Christianity is a weak foundation for Buddhist practice. I now think I was a Buddhist by default, not by conviction. Eventually I returned to see whether the problems I feared in Christianity were really the problems I thought they were.

G. K. Chesterton once failed to write a story. It would have been, he thought, the best story he had ever written had he done so. It would have been about a boy who lived in a farm cottage on a slope of a valley in the sort of landscape that we in England associate with ancient white horses carved into the chalk. One day the boy sets off to find some valuable object in the landscape, perhaps a grave and effigy of a great giant. He walks for a long time over this steep and rolling terrain. Eventually he looks back and sees in the distance below him his little cottage. There he 'saw that his own farm and kitchen-garden, shining flat on the hill-side like the colours and quarterings of a shield, were but parts of some such gigantic figure, on which he had always lived, but which was too large and too close to be seen'.[3] We travel a long way to try and find something of great value. It is only from that distance that we can see that we really had our treasure all along. It was all around us. It was not where we were going but where we came from. Tibetan Buddhists speak of finding a 'jewel in the palm of the hand'. Why did we fail to see it? Why didn't we realise the surprise we would have when we found out where it really was? But we needed the distance. We needed to be elsewhere in order to see it. We failed to discern the great treasure when it was but our familiar surroundings, for it was too close to us. Such has been my journey as well.

Yet how far did I really go? Unlike Chesterton's great figure in the landscape, God is not inert. He is not dead. It seems He followed me. I think I knew it all along. I could hear his footsteps. And I ran. Yet it now seems clear I kept looking back half in fear and half in hope, drawn by that from which I ran. As have others before me, I have been very moved by Francis Thompson's poem *The Hound of Heaven*:

I fled Him, down the nights and down the days;
   I fled Him, down the arches of the years;
I fled Him, down the labyrinthine ways
   Of my own mind; and in the midst of tears
I hid from Him, and under running laughter.
      Up vistaed hopes I sped;
      And shot, precipitated,
Adown Titanic glooms of chasmèd fears,
  From those strong Feet that followed, followed after.
      But with unhurrying chase,
      And unperturbèd pace,
Deliberate speed, majestic instancy,
    They beat – and a Voice beat
    More instant than the Feet –
'All things betray thee, who betrayest Me.'

> Halts by me that footfall;
>   Is my gloom, after all,
> Shade of His hand, outstretched caressingly?
>   'Ah, fondest, blindest, weakest,
>   I am He Whom thou seekest!
> Thou dravest love from thee, who dravest Me.'

Why does God chase us like that? Why will He not let us go? Is this just the residual guilt of a lapsed Christian? There are those who would argue that my return to Christianity in middle age marks an attempt to be reabsorbed into the warmth and security of childhood, or perhaps even the womb. They may be right. But it is not obvious that there is anything wrong with warmth and security. And as I have argued already, whatever the *psychological* origins of my abandonment of Buddhism and return to Christianity it is simply fallacious to think that they have anything to do with the *truth* of Christianity as such (if it is true).

But there is nothing new about what Francis Thompson says. Fifteen hundred years before, St Augustine said the same thing: 'The thought of you stirs [Man] so deeply that he cannot be content unless he praises you, because you made us for yourself and our hearts find no peace until they rest in you.'[4]

Why does God chase us like that? Why will He not let us go? 'Do not be afraid. I am with you. I have called you by your name. You are mine', as the hymn has it. Is it a result in some way of baptism? Baptism has been explained to me as like a tattoo, visible not to us perhaps, but very visible to God. Perhaps it can be removed, but only by drastic and painful surgery. God seeks those with His tattoo. Is this an argument for or against infant baptism?

Albino Luciani, who died in 1978 as Pope John Paul I after a tragically short papacy of scarcely a month, once wrote a ficti-tious letter to G. K. Chesterton (he wrote letters to others too, such as Pinocchio). This letter would have appealed to Chesterton's compassion and wish to bring others to the enormous happiness he had found in the Catholic Church; Pope John Paul I writes:[5]

> What many people fight is not the true God but the false idea they have made of God: a God who protects the rich, who only asks and

demands, who is jealous of our growing prosperity, who spies continuously on our sins from above, to give Himself the pleasure of punishing us.

Dear Chesterton, you know God isn't like that; you know that he's both good and just; the father of prodigal sons, who wishes them all to be, not sad and wretched, but great and free, and creators of their own destiny. Our God is not man's rival, he wants us to be his friends, He has called us to share in his divine nature and in his eternal happiness. And he does not ask anything excessive of us: he is content with very little, because he knows quite well that we haven't got very much.

Dear Chesterton, I'm sure, as you are, that this God will make himself ever more known and loved: by everyone, including those who reject him, not because they are evil (they may be better than both of us!), but because they look at him from a mistaken point of view. If they continue not to believe in him, he replies: 'Well, I believe in you!'

Again and again I have found that the god people reject turns out not to be God at all. Also, alas, I have found already that the god some people worship is not God either.

How far has my growing unease with Buddhism, and attraction towards Roman Catholicism, been reflected in my academic work over recent years? I do not want to say much about this, but I suppose I should say a little. When I first announced that I had decided to become a Catholic I fended off requests for justification by referring those interested to my publications. Unfortunately my recent academic publications have been rather technical and very, very boring.

Although I think I would be the first to separate coherent rational argument from preaching or emotional or psychological description, I have never seen my academic study as divorced from the religio-philosophical quest for understanding. In my 1989 book, *Mahāyāna Buddhism: The Doctrinal Foundations*, there was very little by way of critical comment on Buddhist doctrine. But one of the most important parts of the book for me was the research I had to undertake on the thirteenth-century Japanese Buddhist, Shinran. Shinran's criticisms of the Buddhist tradition of 'self-power', thinking that one could, through one's *own* efforts, attain to the very highest perfection, over the years have had more and more influence on my own religious development. I shall return to Shinran elsewhere in this work.

Until fairly recently I have tended to work more in the history of philosophical and religious ideas, rather than actually engaging in critical and constructive philosophy with my subjects. Early in my academic career I decided that it would not be fair to criticise the philosophical ideas of my Buddhists until I had thoroughly understood them in (as far as possible) their original languages. I now think that approach was mistaken (and I am a poor linguist). Looked at one way, under-standing is an endless process. We can never be sure we have fully understood what we are studying. At what point do we have the right to criticise, even with constructive philosophical criticism? Looked at another way, I am now inclined to think of this endless process of understanding as itself incorporating criticism, perhaps through a sort of dialectic. Through criticism, and then criticism of criticism by oneself or others, one actually comes to understand the subject better. Thus the idea that we have *first* to understand perfectly, and *then* we can undertake criticism, now seems to me to be a sort of idealistic perfec-tionism. It is unattainable and is actually counterproductive to the type of tentative but progressive understanding that (as Popper has shown) we should be undertaking.

In an article[6] I argued that if by 'nonconceptual experience' one meant literally an experience that by its very nature is not conceptualisable, then I could make no sense of the idea of a nonconceptual experience. Such an 'experience' could not have qualities that would distinguish it from no experience at all. Indeed, such an 'experience' could not have any qualities. Thus, I argued, there could be no such experience. Intrinsically nonconceptual experiences are essential, as far as I know, to just about all forms of Buddhism, and certainly to the Mahāyāna forms of Buddhism that interested me.

Absolutely central to my growing unease with Buddhist affil-iation was my paper 'Altruism and rebirth' (reprinted in my *Altruism and Reality* volume of papers). It was while working on this paper that, for the first time, I think I truly appreciated the significance of the Buddhist claim that the rebirth cannot be said to be the same person as the one who died. Indeed, I cited influential Buddhist scholars who have argued explicitly that the rebirth is a *different* person to the one that died.

After reading an earlier draft of this book, one of my Buddhist friends claimed that in my treatment of the Buddhist approach to rebirth here I have misrepresented the Buddhist position. The suggestion is that (since I must know what the Buddhist position is) I must have done so intentionally. I confess that accusation hurt a little. Why should I intentionally misrepresent what the Buddhist wants to say? These arguments are the arguments that encouraged me to change from Buddhism to Catholicism. There could be little point in misrepresenting the Buddhist position *to myself*. But because my argument at this point might be thought to be a little technical I shall put it into an Appendix (Appendix 1).

I began to think that if Buddhism were correct then unless I attained enlightenment or something like it in this life, *I* – Williams, the person I am – would have no hope. For the rebirth of Williams that follows from my not attaining enlightenment would not be the same person as Williams. Clearly I was not going to attain enlightenment in this life. So I (and I suspect all my friends and family) must have in themselves finally no hope. Not only that. Actually, from a Buddhist perspective in the scale of infinite time and infinite rebirths, the significance of each of us as such, as the person we actually are now, converges on nothing. Thus Buddhism for me appeared to be *hope-less*. But was I absolutely sure Buddhism was true? As St Paul knew so well, Christianity at least offers *hope*.

I remember consciously deciding to switch my perspective, to see what things would look like if I saw them *as if* I thought Christianity were true. In that switch of perspective I now think I invited Christ to return. He came.

When I came to write down my ideas on why I became a Catholic – my 'analytic meditations' – I found them taking a fairly simple pattern. I do not have anything very dramatic or original to say, although much was dramatic and original *to me*. Broadly speaking I am going to argue three things:

(i) I have come to believe that God exists. The God I hold to exist is God as a necessary being, Creator of all things out of nothing. All other things are created, and as such are of a totally (unimaginably) different order from God. This God can truly be spoken of as supremely Good, in some sense a Person, and so on. However, we do not know what these expressions really mean as attributes of God Himself (from God's side, as it were). In all this I am influenced by the thought of St Thomas Aquinas. In other words, I have come to believe that God exists, the sort of God that would be recognisable to Christian orthodoxy as represented by the Catholic tradition of Aquinas.

Buddhists do not hold that such a God exists. Thus I can no longer be a Buddhist.

(ii) I have also come to believe that Jesus was indeed bodily resurrected from the dead. That is, I believe Jesus genuinely died, the tomb was empty, and Jesus was subsequently, after his real death, physically alive. He had been physically resurrected from the dead. I repeat the word 'physically' because I gather there are those who accept the resurrection yet interpret it differently from what I would call a literal, physical, resurrection. Perhaps they take the resurrection as a vision, or as a myth, or as a way of speaking about an understanding that the disciples gained concerning the significance of Jesus' life and death. They do not take it as a literal, physical, bodily, resurrection. I understand that scholars working on the resurrection sometimes refer to the sort of literalist approach that I have come to accept by saying that it entails that if someone had possessed a working camera they could have photographed Jesus after the resurrection. Fine. That is what I mean. The arguments that lead me to believe the resurrection happened do not lead me to make a distinction between the resurrection occurring in some watered-down sense, and the resurrection literally, physically, camera-photographably occurring.

Since I believe the resurrection took place, in the sense in which I have defined it, I do not feel I can be any sort of theist apart from a Christian. I cannot be a Muslim, or a mainstream Jew, or a dualist Śaivite or Vaiṣṇavite. None of these, as I understand it, accepts the literal physical resurrection of Jesus from the dead. At least, while it may not follow strictly, it seems to me to make more sense to be a Christian if one accepts the resurrection.

(iii) If I am to be a Christian, what sort of Christian? I want to argue that priority has to be given to the Roman Catholic Church. In other words, I need a strong argument *not* to be a Catholic. While it seems to me that a case can indeed be constructed for not being a Roman Catholic, that case does not seem (to me) very strong. On the other hand there are also counter-arguments in favour of Catholicism. Since I fail to be convinced by arguments not to be a Catholic and – I have to admit – I like the arguments for Catholicism, I shall be a Catholic.

That, broadly speaking, is my argument to myself.

Some of my principles in all of this are: (a) If something is possible (i.e. not a logical contradiction), then God can do it; (b) we cannot say in advance what God will do (but what He does may well be very surprising); and (c) in some things – indeed, some very important things – we cannot know what God has actually done short of Him telling us. His telling us is a revelation. One form of revelation is Scripture. But God cannot be constrained, and that is only one form of revelation. Another major form of revelation is through the tradition and teaching authority (*magisterium*) of an authoritative Church.

A recurrent theme running through much of my argument will be the philosophical and spiritual dangers of basing religion on what I shall term 'subjectivism', or 'subjectivity'. Subjectivism occurs in systems that give overwhelming primacy to certain sorts of private experiences, sensations, intuitions, or emotions, and seek to base all that is ultimately most valuable in the religious (or other ideological) system on those. It is ultimately in those intuitions or experiences (such as the emotion of feeling saved, feeling one with the universe, seeing God, or the experience of *nirvāṇa*, enlightenment) that the rest of the religion concerned is validated. Thus ultimate authority, or validation, or the goal, is essentially *private*. This can be contrasted with the authority of an external body, revelation through the public words of Scripture (literally understood, if that is possible), or the public pronouncements of an authoritative Church. This is a major topic and merits extended treatment. I shall not do so in these meditations. Nevertheless I shall suggest that subjectivism is prone to losing all sense of the objectivity of truth. It has a genuine problem in escaping the privacy of experience, and hence solipsism (the world itself as nothing more than the world of the flow of my own experiences). It thus provides an insufficient base for grounding not only a common world of objective being but also (and therefore) any genuine morality and any spiritual practice apart from self-interest. I shall also suggest that only in Being Itself, i.e. necessary being, in other words God, can the objectivity of the everyday world be grounded. And, correspondingly, only in a divinely authorised and hence infallible Church founded on Being Itself can morality and a spiritual liberation which transcends individual self-interest also be grounded.

To avoid subsequent misunderstanding let me be quite clear what it is I want to argue in all of this. I am not going to argue that I know God exists, I know the resurrection took place, and I know Catholicism is true. I am going to argue only that I can rationally believe these things, as rationally (if not more so) as I could previously believe Buddhism. And in believing these things I believe that they are true. Of course, it would be possible so to define 'know' that we can conclude that we never really *know* anything much at all. This strategy is beloved of sceptics. But I am happy to work with the normal sense of 'know'. Thus I can say I know that I am at the moment working on the computer, or we know Queen Elizabeth II is at the time of writing Queen of England, or Adelaide is not the capital of New South Wales. In this normal sense of 'know', I am *not* claiming to know that God exists, or that the resurrection took place, or that Catholicism is true. Thus I shall not consider that I have (even in outline) proved any of these things beyond reasonable doubt. For if I had proved them beyond reasonable doubt I would take it that in the normal sense of 'know' I could reasonably (if not conclusively) claim to know them.

I want to claim the following.

(A) Buddhism has an 'explanatory gap' that, if it is to be filled at all, can only be filled with a necessary being. This necessary being can also plausibly be taken as the God of theists. It is perfectly rational to accept the explanatory gap and not to seek to fill it at all. But, equally, it is also rational to fill the explanatory gap with God thus understood. Since it seems to me that (i) accepting the explanatory gap and (ii) filling it with God are equally rational, we cannot argue (or I am not here going to argue) that one option is *more* rational than the other. Thus, since we cannot settle the issue either way, we certainly cannot claim to *know* one option is true. But belief in the one option is just as rational as belief in the other. Thus, belief in some form of theism is as rational as belief in there being no answer (or no accessible – or relevant – answer), the option adopted by Buddhists. The two options are equally balanced. One is free to make certain choices, choices which are not forced upon one, but which present themselves as options.

On what might one base that choice? I think there may be a number of reasons, some of which might favour the Christian approach and some the Buddhist. But among the reasons that dispose me now to opt for Christianity is its relative optimism. I am not using the term 'optimism' here in any vague sense. What I mean is that, for reasons I have explained earlier – and will return to later – to do with the nature of rebirth, if Buddhism is correct then this life will be the end for me and for all my loved ones. If Buddhism is right then finally, for almost all of us, our little lives count for virtually nothing. They have scarce meaning and, in the crucible of time, little value beyond themselves. If Christianity is right, on the other hand, our lives – as the lives of the individual persons we are – are infinitely valuable, and we all have the possibility, as the persons we are, of unimaginable perfection. How this can come about is a mystery, but it does not seem to be an obvious contradiction and 'with God all things are possible'. In this very specific sense, related to personal survival, potential and value, I call the Christian scenario 'optimistic'. Relative to that, the scenario of the Buddhist is pessimistic. Of course, if the Buddhist is right in his or her analysis of the nature of things, then they can be portrayed as optimistic in that they at least show a way out of the infinite series of miserable rebirths. But the very idea that this is how it is, is pessimistic. If the universe is such that *ultimately* the only thing to do is to escape an infinite series of rebirths (and ultimately to help others do the same), that is pessimistic. I would argue that all this is pessimistic notwithstanding that the Buddhist goals of enlightenment, or Buddhahood, might be depicted as optimistic (and even, perhaps, positively blissful) *for the persons who achieve them*. And notwithstanding that there have been Christians who could also be depicted as deeply pessimistic.

The optimist has a tendency to live on and in hope. Thus in my case the choice to opt for Christianity, even though for all I know Buddhism may turn out to be correct, given all that I have said, is based on hope. Put frankly, I hope Christianity is true, much more than I could ever say I hoped Buddhism was true.

(B) The evidence for resurrection being the most likely explanation of what happened at the first Easter is very strong. Most people do not realise quite how extraordinarily strong the evidence is. It seems to me that it is up to those who do not accept the resurrection as the most economical explanation to (i) show a better alternative explanation, and/or (ii) show that their objection to resurrection as the best explanation is not a methodological one. In the latter case *nothing* would allow them to accept resurrection as the best explanation. Their objection is, it seems to me, ideological – i.e., they are not open to conviction.

I am not convinced by alternative explanations of the resurrection. Thus I have to accept that as far as I can see it is more rational to believe in the resurrection than in the alternatives. Of course, on all of these issues debate can take place interminably. But at some point in life one has to make a decision – yes or no? (Silence here means 'No', for silence cannot lead to the behaviour that should follow from 'Yes'.) Required to make such a decision – supposing my (eternal) life depended on it – I cannot say 'No'.

I have thus chosen to *believe*. And my belief is based on reasons. I argue that it is a rationally based belief that for me makes more sense than the alternatives. But I would not deny that alternatives like Buddhism are also to a large degree rational. Still, if I am to take my analytic meditations seriously then I have to *act* on the point I consider myself to have reached. Otherwise, like the eighteenth-century Scottish philosopher David Hume, I had might as well remove myself from meditation and retire to the sanity of backgammon. Or devote myself to the National Lottery.

Finally, a word on what I mean by 'faith'. I take it that, in the present religious context, to claim I believe X, where X is a proposition, is the same as to claim that I have faith in the truth of X. And for me faith is not some strange sort of inner feeling. That view of faith is perhaps a Protestant notion. Anyway, I follow Aquinas and the medievals in seeing faith as primarily an act of *will*. 'Will' here is a technical expression. It does not mean forcing oneself, through clenched teeth as it were, to believe something that one might otherwise consider bizarre, or to pretend one holds something to be the case. When the Christian says he or she has faith in the resurrection, understanding 'faith' as an act of will, this does not mean that the Christian *forces* an assent to the resurrection. Rather, faith in the truth of X involves intentionally asserting X as true (i.e., out of one's own free will, not under constraint). As St Augustine puts it, 'To believe is nothing other than to think with assent.' And, 'If there is no assent, there is no faith, for without assent one does not really believe'.[7] This assertion can be made either inwardly, in one's own mind, or publicly in, say, the *credo* when recited at Mass. If one asserts X as true in this way, of one's own free will, one can be said to have faith in the truth of X. Funny feelings as such are nothing to do with it. How one gets to that faith is not at issue in this context. It can be through reasoning, as in the rational faith that interests me here, or through birth, or whatever. But faith in this sense, as expressed in the *credo*, has been historically for Christians pre-eminently a public act, a communal performance, not a private feeling or intuition of illumination (or conversion).

Faith in Christianity traditionally (prior to the Reformation) was a public act of communal inclusion. It meant being a member of the extended family of the visible and invisible Church – the body of Christ – as expressed in the public communal performance of the *credo*.

It is that community, that family – that *faith* which I have now joined.

SUHṚLLEKHA – A LETTER TO FRIENDS

8th November 1999

Dear Friends,

I hope you will forgive me sending a rather impersonal circular letter like this. But I thought I should tell you about a development that to me is very exciting, and which should (at the very least) cause you some amusement.

I intend to be received into the Roman Catholic Church.

This may seem like a sudden development, but for me it is not sudden at all. I was brought up a very committed and active Anglican, and remained so well into my teens. One of my brothers is a Catholic convert. I have always felt a strong draw towards Catholicism. I discovered only recently that on our mother's side the family was historically Catholics until one or two generations ago. Perhaps it is in the genes. I always said that if I returned to the Christian Church there would be no question but that I would become a Catholic. It is all a bit like coming-out, I would imagine. I have been a closet Catholic for years. I have simply stopped running.

Perhaps one or two of you will be delighted with this news, but I would imagine most will – at the very least – consider that I have gone completely off my head! 'Foolishness to the Greeks ...' Some, notably my Buddhist friends, may well feel dismayed and betrayed. Please don't. I have been enormously influenced by Buddhism, and I still retain my affection and gratitude for the Dharma and those who practise it. My academic work in Buddhist Studies continues as before. I am still the same old Paul. You can be sure I will neither thump a Bible nor join the Inquisition. And I certainly shall not lose my sense of humour.

I hope those who think I have gone crazy will allow me that indulgence. At the moment all I can say is that I am very, very happy. For me, like so many others, it really does feel like coming home. Tārā (our daughter) said by way of objection that one has to have *faith* to be a Catholic. Does it make me more, or less, crazy to say that I do? I am told that the honeymoon period soon passes. I do not have any experience of honeymoons. Sharon and I were too busy and too poor to have one. But I do have a wonderful experience of marriage. And this marriage will, I think, last for ever.

With best wishes, and all my love,

Paul (Williams)

I

GOD, BUDDHISM AND MORALITY

An argument concerning what exists (ontology)

Buddhists do not believe in the existence of God. There need be no debating about this. In practising Buddhism one never finds talk of God, there is no role for God, and it is not difficult to find in Buddhist texts attacks on the existence of an omniscient, omnipotent, all-good Creator of the universe.

But there are those who say that Buddhism does not deny the existence of God. It is not *atheist*. It is, rather, *agnostic*. Buddhism does not pronounce on whether God exists or not. Buddhists do not claim to know. God is irrelevant to the Buddhist project of (broadly speaking) final freedom from all types of suffering through the attainment of *nirvāṇa*, liberation or enlightenment. Enlightenment is attained through oneself following a set path of morality, meditation and wisdom. It does not require any help from divine intervention or any reference to a God.

To portray Buddhism as agnostic in this way seems to me a modern strategy. In ancient times Buddhists were quite clear that they denied the existence of a personal creator God as taught in rival theistic systems. Buddhism does indeed hold to the existence of divine beings, rather like the gods of Greek and Roman mythology. But none of these is the one supreme creator God of the great theistic religions such as Judaism, Christianity and Islam. The Buddhist 'gods' (*deva*) tend to be happier and more powerful than we are. They live longer than we do. But they are part of the cycle of death and rebirth. In infinite past rebirths we ourselves have been born as gods many times.

25

Any God as He is understood in a religion like Christianity could not be irrelevant to the path to final spiritual fulfilment. No God as understood by Christians could be irrelevant to final fulfilment. If Buddhism does not teach this God, it either does not teach the path to final fulfilment or it considers that it is not necessary to the path to teach such a God. But a God that is not necessary to final spiritual fulfilment is not God as taught by Christianity. Thus if Buddhism does not need *that* sort of God, it must hold that such a God does not exist. Therefore if Buddhism claims to teach such a path, and yet God is not part of it, then the God referred to by Christians is indeed being denied. From a Christian point of view Buddhism is clearly a form of atheism.

The Buddha is held by Buddhists to have originally been an ordinary human being who discovered the final true way of things, how things actually are. Not understanding this true way of things, and not bringing our behaviour into accordance with it, has been responsible for our infinite series of rebirths and thus our infinite suffering. This true way of things is explained slightly differently in different Buddhist systems. But it is bound up with the impermanent and unsatisfactory nature of things. This is itself the result of their essentially dynamic way of being. All the things we meet with in our unenlightened lives are the results of causal processes. They come into existence. And, since they come into existence as the results of causes, they also cease to be when their causes cease and are thus no longer able to sustain them. We habitually tend to fix things that are by nature changing. That is, we *reify* them, and in reifying them we overrate them – even going so far as to project an implicit permanence upon what is in reality changing. We relate to things, including ourselves and our companions, as if they last for ever. We all think we are immortal, and on that basis we plan our lives. We seek things that we believe will provide us with lasting happiness. We are thus in the world in a mode of fundamental confusion, and misunderstanding invariably brings about unhappiness in the end. Things are actually impermanent, lacking in stability, and holding onto them is bound to lead to frustration and suffering. Like spring flowers, things blossom, fade and perish. We all die.

The remedy to our misery lies in coming to understand at the deepest possible level this true way of things, and in letting go. In letting go of attachment we cut the forces which project, as it were, rebirth. We thus attain *nirvāṇa*, liberation, enlight-enment, and bring to an end all rebirth and hence all suffering.

That, in a nutshell, is a thumbnail sketch of what Buddhism broadly is all about. I was involved for many years with the dGe lugs pa tradition of Tibetan Buddhism, the tradition most familiar in the West from the figure of the Dalai Lama. Tibetan Buddhism incorporates forms of practice known as '*Mahāyāna*'. We might add here to the sketch given above that the goal of Mahāyāna Buddhism is not just to attain liberation for oneself, freedom from all one's own suffering. Rather, it is to attain the state of a Perfect Buddha, which is held by followers of Mahāyāna to be superior to being simply liberated or enlightened. A Perfect Buddha has reached the absolute perfection of wisdom and compassion not just in order to be free from all suffering, but because this state of Buddhahood possesses the optimum facilities for helping others. One who takes the vow to become a Perfect Buddha, no matter how many rebirths that long path might take, for the benefit of all sentient beings (not just human beings), is known as a *bodhisattva*. This bodhisattva is not afraid of rebirth if it can be used to help others, and the bodhisattva is held to use whatever means might be available (even ones we might not expect) if he or she can thus be of benefit. This is known as employing 'skilful means', or 'skill in means' (*upāyakauśalya*). While the bodhisattva will help others in whatever way is needed, ultimately the bodhisattva's concern is with showing suffering sentient beings the way to liberation, freedom from all their sufferings, freedom from the cycle of birth and rebirth.

None of the forgoing needs any reference to God and, as we have seen, any sense of 'God' as understood by the Christian tradition is denied by Buddhism. God is unnecessary. But I have come to believe that there is a gap in the Buddhist explanation of things which for me can indeed only be filled by God, the sort of God spoken of in a Christian tradition such as that of St Thomas Aquinas.

Why is there something rather than nothing? Why is there

anything at all? And why is there a world in which, among other things, the processes (causation etc.) detected by the Buddha are the case? Why is it that this way of things *is* the way of things? As the Buddhist scriptures (*sūtras*) have it: 'Whether Buddhas occur or do not occur, the true way of things (Sanskrit: *dharmatā*) remains.' Why? Why is it like that? The *dharmatā* is not what we call 'necessarily existent'. That is, there is no logical *contradiction* in a world in which things are not like that – no causation, or no causation like that, or the Buddhist path does not lead to liberation etc. Thus the *dharmatā*, the true way of things, is contingent. It could have been otherwise. But in that case there is a hypothetical possible world in which the *dharmatā* is not the case. In the actual world, the world that really exists, on the other hand, the *dharmatā* is the case. Why? We have a contingent fact or state of affairs, how things happen to be in the actual world, for which we are entitled to ask the reason. 'Surely', we could urge, 'there must *be* a reason.' Why are things just like that, and not otherwise?

Note that the question 'Why is there something rather than nothing?' (which comes from Aquinas) is not asking what is the *chronological* first cause of things. Because this is so important to my argument, let me underline the point. We are not asking what was the first beginning of things, if by 'first' we mean the thing which started everything off at some point in the almost unimaginable past – say, the thing that caused the Big Bang. That is not what we are saying at all. We are not speaking about a chronological first cause, something that came chronologically before other things. If someone says, 'I don't see why something was needed to start things off. Why cannot the series just keep going forever?', that would not affect our argument. The argument applies at any point in time. At any point there could have been nothing, but there is actually something. Not any specific thing – just something. Or things could have been ordered differently. But it so happens they are *like that*. Thus whenever there is something, there could have been nothing. The cause of the specific thing is whatever it is that causes it. Thus what is the cause of the specific thing Wensleydale (one of our cats) is Wensleydale's mum, Kettle. But the reason that there are things, or that there are causal sequences, is not answered by appealing to Kettle. This question is not answered by pointing to some other thing and saying, 'Well, it is because of that thing there.'

There is also another quite common way of misunderstanding the sort of question that we are asking here. When we ask, 'Why is there something rather than nothing?', we are not asking why there is the totality of things, as if the *totality* of things were an additional thing over and above all the things themselves. Imagine that there existed in the universe at a particular time just ten things. Each of those things was caused by a preceding thing, and so on, in a one-to-one relationship back for infinity. Then when we ask 'Why is there something rather than nothing?' we are not asking why at time *t* there exists the *set* of ten things, as if the set were something in addition to each of the ten things themselves. Each of the ten things exists because of the preceding thing, its cause, back for infinity. There is no *set* of ten things in addition which requires that we ask after *its* cause. If we have explained the cause of each of the ten things, the 'set' of ten things does not need explaining. It is just another name for the ten things taken together. There is no set that requires explaining over and above the ten things.

But our question does not ask why the set of all things exists over and above its individual constituents. Our question asks why it is the case that there is something – anything – rather than that there is nothing at all. It asks why it is the case that there exists anything at all rather than the nothing that could so easily have been the case. The existence of anything at all is something that demands an explanation.

Supposing (as Buddhists do indeed say) things of some sort have always been in existence, forming a series causally linked from beginningless time. There would thus be no time at which there was nothing and *then* something. Nevertheless the question 'Why is there something rather than nothing?' would still stand. At *any* time there is still this question, worrying us, irritating us. I see no reason to think that this is a question to which there could necessarily be no answer. And it does not seem to be a contradiction. Any answer to that question – if there is one – would have to be a *necessary* being, a being about which it would make no sense to ask the question why *that* exists rather than not. For the theist God is the answer to this question, and God is needed as the ultimate explanation for existence at any time, keeping things in whatever sort of existence things have.

I think I have to agree with the theist.

For me the question 'Why is there something rather than nothing?' has become a bit like what Zen Buddhists call a *kōan*. It is a constant niggling question that has worried and goaded me (often, I think, against my will) into a different level of understanding, a different vision, of the world and our place in it.

It is true that some might incline towards answering our question with reference to something other than a necessary being such as God. Why could not the answer to the question 'Why is there something rather than nothing?' be, say, Mind? I can make little sense of this. There are indeed Buddhist traditions that refer to the primacy of a fundamental non-dual consciousness cut adrift, as it were, from specific mental acts. Thus there is what is known as the 'substratum consciousness' (*ālayavijñāna*), or the 'immaculate consciousness' (*amalavijñāna*), or other types of mentality which play a similar primordial role. But it is difficult to see what we can mean here by referring to these as 'consciousness' or 'mentality' in any sense. I am not sure what consciousness is supposed to be if not a generic term abstracted from particular conscious acts, like seeing a book or tasting a strawberry. And as each of these mental acts could have not existed, I take it that there would indeed be a possible world in which each of them, and therefore Mind itself in whatever meaningful sense we are using the expression, would not exist. In other words, the existence of mental acts and therefore Mind comes within the scope of the question 'Why is there something rather than nothing?'. Why is it such that mental acts exist? Mental acts, and therefore Mind, cannot be a necessary being. Mind can itself be put into question. Even if it were true that all things were reducible to a non-dual flow of consciousness we could still ask the question 'Why are things like that, rather than there being nothing at all?'. 'Why is there a substratum consciousness? There *might* not have been.'

It is sometimes asked of the theist, 'If God causes all things, what causes God?' When God is understood as the answer to the question 'Why is there something rather than nothing?', we can see the absurdity of the question 'What causes God?' If we are going to ask the question 'Why is there something rather than nothing?' at all, then we have to accept that it is a condition of the question that one cannot ask why whatever answers the question itself exists. This is part of what we mean by saying that the answer to this question, if there is one, would have to be a necessary being. Call the answer to the question 'Why is there something rather than nothing?' X. If God were caused – something about which one could ask the question 'Why?' – then God would not be a necessary being and therefore would not be X. God would be something contingent. But if God were not X then something else would be X. Since God *is* the answer to the question 'Why is there something rather than nothing?' (i.e., God by definition is whatever is X) it would follow that God would not be God, and something else would be God. Since God is not God and something else is God, it follows that God must have been misidentified. That 'something else' is actually God. Once we understand what God is, we can see that it is not *logically* possible to ask the question 'Why God?' We cannot get rid of God by asking, 'Why God?' Thus God, if there is a God, must be what is called technically a 'necessary being'.

Buddhists claim that there is no chronological first beginning, no first cause in the sense of something that came earlier and initiated the whole process of creation. Thus there is no first cause, no God. But this does not touch Aquinas's question, which applies not at the chronological beginning but rather at *any* time. The Buddhist simply never addresses that question, and in never addressing the question the Buddhist also leaves aside the question why 'the way things really are' (the *dharmatā*) – the seeing of which is so central to the Buddhist project of liberation, enlightenment – should be that way.

In terms of the logical options one could say (i) that with the Buddha's detection of 'the true way of things' (*dharmatā*) we reach a bedrock position. Perhaps this bedrock position is, it is claimed, a presupposition of all inquiry. We could simply refuse to go further in questioning why that way of things should be the way it is. Or (ii) one could nevertheless probe further and ask why 'the true way of things' actually is the way it is. Adopting (i) with the Buddhist is not necessarily irrational. But equally it is no *more* rational than adopting (ii) with the theist.

Of course, a claim that it is more rational to adopt (i) than (ii) could be based on the pragmatic grounds of the common Buddhist argument that such 'speculation' is not conducive to the Path to liberation. It takes us off into spiritually irrelevant metaphysics. Thus in the context of a presupposed spiritual project (i) becomes more rational than (ii). But what is, or is not, conducive to the Path depends on a prior acceptance of the *Buddha's* vision of how things are, what the goal is, and therefore what the Path should be. It requires the *Buddha's* vision of what is spiritually relevant, not Christ's. With perhaps the exception of Aristotle, no theist would say God is spiritually irrelevant. To adopt (i) on the basis of a prior acceptance of Buddhism is possible, but not more rational than adopting (ii). And if one adopts (ii) one must be adopting an approach which goes beyond what the Buddha himself actually taught. Any answer to (ii), 'Why is there something rather than nothing?', would have to employ the concept of necessary being, upon which all other things depend. It seems to me that in insisting on asking the question and, with Aquinas, answering it theistically, I can no longer be a Buddhist.

A Buddhist friend has protested that in choosing to accept God as an answer to the question 'Why is there something rather than nothing?', I am in fact having recourse to nothing more than a 'God of the gaps', and a God that is too vague to be informative. I do not agree. The expression 'God of the gaps' tends to be used in cases where theists appeal arbitrarily to God in order to create a complete explanation where otherwise the explanation would have something missing, a gap. Thus, for example, a theist might appeal to God's activity in order to fill various gaps in an account of evolution. God is used in an empirical or scientific theory to make up for any present inadequacy in our scientific understanding. Eventually, as our knowledge expands, the gaps left for God to plug become fewer and fewer.

My use of God to answer the question 'Why is there something rather than nothing?' is not an example of a 'God of the gaps'. This is not a scientific question. It is metaphysical. No future scientific investigation will ever produce an answer to a question of this sort. Anything that answered the question, that was not a necessary being of the type I have introduced, would itself be subject to the question. Why does *that* exist, rather than not exist? No scientific investigation through hypothesis and experiment could discover a *necessary* being as an answer to our question. And any necessary being which is postulated through abstract reasoning as an answer is indeed the being I am calling 'God'. But I have argued already that this is not intended as a proof of the existence of God. No one is forcing the Buddhist to have recourse to this necessary being. We still have two viable alternatives:

A. The fact that there is something rather than nothing, and the way things are, in terms of causal processes and so on, as discovered by the Buddha, just *is* how it is. End of the matter.
B. The reason why there is something rather than nothing, and things are the way they are, is because they are grounded on a necessary being who has in some sense brought it about.

No one forces assent to B rather than to A. B is not here more rational than A. But equally, A is not more rational than B. *That* is my point. If Buddhists do not want to assent to B then no one says they have to. But they cannot claim greater rationality in not doing so, since for them the question still stands.

Of course, I have assimilated our necessary being to God. But that involves a leap. As Aquinas stressed, this necessary being is not in itself identical with God, having all His features (such as love, beauty, mercy, justice, active engagement and so on) as understood in e.g. Christianity. Indeed, a mere necessary being seems rather contentless. Aquinas holds that having got to a necessary being, while we might be able to discern some features of that being from reasoning alone, revelation is necessary in order to have a full account – in order to get to the Christian doctrine of God. Christians hold that this necessary being is also a being that *cares* enough to tell us about Himself. I shall suggest that it is reasonable to think that the necessary being cares, although, beyond self-revelation, what that care

33

amounts to is not yet decided. What it means from God's side to say all this we have no idea. But because we have very little idea of what this God is from its own side, it does not follow that we would therefore be *more rational* in adopting strategy A above and saying that there is no answer to the question, 'Why is there something rather than nothing?' If we do that, the question still stands. If we adopt strategy B and say that the answer is a necessary being, then we *do* have some information about that being. We know that it is the answer to the question, 'Why is there something rather than nothing?' It does not become less of an answer, or an inadequate answer, because of paucity of further information. Paucity of information should be just what we would expect of any answer to a question of this sort. So, again, it is still no less rational to adopt B than it is to adopt A.

It is admittedly perfectly possible that the being on which all things depend has no interest at all in His (or 'Its') creation. Aristotle's God, the unmoved mover, is held by him to be totally uninterested in the world and the doings of its denizens. An engaged God with a concern for his devotees comes into our picture through Judaism. But it is not easy to reconcile such an engaged God with the necessary being (as such, outside time) that is the answer to the question, 'Why is there something rather than nothing?' This is not the place for me to try and argue systematically and in detail from necessary being to God, with all the qualities such as love and active engagement with creation that God is said to possess in Christianity. Theologians such as Aquinas offer ample material for consideration. And if I am going to accept a God there does not seem much point in accepting a spiritually sterile God like Aristotle's unmoved mover. A God who is totally uninterested in us would be a God with no contribution to make to meaning. That may be how it is, but I see no reason to have to adopt that scenario. And I see no problem in thinking that there *might* be a bridge from our necessary being to the point at which it becomes reasonable to allow revelation to take over.

Perhaps the following argument might have some potential.

For Aquinas a necessary being that explains why there is something rather than nothing is the final cause of things. But it seems clear (at least to me) that things do not just *happen* to depend on such a being. If things just happened to exist in dependence upon a totally 'blind' necessary being then the occurrence of something rather than nothing would in the last analysis be pure chance and the necessary being would not finally explain anything at all. That is, inasmuch as there is something, a necessary being would be the answer to the question 'Why is there something rather than nothing?' But with a blind necessary being we would still have no explanation of why there ever was anything at all. Of course, that could indeed just be how it is. But it is no more rational to think that that is the final way of things than to argue that the relationship between the necessary being and things is one of (in our terms) *intention*. If we want to say that the necessary being is not blind, then (I suggest) the only way we can speak here is to say that (in some totally mysterious and analogous way) the necessary being *wants* something rather than nothing. It *wills* things. That way, the necessary being becomes a final explanation not just ontologically but also in terms of volition, intention.

In support of a necessary being that is not blind we might offer the argument from fine-tuning, which is a modern version of the classical argument for the existence of God from design:

> Almost everything about the basic structure of the universe – for example, the fundamental laws and parameters of physics and the initial distribution of matter and energy – is balanced on a razor's edge for life to occur. . . . it seems enormously improbable that such a coincidence could have happened by chance.[1]

That is, there is some plausibility in the claim that things being how they are is a condition of life and enormously unlikely by chance. Intention is a more plausible option. In other words, a necessary being that just happens to be the answer to the question 'Why is there something rather than nothing?' is not going to explain features of what there actually is as satisfactorily as a necessary being that wills, that has intentions.

As we shall see, this point is pertinent to our consideration of the Buddhist's position too. If we are going to appeal to a necessary being in order to explain why the *dharmatā*, the way of things, is indeed the *dharmatā*, we are going to need to do more than just answer the question, 'Why is there something rather than nothing?' We are going to have to explain why things actually are the way they are. Why, for example, do things always operate in causal sequences? Why, in accordance with the 'law of *karman*', do good deeds produce happiness and bad deeds produce suffering? In other words, if we are to appeal to final explanations then we shall need more than just a blind necessary being. We shall need a being that wills, a being that cares. A being, in being the source, the Creator, actively wills that things exist in dependence on It (or, as we say 'Him'). We can say that He wants them. To that extent, as the source of things, He is Good and thus they are good. In wanting them, inasmuch as they are good, He can be said to love them. He therefore wants not just their existence, but also their flourishing.

But where does the *justice* of the necessary being come in? I wonder if something like this may be of any use? Suppose we do opt for a necessary being as the answer to why there is something rather than nothing, and supposing we do accept that this necessary being is not blind, but wills that there be things, and is to that extent good. Yet, if there is not also a sense in which all things will be, or are, reconciled in God, our necessary being, while not blind, would perhaps be only one-eyed. That is, God may be the origin of things, but inasmuch as He wills (that there be) things which are yet capable of diverging from His will (His intentions as Good for their good, their flourishing), He must also be their end as well. Things return to their source – for they could never really escape the source of the very being of things – and their source is Goodness itself. Of course, perhaps God is indeed one-eyed. Perhaps God is the origin of things, wills them and to that extent is good, but has (like the watchmaker) simply sent them on their way and let them go. That God is also the end of all things, that things return to Him, that creation is therefore *teleological* (has a point, moves towards a final aim), does not as such follow. But it is what the theist, or at least the Christian, hopes for. It is what seems most appropriate to his or her vision of where the essential goodness of this necessary being lies, a being that is neither blind nor one-eyed. It is the hope that gives all this meaning. And when those things that diverge from Good return to the Good, that meeting is called 'Justice'. God is the end wherein all meet Justice. And when things meet a Justice that is also Goodness itself, then their readjustment to Goodness is called 'repentance'. And inasmuch as repentance is still possible, Justice on the part of Goodness becomes Mercy.

At least, something like these arguments may be plausible. Or perhaps other arguments may work better. I can leave it. It does not affect my choosing God.

Of course, if we do not wish to appeal to final explanations, if we wish to leave things hanging in the air, then so be it. But not to make that appeal is not *more rational* than to do so. And in so doing the way is then open for a sympathetic appropriation, with Aquinas, of revelation as the means by which one can supplement our bloodless reasoning by an account that renders Being into God. It is revelation that explains fully what it means to say that the necessary being is God, a being who cares and is therefore not just the origin but also the end of all things, a being who is perfect Goodness, Justice and Mercy.

A necessary being, or God as a necessary being, is outside time. It (or He) does not change. There is no sense of 'before', 'after' or 'when' in reference to God. Thus it makes no sense to ask, as Buddhists sometimes do, 'What change occurred in God such that He created when He did create?' Supposing we were to speak hypothetically of 'before creation'. There is no time 'before creation'. Therefore there is no change, no 'when'. We cannot even say that creation occurred when it occurred. Rather, all 'when' began with creation. And in a strict sense there cannot even be a *'before* creation'. We also cannot ask why God did not create earlier than He did. Or why, if God is eternal, creation is not eternal. God is not eternal in the sense that He lasts throughout all time. He is eternal in the sense that He is outside time. Thus it does not follow from the eternality of God that creation, as in time, should be temporally eternal. But even if creation were eternal it would still be creation, in that it would still be contingent and would depend on God as a necessary being.

Buddhists commonly suggest that if we can speak of God acting in the world, intending, or responding to prayer, and so on, this must entail that God changes and is therefore in time. From a Buddhist point of view, if God changes then He would be a continuum. 'God' would become a word used for practical purposes to give a unity to what is in fact multiple. And (in a very technical sense that I do not want to go into) it would follow that God is an 'impermanent being'. Well, first, some theists (such as Jürgen Moltmann) could live with the idea of God as a changing being in time, and even of God as a being who undergoes suffering. Indeed, I remember some Mormons telling me many years ago that 'God has a body of flesh and bones like you and me'. I thought at the time that that was weird, and I still do. But it need not follow that He is anything other than God, a being on whom all things depend, omnipotent, omniscient and all-good. Thus even if God were like this, no conclusions favourable to the Buddhist position need follow. But this would not be an acceptable strategy to traditional mainstream Catholic thought. Instead, it simply does not seem to follow in any obvious sense that if God acts in the world, intends, or responds to prayer, then God needs to undergo change. Of course, from our side, as beings in time, we see God as acting in time and explain it in these various ways. But there does not appear to be any obvious contradiction in saying that what we call 'God responding to Archibald's prayer', or 'God guiding the good works of Mother Fiona', is from God's side the case, as it were, from all eternity. No change occurs in God when He responds to Archibald's prayer. I say 'as it were' because if God is outside time then it would *not* follow that God was always guiding the good works of Mother Fiona, say a million years before she was born. This would be to see God's eternity wrongly as a state of eternal prolongation, rather than as outside time. There would seem to be no contradiction in a being outside time bringing something about and, as a being outside time, it follows that this being could not change. Change can occur only in time.

There are philosophical problems in all of this, of course, well known in the philosophy of religion. For example, if God is outside time, what sense can we make of God knowing things that occur in time? And how can we relate to a being that is outside time? These problems are not, I think, insoluble providing no contradiction is involved (although the solution may have to remain for us at present a mystery).

My Buddhist friend has suggested that I am guilty of arbitrariness in my constant defence of God simply by arguing that something is not a contradiction. That, I think, is unfair. We define God as, among other things, having the feature of omnipotence. This is normally understood in Christian theology as entailing that God can do anything that is not a contradiction. Even God cannot do a contradiction, not because it is too difficult for God to do but rather because a contradictory act cannot be specified. There can be no such act. It is a bit like asking someone to walk in a perfectly straight line all the way to London with one step forward and an equal step back. That would not be a very strange or very difficult way to walk to London. It would be no way to walk to London at all. Even God could not do it. One may not believe in God, but there can be no arguing here over what the orthodox mainstream Christian *means* by God. The Christian is perfectly entitled to say that the God he or she believes in has not been disproved if the postulated actions of that God do not involve contradiction. It is up to the theist to specify what he or she means by 'God'. Someone may then want to refute it, but they cannot do that by objecting to the definition.

I want to mention here another common argument in Buddhist sources against the existence of God. This argument urges that an unchanging thing could not act as a cause, and certainly could not be the cause of the actual world with its manifold changes. But is this right? The argument seems to work with a very restricted idea of what it is to be a cause, and also what it is to be God. Causation and the creative function of God are here being specified in terms of *doing* something, rather than simply *being*. Paradoxically, the paradigmatic formula for causation adhered to by Buddhists is 'This being; that occurs. With the nonoccurrence of this there is the nonoccurrence of that.' This means that for the Buddhist too it is quite possible for causal function to be exerted simply by being. The paradigmatic formula states that we speak of causation occurring when, with the existence of X, there is Y. And with the nonexistence of X, there is not Y. The formula is perfectly fulfilled by the existence of God. The theist wants to claim that God, as the answer to the question 'Why is there something rather than nothing?', is the very condition of there being anything at all. Thus with the existence of God there can be things. With the nonexistence of God there would be nothing at all. This must be for the Buddhist too a perfect description of God's *causal* function. God does not need to *do* anything in order to be the cause of things. He simply needs to *be*.

Moreover, the idea that God would have to change in order to be the Creator of a changing world also misunderstands the claim the theist wants to make. As we have seen, since God is outside time it makes no sense to think of God changing at some (temporal) point in order to bring creation into existence. And God does not need to change continually in order to generate and sustain a changing creation. If God is the condition of there being something rather than nothing, then God is the cause of all and every thing simply by being, by being God in the way that God is. Whatever we want to refer to, God must be in order for that thing to be. God must be in order for things to come into existence or to perish. It is not necessary that God acts, that God does something. God is not continually doing things, like an ever-busy bumblebee. All that is needed for God to be the Creator is for God to be God. And God is God unchangingly.

Is the atheism (or 'non-theism') of Buddhism more *rational* than theism? Perhaps unknowingly in becoming a Buddhist I threw out the Holy Baby with the bath water.

ANOTHER ARGUMENT, RELATING ORDER – PARTICULARLY MORAL ORDER AS UNDERSTOOD BY BUDDHISM – TO ONTOLOGY

Absolutely fundamental to Buddhism is not just order, built into the very fabric of things, but moral order. By 'moral order' I mean that good deeds produce happiness and bad deeds produce suffering. This is the well-known 'law of *karman*'.

A. But, we can ask, is moral order (i) necessarily the case or (ii) merely contingently so?

If (i), then the statement 'Good deeds do not produce happiness' would be logically contradictory. There *could not* (where 'could not' indicates logical impossibility) be a world in which good deeds did not produce happiness. But this does not seem to be the case. It may not be *true*, but it is certainly logically *possible*, that good deeds do not produce happiness. There is no contradiction involved in good deeds not producing happiness.

Therefore the only option is (ii). Moral order must be merely contingently so. That is, moral order may be the case in all actual worlds, although there could logically (i.e. without contradiction) be a world in which it was not the case. Its not being the case is possible. But if (ii), there must be a hypothetical *possible* world (although not, the Buddhist urges, an actual world) in which moral order as understood above does not apply. This is because the moral order that applies in the actual world is merely contingently the case.

If that is true, then the crucial question is why it is the case that moral order, the 'law of *karman*', applies in the *actual* world.

B. Moreover, moral order is a particular application of (causal) order. Why does (causal) order apply in the actual world at all? If X causes Y, is this necessarily the case or merely contingently so? The same argument as above applies. Also, as David Hume pointed out, we cannot abstract from previous cases of X causing Y to future cases, and therefore to any *law* that X causes Y. It does not follow that just because X has caused Y in the past, this will continue in a *lawlike* way into the future. The application of causal law to the past and present is only contingently the case, and is also without grounds for the future.

Reapplying this to A, we have no grounds for arguing from, e.g., good deed X to pleasant result Y, as a *law* – i.e. it must occur in the future – even in the actual world.

If you think about it in this way, that things occur in accordance with causal laws is amazing. That moral order (justice) prevails is quite astonishing, if the Buddhist is right and it does prevail.

Let me underline this last point, because I think it is

particularly important. If asked, if pushed, the Buddhist must want to claim that it just happens to be the case, and could equally logically have not been the case, that things exhibit a certain order and part of that order is moral order as defined above. Nevertheless things will always exhibit that order, no matter how far into the future one goes, or how far away in space. This just happens to be the case. There is no explanation of why it is the case. That is just how it is.

Well, that may be. But it seems to me astonishing that things should happen to exhibit order. It is much more astonishing that we can say with confidence that this order will continue into uncharted space and time (on what grounds could we say that?). And it is almost beyond belief that this order is not just physical and psychological order but also just happens to be *moral* order. Thus, if it is rational to believe that this just happens to be the way it is, it seems, to say the least, equally rational to believe that it is like this because it is a product of a Creator. Even on Buddhist premises one might argue that a Creator would seem to be needed to bestow order and morality, and the nature of that Creator must be such (e.g. Just) that it can bestow order and morality. Appeal to the regularity of causation alone simply will not do it, since we still need to know why causation is regularly ordered.

C. Moreover, if moral order is simply contingent, what is its final purpose? Does it just happen to be the case (if, as Buddhists claim, it is the case) that the 'law of *karman*' – good deeds produce happiness, bad deeds produce suffering – applies in the world? One can argue that moral order does apply but that it has no final purpose, although as a matter of fact it can be *used* for the purpose of transcendence, attaining liberation. But why is it that this is as a matter of fact the case? Is it all simply just how it is?

Alternatively, one can see moral order as teleological – it exists for a purpose, a goal. But, again, such a purpose suggests the possibility of a Purposer.

There is a gap in Buddhism which can (for me) only be filled (if it can be filled at all) with God. This gap has a knock-on effect for the rest of Buddhist thought – as in

Buddhism's largely negative evaluation of the everyday world. It looks to me as if there has to be a Creator, a cause which is Rational (i.e. a source of order), Good and Just (i.e. a source of moral order), and a Purposer who has a purpose in which morality plays a part. One can of course question the presuppositions here – of causal and moral order in the universe, for example – but only by questioning Buddhism as well.

Of course the Buddhist will say that in taking this 'transcendental turn' I am spinning off into endless metaphysical speculations that will immeasurably block my ability to take advantage of the Buddha's very practical teachings and avail myself of the medicine of his Dharma (doctrine).

The Christian, on the other hand, is entitled to hold that without taking this transcendental turn I may well have failed to discover God, the be-all and end-all of everything. In failing to discover God I would not have discovered my real purpose, end, and happiness.

Who is right? I have made the choice I have made.

And if God created the world, and if God is good and just, then the created order *as such* is really existent, good and just. Of course, this gives rise to issues of theodicy – reconciling the existence of God with the existence of evil – but that is another question.

GOD AND EVIL

A common argument against God is that an omnipotent and wholly good God *could* only have created a wholly good world. The world clearly is not wholly good. Evil exists. Therefore there could not be an omnipotent and wholly good God. In my experience this is *the* argument that appeals most to Western Buddhists in their opposition to Christianity. It did to me too. Apparently also, for my sins, when we were much younger I finally destroyed any lingering faith my wife Sharon might have had in the existence of God with a version of this argument. That I now bitterly regret. It just goes to show how seriously we should take these issues. *Pace* Wittgenstein and the young, we are not playing games.

One response would be to say that at the very most the argument shows only that there is not an omnipotent and wholly good God. It does not show that there is no God at all, and if there is a God who is the Creator of all that is, then our dependence and duties towards this God still stand. How powerful and how good does a being have to be in order to be that upon which all things depend? God is God. What, in real life, here and now, is it to me whether God is *literally* omnipotent and *wholly* good?

This response, however, while worth considering, would not be that of mainstream orthodox Christianity. It should certainly make a theist think twice before abandoning theism in response to the presence of evil, but perhaps we can do rather better.

The argument from evil is still based on presuppositions to which the orthodox Christian need not be committed. Since there must be an infinite number of possible worlds, a better world than any one actually made would always be possible. Thus Leibniz's 'best of all possible worlds' would seem to be a logical contradiction. Since God cannot do a logical contradiction (not because it is a limit on His power, but because there is no 'doing' of a logically contradictory act – it is gobbledygook) God *could not* have made the very best of all possible worlds.

Moreover, can we say that God has moral obligations? I very much doubt it.[2] We cannot say that God has failed to perform His duty properly, that He has not given to beings what He owed them. Thus we cannot say God should in spite of that have made a better world than He has. God has no moral obligations to beings in which He could have failed.

It has been suggested to me that if we say God is good, or just, God must have moral obligations. But this does not follow. I take it that if someone is intentionally a source of good things, we say that that person is as such good. We also say a person is good who fulfils his or her obligations, his or her duties. But it makes no sense to say that God has duties and obligations. Thus we cannot say God is good in the sense that He fulfils those obligations. But we can certainly say God is good, and genuinely good, in that He is intentionally a source

44

of good things. Or that God is just in that He is intentionally a source of fair rewards and punishments.

Why has God, nevertheless, as a matter of sheer contingent fact, not made at least a better world than the one He actually has made? I have no idea. How could we answer a question like this? We cannot accuse God of moral failing, in failing to make a better world than He actually did. I once thought that if God existed I would stand up at the Last Judgement and accuse God of appalling mismanagement. I now realise that I would not have had any rational grounds to stand on. I thought that at least I should have morality and reason on my side. He would have only power. Thank God, I have lived long enough to realise that I would not have even morality and reason.

God has made the world He has made. He could have made a better one (although not the *best* one), but He has not. The rest is a mystery. And there is no reason why He should explain it to me. This, I think, is the final meaning of the book of Job in the Hebrew Bible. And whether or not we could answer the question 'Why has God, nevertheless, as a matter of sheer contingent fact, not made a better world than the one He actually has made?', it presupposes God as Creator and can serve as no argument against the existence of God. Thus the issue of evil in the world becomes an issue of a particular type of mystery for the *believer*, rather than an argument against the existence of God.

We can truly say God is good. But for us His goodness is bound up with His being the source of all good things (Aquinas). Apart from that we cannot know what we mean, as it were 'from God's side', by saying God is good. There is indeed an issue here as to whether we should also say God is evil, as the source of all evil things. There is a sense in which it may be correct that God is the source of all evil things, in that the existence of the world is a condition of the existence of evil, and God is the source of the existence of absolutely everything that exists. God is *in that sense* the cause even of our free acts.[3] Yet it need not follow that God is in some sense morally responsible for evil, and His relationship to evil things need not be the same in all respects as His relationship to good things. He saw that His creation was good. Following a certain stream of Catholic tradition found in Augustine and Aquinas, Herbert

McCabe has argued[4] that sin is a deficiency and as such a failure on the part of the sinner to be what he or she could be. Failures are negatives, and God does not make negatives. For example, the wickedness of Hitler consisted in his failing to be what he could have been, and manifested in *Hitler's* acts that fell short of his potential as a human being created in the image of God. But while the 'failing to be what he could have been' and the 'falling short' of Hitler were dependent upon the existence of the world and were thus in that sense dependent on God, they were not created by God. A 'failing to be' and a 'falling short' are negatives, negative properties of Hitler's own acts. They are thus not existent, i.e. created, things. They are not the responsibility of God. Thus sin as such is not made by God. And it is debatable how far so-called 'natural evil', like volcanoes or tornadoes, are actually in themselves evil at all.

Because of its importance, let me summarise my argument here.

(i) God could not have made the best of all possible worlds, for with infinite possible worlds no world actually created could be the best possible world.

(ii) God has clearly, as a matter of fact, not made a better world than the one He has made. Should He have done so? If we say yes, it is difficult to see what the force of 'should' is here apart from a moral one. In other words, if God is good He is morally obliged to make a better world than this one.

(iii) But if God is morally obliged to make a better world than this one, God has fallen down on His moral obligations. That is, God has failed in His duty. Since God has made this feeble world when, as an omnipotent being, He clearly could have made a better one, God has behaved wrongly, immorally. God is thus not good.

(iv) But when the theist says that God is good, indeed Goodness itself, he or she is by no means necessarily committed to the idea that this entails God having moral obligations. All good things flow from God. God cares for us (analogously) as a Father cares for his children. And so on. All these things entail that God is indeed

46

genuinely good. But God does not do all these things out of moral obligation, out of duty.

(v) Since God does not do these things out of moral obligation, we cannot say that God can fail in His obligation. How can we say that God is under any moral obligations, such that He could fail in His duty? It seems that as God, God is under no moral obligation at all to make a better world than the one He has made. He is good, He is omnipotent, but He has made the world He has made. There is no incompatibility in any of this.

(vi) Granted this, why, nevertheless, has God made this particular world and not a different, better, world? We have no idea. It is at the moment a mystery. It might be that this is the best world for His purposes. It might be that eventually we see that all will turn out for the good. But it might not. God is under no obligation to divulge all to us. But God is still God. End of the matter.

In a copy of the Catholic journal *The Tablet* (18 December 1999) a Benedictine monk, Fr Mark Barrett, confesses to a friend in grief who asks 'Where is God in all this?' that he has no idea, and that 'God's a bastard and I shout at him a lot.' Is this shocking? Does it mean that one would be foolish to believe in God? Fr Barrett himself adds that 'Sometimes I don't believe in God.' Yet if we think about it, this is not shocking. It is very human and quite consistent with the God we find not only in the Bible but also in the thought of someone like Aquinas. I seem to recall a story of Jews in a concentration camp who, having convicted God of inexplicably and hideously abandoning His people, returned to the evening prayer. That was supremely consistent. None of it, I think, is incompatible with the God I have come to believe in. Hugo Gryn, later to become a famous rabbi in Britain, offered to devote his life to God if He saved Hugo and his family from Auschwitz. Gryn kept his side of the bargain. God did not. But who said God should keep bargains? And, really, what would it be to enter into a bargain with God? What could we possibly understand by it?

God has created the world He has created. He certainly

could have created a better world. For *any* world he created, he could have created a better world. We do not know why He did not create a better world than this one. From our side we would be perfectly consistent in bemoaning the way the world is when horrible things happen to people apparently through no fault of their own, because 'that is the way the world is'. From our side, accepting the existence of God, we could say (metaphorically, of course) that 'God is a bastard', for He has not done what we think He should have done (i.e. make a better world). Or we could sometimes think that perhaps God does not exist. Yet we can also consistently – and I would argue, rationally – return then under the force of our arguments and experience to a belief in God again. We might compare here the wonderful humility and wisdom concerning the problem of evil found in the late Cardinal Basil Hume:

> In this world I can't understand it. But that doesn't affect my belief. I believe we are a fallen race, that human life is always in the hands of fallen people and when I am faced with the ghastliness of concentration camps and so on, I can't put it to God at my level.[5]

I used to think that this sort of thing was a cop-out and missed the point entirely. I couldn't imagine how anyone could still believe in God under such conditions. I now think that the sort of thing Basil Hume says is exactly right. The God we believe in is truly good and cares about us. He is the source of all good things and He is involved with the world through Jesus, His Son, who died so horribly. God is indeed omniscient, omnipotent and all good. But He is incomprehensible. We know God is good and cares about us. But with Aquinas we do not really know what we are saying – what it means 'from God's side' – when we say God is good and cares for us. We are owed nothing. That there is anything at all is a miracle. That it is good is a wonder.

The nature of God is inexplicable mystery. We know Him only by His effects. From our side He could have created a better world. We say 'God is a bastard'. We shout at Him a lot. We worship and love God, as we should. And He loves and saves us. But freely – not 'as he should'!

48

MEDITATION ON A DOUGHNUT

When we read the account of Basil Hume's life we find (as with all religious) times of faith and times of doubt. He too went through a 'dark night of the soul'. I still find an almost irresistible tendency to think that doubt shows truth; faith shows wish-fulfilment. But this is unwarranted. Why should the times of doubt reveal truth? Why should this be truth any more than times of faith that reveal the comforting feeling that we are cared for? That I adopt the darker option surely says more about me than about truth.

> Twixt the optimist and the pessimist the difference is droll –
> The optimist sees the doughnut; the pessimist sees the hole![6]

Basil Hume preferred doughnuts. He preferred faith. And he was right to do so. A world of pessimists (like a world of doughnut holes) would be no fun at all.

But would it be more in harmony with reality?

A distinguished Tibetan teacher once came over to me while I was looking out of a window at wonderful British patchwork country scenery. The flowers were out; the birds were singing. Sheep meandered gently across the turf. In the distance were steep hills fragrant with old ruined abbeys and castles, the mythology of ages. 'Ah, beauty', he said to me softly. 'Yes, I saw beauty once. Now all I see is death and destruction.'

Of course, my Tibetan teacher was frequently very kind and compassionate. This compassion is that of one who sees what others do not. Ultimately, Buddhist compassion seeks to save *all* sentient beings, even wiggly worms and clammy cockroaches, from the treadmill of suffering, death and destruction. But pointing to the possibility of liberation, and compassionate concern for others, is not the answer to those who would speak of Buddhism as pessimistic. For it seems that these features of Buddhism are an implication of that pessimism.

Certainly doughnuts *do* have holes. Perhaps realism here is not pessimism? But was our Tibetan's perception truer to reality? Is this a better way of seeing things? And is it a deeper, profounder, more spiritual vision of the world? Should I wish to be able to see things that way? Should I lament that my

Buddhist practice was so weak that, try as I might, I simply could not seem to do so? Which is better, to see the doughnut or the hole? Surely the truth is to see both. But in seeing the doughnut we all *do* see both. Which should we focus on, which should determine our life (and our death)?

> Today, I call heaven and earth to witness against you: I am offering you life or death, blessing or curse. Choose life, then, so that you and your descendants may live, in the love of Yahweh your God, obeying his voice, holding fast to him; for in this your life consists...
>
> (Deuteronomy 30:19–20)

Choose life. This passage was a particular favourite of Rabbi Hugo Gryn, who died of cancer a few years ago after having lived through the horrors of Auschwitz, which saw the deaths of his father and brother as well as innumerable family and friends. 'To life!' was his frequent toast. And he was active in campaigning against the forces of intolerance, misunderstanding, and sheer evil that had led to Auschwitz. *That* was realism.

Is it wiser to concentrate on the hole, because soon all that will be left of the doughnut is its absence, its consummation? I don't know.

In one of the early Indian Brahmanical ('Hindu') texts, the *Upaniṣads*, we are told of two birds seated on the same tree. One eats the fruit, the other simply observes. Unlike what you might expect, the point of the image is that the bird who observes is better off. It represents the true Self, rather than the engaged, everyday person we think we are. This Self is liberated from all attachment, free of all desires. It has no need for the fruits of everyday life. This Upaniṣadic text dates from perhaps a little before the time of the Buddha.

In the ultimate last analysis, a great deal of Indian thought, I think, sees the final spiritual goal in terms of this self-sufficiency, whether it expresses that fact in terms of the true Self (*ātman*) – as do most Indian traditions – or in terms of not-Self (*anātman*), as does Buddhism. This is not surprising. Indian society was (and is still, to a large degree) rigidly structured in a network of reciprocal duties, the duties of caste and class, that strictly governed everyday behaviour. Social involvement, social behaviour, the network of duties and constant rebirth were closely related. Rebirth was into a network of obligations and duties. In social terms the Indian seeking after final liberation from the cycle of rebirth precisely renounced society and the duties that went with it. He (or she) 'went forth from home to homelessness', as a common Buddhist expression has it. Dependence on others is finally to be avoided. Liberation from rebirth is intimately related to finally, most perfectly, being oneself. One finally no longer needs the food of others. Food and its preparation is closely associated not only with the duties and roles of society but also, in India, with the possibility of ritual pollution and therefore lowering of caste and class status. Buddhism is no different from all this. Buddhism too is a religion of space. In terms of final spiritual achievement, for the one who attains it the goal is that of absence. *Nirvāṇa* in Buddhist texts is often likened to space. In earliest Indian Buddhist art the Buddha was not portrayed. We might see people prostrating and making offerings to an empty seat at the base of a tree, the seat on which the Buddha was finally enlightened. But they are not worshipping a seat. They are worshipping the Buddha. The Buddha is portrayed through his absence. He is present, as the Absent One, the space – the rip – in the mesh that is unenlightenment, the mesh in which those around him are still involved. Final liberation here is simply the absence, and that absence is an absence of dependence. It is essentially an absence of dependence on others, and also on an Other, God.

Buddhism is vividly portrayed here as essentially a religion of the hole rather than the doughnut. For all its advocacy of compassion – a compassion which will take those who suffer to the bliss of freedom – the state of one who is enlightened, or the state of a Buddha, from his or her own side is one of complete and utter self-sufficiency. In terms of one's own needs and aspirations it is complete immutable independence from others. The compassion of the Buddha is a natural – indeed, it is said to be spontaneous – expression, a natural overflow, of his fully enlightened state. It is compassion for those who still suffer, compassion that will bring those who are suffering to the bliss of liberation. But the Buddha, *qua* Buddha, has no *need* of those others. He could still be a Buddha if it turned out that, in the omniscience of his enlightenment, he was the only being in existence.

In the ultimate last analysis, it seems to me, the final goal of orthodox Christianity as it has existed in history is quite different from this. It is envisaged in *communal* terms. It is a community, the Church, a *body* with Christ at its head and its saved members as the limbs. Not surprisingly, this communal dimension of Christianity is expressed daily in the Mass, the sharing of food, the sharing of the body of Christ. Christianity expresses its very being, its very vision of itself, in terms of complete and perfect dependence, dependence on God (the Other) and dependence on each other, the fellow members of the community. Christianity is the religion of the doughnut, not the hole. It is the very diametric opposite of the Indian vision of the spiritual goal expressed above. Christianity is essentially a communal religion, the religion of a family. The community of the Church, perfected, *is* the goal. And the Church is not a means to some higher, final goal expressed perhaps in terms of mystical experiences. If there were only ever one person in existence the goal as conceived by Christianity would be impossible. Maybe this is why (as far as we can ever tell) creation occurred. It is sometimes asked in Buddhist texts what a hypothetical God lacked, in order that He created. The answer, perhaps, is that God lacked nothing. That is why He created, from the fullness of His nature. It is because God is God that He creates. God's very nature is love, and love's very nature is communal. For Christians even God Himself is a community, a trinity.

If I am right here, then it has implications for certain broadly 'mystical' ways of reading the Christian goal *vis-à-vis* that of Buddhism. We sometimes find the view expressed that the goal of Christianity is finally, ultimately, a state of union with God. Frequently what is meant by this nowadays is a psychological state, a mystical experience, of oneness with God. Indeed, it is sometimes urged that this is a *nondualistic* and *nonconceptual* state. As such it is comparable with, and perhaps identical with, the nondualistic and nonconceptual experiences found in other religions, for example in Hindu Advaita Vedānta or certain forms of Buddhism like Zen. Perhaps, it is urged, all religions ultimately converge in this final nondualistic and nonconceptual experience. Certain people – mystics – have such experiences in *this* life. But the rest of us, it is argued, if we are to attain the goal, will have the experience in some sort of *post mortem* state. I have heard it said that Christian mystics like St John of the Cross themselves experienced such nondualistic states and struggled to express what they had experienced within the language of Christian orthodoxy, which is essentially dualistic (God and us – 'I and Thou' – and ne'er the twain shall truly meet). The implication here is that the experiences of mystics like St John of the Cross were similar, if not identical, to those of e.g. Buddhists, but the Buddhists were better served by their vocabulary of nondualism and nonconceptuality. In other words the Buddhists expressed more precisely the truths experienced by the Christian mystic. The Christian was hampered by his conceptual vocabulary, his dogmatic theology.

For all I know this account may be true, and we may all eventually (probably in some *post mortem* state) come to discover that fact. But from our side as the unenlightened individuals we are now in this life, we have no reason to think that the account above is true. More importantly, if it were true I would argue that it would be completely destructive of orthodox Christianity. For to implicate God in nonduality is to destroy God. It is to destroy love, and *ipso facto* to destroy the community, the family.

Perhaps the Christian who favours some sort of account like that given above is unaware just how fatal it is not only to traditional Christian theology but also to any notion of Christianity as it has existed in its origins and history. I have urged that the final goal of orthodox Christianity must be understood essentially in communal terms. It is simply contradictory to speak of a religious goal both as communal and in terms of nondualism and nonconceptuality. One must give way to the other. A community essentially requires difference, and difference essentially involves dualism and conceptuality. It is not just Christian theology that insists that the Christian goal cannot be seen in nondualistic and nonconceptual terms. It is not just the prejudice of the Vatican, or the preservation of the notion of God as a Grand Inquisitor in the interests of patriarchal church politics. That the Christian goal cannot be seen this way is a matter of logic. If Christianity essentially sees its goal in communal terms – and it does – then this cannot logically be defined in terms of nonduality and nonconceptual experiences. The final goal of Christianity is not just a state of perfection. It is not just a seeing of God. It is not just (to use a central expression of Eastern Orthodoxy) 'deification', with this term understood in whatever way is currently fashionable. Indeed, deification for the Catholic occurs through the integration of Christ into one's very being through participation in the Mass. Christ is food. What one eats, that one becomes. The final goal is a community, and this community of Christianity is spoken of as 'new heavens and new earth' (2 Peter 3:13). The final goal is essentially communal, for the Christian vision of history is as a love-song, the love between God and His people.[7]

The Jewish vision of history, which was certainly shared by Jesus and which the early Christians inherited, always saw the final goal in terms of community, God's relationship to His people, and not in terms of mental states, mystical experiences. Experiences are, *qua* experiences, essentially private. Privileging experiences in this way is to privilege the individual over the community. If the goal is expressed in terms of nondual experiences this must finally be to privilege self-sufficiency – indeed self-absorption – over a position where one's very being is essentially bound up with a community, with others. It is the goal of an essentially subjectivist, rather than communal, vision of religion. It is not surprising perhaps that the English Buddhist Stephen Batchelor chose to call one of his earliest books on Buddhist philosophy *Alone With Others*. From this point of view even when one is with others one is still alone, wrapped, absorbed, in self-sufficiency. In modern Christianity, I suggest, more often than not a mystical, nondualistic vision of the Christian goal itself draws on Indian sources where, as we have seen, the goal is indeed expressed in terms of self-sufficiency. But actually the Christian perspective is the exact opposite. For the Christian vision, even when one is alone one is essentially with others, the community of the visible and invisible Church.

Final consummation in love (not just compassion for those who now suffer) requires difference. God, for Christians, is perfect love. And I would argue that love simply cannot exist for one who experiences in terms of nondualism and noncon-ceptuality. Indeed, if we understand by a nonconceptual experience an experience that by its very nature is nonconcep-tualisable (and not just an experience that does not involve the conscious application of concepts while it is occurring), and a nondual experience as an experience in which it makes no sense to distinguish a subject and an object of that experience, then I am not actually sure that anything could exist in a mental state characterised by nondualism and nonconceptuality, or indeed why anyone should want such experiences. Nonconceptual experiences would by their very nature be quite meaningless. Indeed, it is difficult to see what would qualify an experience which is nondualistic and nonconceptual in that sense as being an experience at all.[8] Forced to say something about it, supposing one can make any sense of these 'experiences', all that one could say is that what exists there is one's own self-sufficient self-absorption. But perfect love involves recognition of and respect for difference in perfect harmony. All lovers know that. Difference *by definition* is dualistic, and its expression *by definition* involves conceptuality. 'Our final salvation will be not only individual, but together in perfect unity with Christ and the whole of the human race united in him.'[9] 'Heaven is eternal Easter.'[10]

Thus the Christian idea of the goal as essentially communal (derived from the Jewish vision and theology of the final goal, i.e. its eschatology), and the Christian idea of God as love, are intimately related. Both involve the complete impossibility (contradictoriness) of an interpretation of the (orthodox) Christian goal in terms of mystical experiences of nonduality and nonconceptuality. To urge such an interpretation would be to destroy orthodox Christianity as it has existed in its origins and history. If St John of the Cross enjoyed such experiences they had nothing to do with the goal of Christianity. There can be no relationship, and hence no relationship with God or one's fellow human beings, in a state of nonduality and nonconcep-tuality. Love of God and love of one's fellows – the first two commandments – would become impossible in anything like the sense they have been understood by Christian orthodoxy from the very beginning.

A goal of a perfected community, it seems to me, offers the

possibility that I and those I love and value for themselves will survive in some unimaginably wonderful state wherein we see and love each other, and God as He is, for ever. It offers hope. Even if I could attain the experience of perfect self-sufficient self-absorption in an experience that is nonconceptual and nondual, I am not sure I should want it. What would that be to *me*? Such a state is also unimaginable, but unimaginable because I am not sure what I am supposed to be imagining. What would it be like? Surely it would be like *nothing*?

We can take our choice. We can have as final goals a perfect community in a relationship of love with God and our fellows, or we can have nondual and nonconceptual experiences. But one cannot have both as equal final goals. I have argued that this is a matter of logic. Thus we cannot have both Buddhism and Christianity, if we understand 'Christianity' in anything like its traditional meaning. Once more, we face a choice.

CONSCIOUSNESS, SELF, MORALITY
AND OTHERS

In the last analysis Buddhist ontology always comes back to the dependence of everyday things in some sense on consciousness. Everyday things are conceptual constructs, and the process of conceptual construction is (of course) essentially mental. It follows that from this point of view others too are in some sense dependent upon consciousness. *Whose* consciousness? Buddhist thought has a very real problem in avoiding solipsism. Inasmuch as I accept that there are others at all, they must exist in dependence upon *my* consciousness. And corresponding to the primacy of consciousness in Buddhist ontology is the primacy of *sensations* in Buddhist soteriology. In the final analysis, Buddhist soteriology comes back to either the achievement of positive, or the avoidance of negative, sensations (i.e. experiences). Again, the whole direction is towards the essentially private. It involves gnosis (*jñāna*), or insight (*vipaśyanā*), or indeed awakening (*bodhi*), from which we get words such as *bodhisattva* and *Buddha*.

The Buddhist would of course disagree. The primacy of

consciousness is not that of *my* consciousness. The soteriology is not egoistic, for Buddhism is based on the centrality of *anātman*, not-Self. Yet it is difficult to see how things as given to me can depend on consciousness if not on my consciousness. It has to be the consciousness of *someone*. It makes no sense for me to talk of things as given, except as given *to me*. There is no such thing as consciousness in abstract. Likewise, what is Buddhist soteriology based on if not finally the achievement of positive sensations (understood in the sense of any experiences), or the avoidance of negative sensations, by *someone*? Liberation, Buddhahood, or whatever, is achieved by someone. And who could that be, therefore, if not me? Buddhism places great emphasis on the concrete, the here-and-now, an individual in his or her suffering and potential. Either Buddhism is stressing the primacy of individual consciousness and its sensations, or it marks a move away from the individual towards abstractions. But as Descartes realised, abstractions in the case of experiences are difficult to justify in reality. There is no such thing as a pain in abstract.

So whether or not the experiences involved are of nonduality or nonconceptuality (whatever they might be), these still must be experiences of individual persons. Otherwise they could not be expressed in consciousness-terms. In actuality there cannot be experiences in abstraction from beings undergoing experiences. Thus, in the sense in which I am using the term here, they must come under 'self' (i.e. this experiencing person (*pudgala*) here), if not 'Self' (*ātman*). One way or another the goal involves working on oneself, and is expressed in terms which are self-implicating. This is indeed often claimed as the glory of Buddhism. It comes right down to earth in the most immediate of individual experiences.

The same is the case even where, in Mahāyāna Buddhism, the goal is expressed in terms of attaining Perfect Buddhahood for the benefit of all sentient beings. Attaining Perfect Buddhahood can only be in terms of one's own mind, and finally the benefit of all sentient beings involves the minds of others too. Thus, in the sense in which I am using 'self', 'other' – inasmuch as we mean other sentient beings – can also be expressed under 'self'. Both self and other are important for Buddhists in terms of their pleasant or unpleasant experiences.

Perhaps in Buddhism it was only the great Japanese Buddhist Shinran (1173–1262) who saw the implications of all this. Concern with one's own experiences – all that meditation – cannot finally escape charges of egoity. Indeed, all concern with experiences implicates egoity. For Shinran this means that *nothing* one does can bring about enlightenment, for enlightenment is essentially beyond egoity. In finally realising one cannot do it, in finally letting go of one's own ability to attain enlightenment, the Other who is Amitābha Buddha shines forth from within one's very own depths, where he has been shining fully enlightened all along. One turns from self-power (*jiriki*) to Other-power (*tariki*). This is what Shinran calls 'faith' (*shinjin*). 'Faith' is that letting-go which occurs at the deepest level when one finally goes beyond all egoity in realising that even trying to bring about enlightenment for oneself is also a subtle form of egoity. In my terms, any basing of ultimate concerns on self-implicating experiences, subjectivity, finally veils egoity.

Yet in the last analysis Shinran himself still thinks of the goal in what I would call 'self-terms'. For Amitābha shines forth from one's own inner depths. This Other has always been there, enlightened. The Other is the Buddha-nature but, inasmuch as it can be expressed using psychological terms, it is *one's own* Buddha-nature. In one's innermost depths, so far beyond egoity that one cannot even speak of it as 'one's own', lies the Buddha-nature, forever unsullied. Its radiance has been blocked by the strivings of egoity, including of course the striving to attain enlightenment. But it is in some sense implicated in mind-terms, consciousness, psychologism. And it is in some sense *one's own* attainment of liberation.

Shinran is right to see that transcendence of self and other involves the shining-forth (grace) of an Other. But self and other, myself and other sentient beings, are all contingent and hence created. Concern with their welfare alone finally involves the primacy of experiences, and primacy of experiences involves hedonistic (egoistic) concerns. The Other who is God, the Creator, is of a completely different order, and I would argue that orientating onself to God is salvation from any primacy given to experiences, to sensations, even to the most refined mystical experiences.

How are we to get out of the egoistic circle towards others?

I agree entirely with a comment made by Pope John Paul II who, in the course of a trenchant critique of contemporary relativisms, observes that:

> It should never be forgotten that the neglect of being inevitably leads to losing touch with objective truth and therefore with the very ground of human dignity. This in turn makes it possible to erase from the countenance of man and woman the marks of their likeness to God, and thus to lead them little by little either to a destructive will to power or to a solitude without hope. Once the truth is denied to human beings, it is pure illusion to try to set them free. Truth and freedom either go together hand in hand or together they perish in misery.[11]

What the Pope calls 'being' here is what is outside the circle of subjective impressions. In basing itself on subjectivity, Buddhism has always had great trouble in transcending the subject towards the other. Only in escaping the privileging of personal experience can one find God, and only through being based in God as Other can one find others in their own terms. Only in finding others in their own terms, in the light of duties and responsibilities founded ontologically and morally on God, can one finally ground morality (just as one can only finally ground beings in Being).The other is reached morally by a leap towards the Other ontologically and soteriologically. Things are based not at all on consciousness but on the essentially Other, God. As others based on an Other, things escape me and mine. We transcend subjectivity, solipsism, and its accompanying egoity, by appeal to something else, something unimaginably different, in which self and other are both grounded. We ground others in God, and in others true, objective morality becomes possible.

This is a leap because it is the leap outside ourselves. That is very difficult in a culture based on the primacy of individual sensations, self-gratification. I wonder sometimes if the current popularity of Buddhism is simply an expression of this stress on personal experiences, and thus a symptom of the problem rather than its answer.

The truly Other, outside me and mine, is God – the finally Wholly Other – the answer to the question why there is something rather than nothing, the God who has revealed

Himself. This is not an abstraction but the most really Real. As such He is Being itself. As grounded in God, others cease to be abstractions too, and morality ceases to be mere talk veiling my egoity.

THE UNDESIRABILITY OF SUFFERING

The very starting point of Buddhism, historically and conceptually, is the undesirability of suffering. Actually, it is for this reason that Buddhism is based on the transformation of consciousness. Suffering is a matter of experiences. The key to the transformation of experiences from those held to be negative (suffering) to those held to be positive is the transformation of the mind from the three negative states of greed, hatred and delusion to their opposites: altruism, loving-kindness and wisdom. The result is happiness, the overcoming of all suffering. Thus if an omnipotent, omniscient and all-good God were to create a world, it would seem inconceivable that He would create a world with suffering in it.

The Dalai Lama often starts his teaching with the axiom that we all desire happiness and the avoidance of suffering. This utilitarian principle provides for him a common human basis in his approach to religion and religious pluralism. The very *purpose* of religion is to bring about happiness and the avoidance of suffering.[12] Religion exists for humanity, not the other way round. It is this approach which is behind the Dalai Lama's much admired direct focusing on kindness and compassion, cutting through the differences between religions that all centre on what he sees as inessentials. Doctrinal differences between religions, like what he calls the 'God-theory', are unimportant.

Yet is all this so obvious? I have suggested that it is possible to defend belief in the existence of God as being at least as rational as His dismissal in Buddhism. And we have seen that we have no grounds for saying that it follows *necessarily* that an omnipotent, omniscient, and all-good God would not create a world with suffering in it. That being the case, we cannot know in abstract what sort of a world an omnipotent, omniscient and all-good God would create. All we know is that we have the world we actually have. It is *this* world we have to make sense of, with or without God. Some have chosen God.

Given that, it seems to me that we can also attack the presupposition of the undesirability of suffering. I have just been reading Evelyn Waugh's biography of the Elizabethan Catholic martyr and saint Edmund Campion. It seems clear that these Catholic priests, who returned to Protestant England to minister in secret to their fellows, expected and indeed courted martyrdom. They desired to witness to their faith by patience while being hung, drawn and quartered. That, I should imagine, hurts. Campion and his friends thus desired the witness of suffering.

The obvious response to this is that they did not desire the suffering involved. They desired the reconversion of England, or the martyr's crown, or whatever. Anyway, what they desired would be a happiness. The suffering was just the unavoidable means to that end. The motive for their action was actually happiness. But is that right? It doesn't seem to me to be obviously so. This is certainly not how a Christian would see the motives of the martyrs. Their motive was to do God's will. *Not* because doing God's will would lead to happiness. For a theist to do God's will is axiomatically an end in itself. To think that one does God's will for some other reason is to misunderstand in a very fundamental way the theology and also the psychology of theism. A Christian does not (or should not) do God's will for some future gain, some pleasantness, for him- or herself. If God's will was done out of a motive of hedonistic gain, God's will would not actually be done.

So what I want to argue is actually quite simple. It is this: *If God exists – God as He is understood in Christian tradition – and if one is a Christian, then there is no possible circumstance under which doing God's will would be the wrong thing to do. In that sense, for the Christian doing God's will is an absolute imperative. This is illustrated many times in the Bible. God's will is ethically non-negotiable. If that is right, then any question of what follows for oneself, or indeed for others, from following God's will is incidental and as such irrelevant. Thus it follows that the issue of happiness is also irrelevant. If happiness follows from doing God's will, that happiness is an unpredictable and thereby totally unmerited act of God's grace. Christianity is not about happiness. Christianity is thus not for humanity at all. Christianity is about *God*.

Supposing God had created a world where, every time His will was done, suffering followed. Under such circumstances, because He is God, and because He is the Creator, God's will would still have to be done. A Christian as such simply wishes to do God's will. When the Christian does God's will, he does God's will because he believes in God, and God is *God*. That is the end of the matter. The Christian has moved outside the circle of his or her own experiences. The Other that is God, a necessary being, is also itself a complete and sufficient explanation. Edmund Campion was prepared to suffer, and to that extent desired to suffer, simply because he considered (rightly or wrongly) that this was what God wanted. If God had created a world where there was only suffering, and placed Campion in that world, Campion would want suffering if that was what God wanted. It is simply not true that we all want happiness and the avoidance of suffering. There is something more fundamental than pleasant sensations. The theist tries to express this in terms of the rather unfashionable concept of duty – duty first and foremost to God, and then duty to our fellows. We owe God obedience, and in the light of God we have a duty towards our fellows of concern, care, and respect.

Perhaps there is indeed some connection here between the hedonism of the modern world – the axiomatic assumption that everything comes back to pleasant experiences and the avoidance of suffering – and the moral collapse which many feel in contemporary society, the collapse of respect for others. Morality, it seems to me, balances talk of rights with talk of responsibilities, of duties. But whereas rights are susceptible to egoistic reduction ('*my* rights to *my* happiness'), duties and responsibilities require an appreciation of others and a concern for their welfare. Rights and duties are bestowed by membership of a society, and a hypothetical person with no duties could also have no rights. It also seems to me that there is some sort of correlation between rights and duties such that if a person appeals to his or her rights in a particular case, one can also look to the corresponding duties. If there has been a failure in duty then to that extent there may be an amelioration of rights.

If there is some sort of reciprocal relationship between rights and duties for members of a particular social group, and rights and duties only make sense in terms of membership of *a* social group, then this might have some interesting implications in our present context. For it would follow that since God is not a member of *any* social group, God cannot be said to have either duties or rights. Thus, as we have seen, we cannot accuse God of falling down in his duty in not making the world different from the way it is. God is thus not immoral. He does not have a duty towards us. Equally, it follows that we do not have a right to expect the world to be any different from the way it is. But it also follows that, since God has no duties, He does not have a *right* to expect worship and obedience from us. Is that a problem? I do not think so. We can certainly have duties towards those who are not members of our community (hospitality to strangers, for example) and who as such cannot be said to have rights. Thus it seems to me that while God has no right to worship and obedience, we still have a duty of worship and obedience towards God.[13]

I should note in passing another implication of seeing a correlation between rights and duties for members of a particular society. It seems to me that we cannot speak of animals having duties. If we cannot speak of animals having duties then it would seem to follow that we could make no sense of animal *rights*. And if we *can* make sense of animal rights, then correspondingly we should be able to make sense of animal duties and animals failing in their duties, i.e. behaving immorally. And there is another implication of relating rights to duties. It should also follow that we cannot properly speak of the *rights* of the unborn child, or those, for example, in irreversible coma. For neither of these can possess duties. But we ourselves can have *duties* to animals and the unborn child, without animals and the unborn child themselves having rights. We fail in our duty if, for example, we microwave a kitten. We behave appallingly immorally because we have very much fallen down in our duty not to harm the innocent, not because we have infringed the kitten's right not to be hurt. A duty not to harm the innocent is fundamental to being in society, and we are in society. And we can argue that all the behaviour towards animals and foetuses that we wanted to secure with talk of rights can in fact be secured by appealing to our duties. I am influenced here by the way that in classical India the entire social system was also based on duties (*Dharma*) rather than rights. It seems to me preferable to refer to our duty towards e.g. animals, than to speak of the rights of animals. This is because rights are much more difficult to pin down and ground than duties. It is not clear to me what we mean by speaking of animals' 'rights', or from where animals as such could get their rights. But it is possible to see how one might argue that members of a society, as members involved in society, gain *duties*. It seems likely that it would be much easier to argue for our duties as members of a community, or as the sort of beings we are, or as the sort of beings we should want to become (i.e. virtuous) or whatever, than to argue for creatures that are not human, or are not functioning members of our community, or are not able to engage in the duties of members of the community, having *rights*. Thus it ought to be possible to explain how, as human members of the particular group we are members of, we have duties towards animals, the unborn child and people in irreversible coma. We could argue, for example, that we have duties towards weaker members of our own species and other species. Talk of duties is clearly using the language of morality, and the language of morality can only be used of beings that can enter into specifically moral relation-ships. But in that case talk of rights can also only be used of beings that can enter into specifically moral relationships.

Giving primacy to others (after God) requires a complete escape from concern with the importance of personal sensa-tions. It requires a complete transcendence of the egoistic circle that privileges consciousness, experiences and approved sensa-tions. In the last analysis I suspect that such a complete transcendence, which securely bases morality on duties and responsibilities and thus provides a framework for appeal to rights, can only come from a complete switch from self to Other. This Other is expressed in the will of God. Christianity exists for God. It all begins and ends, not in humanity, not in happiness, but in God, the Other.

The many Buddhist strategies for mind-transformation

Once we take it as axiomatic that what religion is all about is the transformation of the mind from greed, hatred and delusion into their opposites, it seems obvious that what is religiously most important in day-to-day terms is *becoming a nicer person*. This too is central to the message of the Dalai Lama. In concrete practical terms religion is about goodness, kindness. Few people are willing to disagree, for who could disagree with virtue?

Buddhists often state that one of the great contributions that Buddhism can make to this project is its vast array of strategies for mind-transformation. Buddhism has many meditation techniques, practices and teachings, all with this one aim in mind – to make people nicer and eventually also fully happy, enlightened beings. 'All the teachings of the Buddha have one flavour, that of liberation', as one Buddhist text has it. Followers of other religions, while not needing themselves to become Buddhists, can learn from Buddhists, adding to their own religious practices Buddhist techniques of, for example, meditation.

But it seems to me we need to be careful that in doing this we do not accept uncritically the presuppositions of the Buddhist rhetoric in their advocacy. We can question the obviousness of the axiom that what religion is all about is the transformation of the mind, and that in day-to-day terms what is important is becoming a nicer person. We can also question the idea that Buddhism is superior to other religions in its vast array of strategies for transforming the mind. For all of this is based on the assumption of the *Buddhist* vision of what religion is all about, and therefore the Buddhist vision of how to go about achieving those aims.

The Buddhist presupposition tends to be that mind-transformation in the appropriate way is something *one brings about*, pre-eminently through working on one's own mind in the solitary privacy of meditation. In my experience Buddhist rituals, for example, are themselves approached in the spirit of meditation (as in the case of Tibetan tantric rituals) and are therefore, in the last analysis, even though communal, subordinate to the goal of personal, private transformation through the appropriate experiences. The individual who has undergone the appropriate experiences, that is, who has transformed the mind, of course then expresses that fact outwardly in care and concern, benefiting others, as did the Buddha himself. But one works first and foremost on oneself to bring about the appropriate experiences. Thus when the Buddhist says that Buddhism has a superior array of mind-transformation techniques, it is within this framework that he or she is speaking. Since e.g. the parallels in Christianity are identified with Christian meditation, it is commonly taken by those who would adopt this approach that the people who are really articulating what (the Christian) religion is all about are therefore Christian meditators, contemplative monks and nuns, or the so-called 'mystics'.[14]

What Christian mystics are engaged in, it is thought, is broadly the same project as that of the Buddhists: mind-transformation aimed at becoming a nicer person, and finally some sort of 'enlightenment' through the appropriate experiences. Indeed, there are those who would want to argue that this is what all religions are really about. And as regards the essence of each religion – the appropriate mystical experiences, usually expressed as nonconceptual and nondual experiences – all religions are really saying the same thing.

But it seems to me that much of this could be questioned and is of doubtful value in approaching Christianity.

If we read the New Testament we do not find any clear suggestion that Jesus had the sort of experiences commonly thought of as 'mystical experiences': feelings of loss of self, nondual absorption or oneness with the universe, experiences of divine bliss, visions of God, radiance, or whatever. Nor did He base His message on the centrality of particular supranormal experiences or sensations. We read that Jesus prayed to God. Others saw Him in light conversing with ancient prophets. He spoke to God as to a Father. He spoke of His oneness with God. He spoke as one with authority. But there is not much on His *mind*, or His experiences, as such. And we find no clear description of experiences like those associated with the great mystics of the world religions. Jesus simply does not speak of meditation or advocate the way of a mystic for His followers. His message seems to have been one of salvation for all, associated with repentance and newness of life – an essentially moral behavioural transformation – not with skill in meditation for a small capable elite.

And it is simply not true that all religions are saying the same thing, either in their doctrines or practices. Nor is this true on the level of the experiences associated with being a Christian, being a Buddhist, being a pagan, or being a shaman. The fact that a certain minority of members of each major religion – 'mystics' – speak in common of an overwhelming, inexpressible experience that they each identify with the focus of their religion (God, emptiness, or whatever) does not entail that they each experienced the same thing. Let alone does it entail that this experience is the essence of the religion, what it is really all about. To say this is to deny the very differences between religions that actually form the identities of the religions that most members follow and value. It is those differences that contribute to the essences of the religions, in any meaningful sense of 'essence'. The alternative is to say that the majority of members of a religion do not understand what their religion is really all about. Those who would seek the identity of all religions in a nondual, nonconceptual and inexpressible experience end up adopting a position that embodies a considerable degree of intolerance, intolerance of what believers themselves say about their own religions.

If two people say that they have each had an experience of X and that it was nondual, nonconceptual and inexpressible, they precisely have said nothing as such about either X or the experience of X. The experience of X has no content. Thus they cannot say that both experiences were of the same thing. That would be a contradiction. They can, of course, attempt to say that they are the same type of experience, but only on the basis that both were expressed – conceptualised – as experiences, nondual, nonconceptual and inexpressible. They are both the same type of experience inasmuch as they are members of a class of experiences that lack all content, even the content that will allow them to be called experiences. To claim that this is the essence of all religions, and that it is conceptualised in different ways depending on cultural expectations, seems to me vaguely absurd. Those who would read Christianity this way are precisely adopting a model derived from a particular understanding of certain forms of Buddhism, or perhaps of the Hindu Advaita Vedānta. That this is the essence of all religions expresses their *faith* – and it is a rival faith to Christianity as it has existed in history and orthodoxy.

The founders of each religion do not all agree in a nonconceptual experience. They do not each hold that this experience articulates the essence of what they are trying to say. It is simply not true on any level that what the Buddha taught and what Christ or Mohammed – or the pagan, or the shaman – taught is essentially the same, expressed differently simply due to different cultural contexts. Indeed, if there is one feature in which the Buddha, Jesus and Mohammed do agree, it is that what they taught was precisely not in accordance with cultural contexts and expectations. Each in their different way taught something radically unexpected and challenging. As the Buddha put it, his teaching 'went against the current'. Mohammed had to fight. Jesus got Himself killed.

In the case of Christianity all this is what we would expect, given Jesus' Jewish background. Judaism at that time was not a religion of mystical experiences. It was a religion of covenant with God. Prophets recalled those thus covenanted back to their commitments and appropriate communal behaviour such as ritual purity. In spite of what is sometimes thought, this return to ritual purity and the strict requirements of the covenant was precisely the principal concern of the contemporary Essene community responsible (if they were) for the Dead Sea scrolls. Meditation was also part of their practice, but meditation understood not as a quest for direct experiences of God ('no human being can see me and survive': Exodus 33:20). 'Meditation' here, from Hebrew *hagah*, or *siyach*, both words also relating to speaking or uttering ('murmurs [King James version: 'meditate'] his law day and night': Psalm 1:2), meant study of the *Torah*, the Hebrew scriptures, and its understanding and application to historical events. Meditation, as in the Hebrew Bible, also meant considering, pondering, the greatness and works of God. It would have been very surprising in such a world to find Jesus lauding nonconceptual mystical experiences of God Himself. Well, much that Jesus said was indeed surprising. But advocating nonconceptual mystical experiences was not one of those.

If we think about it, what could be an experience of God? Could there really be an experience of God as He is in Himself? How could any created being have such an experience? Those who speak like this can have no idea what they are talking about. No created being can have any idea what it would be like to be or even to experience God as He is in Himself. Words cease to have any meaning. And I do not mean words cease to have any meaning because this experience would be beyond all language, all conceptuality, or whatever. What I mean is that no created being could have that experience. There could be no such experience. Anyone who thinks it could be possible to experience God as He is in Himself cannot be speaking of God. They do not know what God is.

And what concerns me is precisely the absence of God in our 'Buddhist' vision of what Christianity is all about. God as He is in Himself cannot be experienced, or be an experience. God, as He actually is, is therefore omitted altogether. The presupposition is that of the centrality of experiences, and as experiences these are thought of as coming from one's own volition. The meditator *brings about* the meditative experience. God becomes incidental, or disposable, if not of 'practical benefit' in bringing about the desired experiences. Thus the Dalai Lama tells us:

> There are many different religions in this world. Each of them has its own special qualities, its own unique way of presenting the spiritual path. We Tibetans chose Buddhism as our national religion. Buddhism is an especial tasty and profound religion because it is not a path of faith but a path of reason and knowledge. Buddha himself stated that his doctrine should be accepted not on faith but only in the light of reason and logical inquiry. ... Had Buddha not relied upon truth in his teachings, were his teachings mere superstition, he would not have advised us to critically judge his words in this way. Instead, he would have given us a dogma like, 'Believe what I say or else you will come to experience misery'. ... Many religions begin with the idea of a God ... Although this is an easy answer, it is not logically proveable [sic]. Therefore Buddha avoided it and tried to present a doctrine that in every way could be established through reason. ... By

> avoiding the use of the God-theory, Buddha also avoided the many
> problematic side-effects that come with it. . . . [R]eligions based on
> the 'God-theory' usually do not permit rejection of the 'Words of
> God', even should they contradict all reason. This can very easily
> stunt the growth of philosophical enquiry. . . . Buddha tried to
> present a path based purely on reason, and a path expressed solely
> in terms of human problems and human goals.[15]

This, I think, sums up a great deal of what I have been trying to
say in this book about why I came to question the Buddhist
approach. It is indeed an honest expression of the Dalai Lama's
personal perspective, and as his personal perspective it has not
changed over the years. Here it is taken from a relatively early
work given originally in Tibetan to Tibetan refugees in Delhi
and published in India. It is described as representing 'the direct
and personal nature with which His Holiness communicates
with his people'.[16]

But I have argued for the rationality of belief in God (the
actual existence of God, not just adopting the 'God-theory'). I
have argued that if the Buddhist is rational in not believing in
God, the theist is equally rational in believing in God. If the
theist is subject to 'faith' in opting for the necessary being, the
Buddhist is also subject to faith in saying that the way things
are simply has no final explanation. If the theist is subject to
'blind faith' in adopting God and not questioning his or her
upbringing and cultural adherence to God, or subjecting it to
minimal questioning, it seems to me that the Buddhist is also
subject to blind faith. For just as often the Buddhist too tends
not to question his or her upbringing and cultural adherence to
there not being a God, or subjects it to minimal questioning.

The Christian presuppositions are the exact opposite of those
enshrined in our quotation from the Dalai Lama. That should
be enough for the Christian to question the Buddhist approach
here and therefore to question whether it is simply a matter of
Buddhism having more strategies for mind-transformation,
strategies that can merely be taken over by the Christian
without commitment. The fundamental Christian presupposition is that what religion is all about is not experiences. What
Christianity (and Judaism and Islam) is all about is *God*, and
God's approach to humanity. Not the Dalai Lama's irrational,

superstitious 'God-theory' which stunts philosophical enquiry, but the living God. God's approach to humanity is called 'grace', and inasmuch as Christianity favours virtue and condemns vice, inasmuch as Christianity looks for mind-transformation from a sin-filled mind to a virtuous mind and the acts that flow from that mind, for the Christian this transformation is initiated by God in grace. The recipient does not at all bring it about through strategies aimed at directly changing the mind, strategies that for the Buddhist are really based on theistic superstition and a fear of rational enquiry. If we start by thinking that what is important are particular sorts of experiences, then we may indeed eventually decide to adopt the direct experiential way of Buddhism. In presupposing with the Buddhist the primacy of experiences, the 'Buddhist' approach will, I fear, lose God altogether.

The fact that Christianity here starts with God and grace is, of course, one reason why those nowadays who have difficulty with the concept of God are inclined to switch to a religion like Buddhism that starts from a very different point and that promises direct, practical, experiential benefits. But we need to be clear about the magnitude of that switch. It is the presence of God in Christianity that makes Christianity so often the exact opposite of Buddhism. And God is not some sort of bolt-on optional extra. It is not that basically, fundamentally, Buddhism and Christianity are alike, with Christianity adding something called 'God' (the Dalai Lama's 'God-theory') which Buddhists consider that, on balance for practical reasons, they are better off without. The presence of God, God Himself, is what Christianity is all about. God pervades Christianity as He does all things. In the light of God, even those aspects of Christianity that seem similar to Buddhism are really quite different. There is no avoiding the choice.

Thus it is not simply a matter of the glory of Buddhism being that it has many strategies for transforming the mind. The Christian presupposition of God coming to humanity in grace, rather than the meditator working on his or her own mind, is naturally reflected in Christian *practice*. I used to think that Buddhism scored over Christianity in its stress on the actual personal experience of what it teaches. I used to think that, compared with Buddhist meditation sessions, church services

71

somehow missed the point. How could all this standing in draughty buildings singing hymns really reach the Truth, compared with going within in meditation and the experiences that engendered?

I suspect that this has been a common experience among those ex-Christians in the West who converted to Buddhism. But all of this presupposes the Buddhist orientation outlined above, and not that of Christianity. Why should God be found in meditation? Why cannot God be found in draughty churches while singing hymns? If we hold that God is not an experience and that God comes to us – we do not, cannot, force Him – then it seems clear that 'finding God' is not what it is presupposed to be in our 'Buddhist' account. In fact, for the Christian finding God is finding His Church and doing what He requires of us. This means that one is said to have found God if, paradigmatically, one loves and worships God in the prescribed way and manner, treats one's neighbours as oneself, and so on.

This worshipping God in the prescribed manner and so on is 'having faith'. *That* is what finding God is. 'Having faith' is not simply saying casually, 'I believe *X*', or Y, or Z. Thus again we see that for the Christian finding God is not a matter of experiences as such, but is a matter of communal behaviour. Of course this includes prayer and perhaps contemplation, meditation. And of course, we are also promised that this will include *post mortem* experiences of God. One cannot be in a perfect relationship with God and one's fellows, and see God as He is, without involving experiences. But none of it is a matter of the primacy of experiences as such.

> I seek no more experiences, but only to do your will, O Lord, my God and Saviour. And how can I do even that? Who then am I to seek experiences of You?

I have been told by a Christian friend that the problem with my approach here is that I downgrade the importance of the search for perfection and holiness. Why, however, should it be thought that I am doing that? I agree entirely with the document of Vatican II, *Lumen Gentium*, which tells us that 'all the faithful, whatever their condition or state, are called by the Lord, each in his own way, to that perfect holiness whereby the Father Himself is perfect'.[17] But in what does holiness and perfection lie? The same Vatican II document tells us that holiness 'is expressed in multiple ways by those individuals who, in their walk of life, strive for the perfection of charity, and thereby help others to grow'.[18] And:

> Each must apply himself constantly to prayer, self-denial, active brotherly service, and the exercise of all the virtues. For charity, as the bond of perfection and the fulfillment of the law ... rules over all the means of attaining holiness, gives life to them, and makes them work. Hence it is the love of God and of neighbor which points out the true disciple of Christ.[19]

In other words, the call to holiness and perfection is a call to particular types of behaviour, a way of living, which springs from ever-increasing union with and conformity to the will of Christ.[20] It is for us a way of being in the world, in the community, with others – a mode of virtue – not the privacy of experiences. And this is what we should expect, for it corresponds with ideas of perfection and holiness in the Bible and the early Church. In the Hebrew Bible holiness (Hebrew: *qodesh*, associated with God's difference, His set-apartness) is pre-eminently an attribute of God, not of humankind. It can be used of others, like Israel itself, inasmuch as others share in that set-apartness through association with God, and this sharing is seen in purity of behaviour, faithfulness to the covenant. Perfection[21] is an attribute of completeness, wholesomeness, lacking impairment, or moral uprightness. This is reflected also in the crucial verse of the New Testament, Matthew 5:48, 'You must therefore be perfect, just as your heavenly Father is perfect' (cf. Matthew 19:21). The Greek here is *teleios*, related to *telos*, the end, as that which has come to its end, which has reached its natural aim and is therefore complete. One should be what one was meant to be, as Aristotle would have it, in 'conformity to the divine ideal'.[22] Clement of Alexandria, writing in about 195 CE, glosses Matthew 5:48 with 'One does this by forgiving sins, forgetting injuries, and living in the habit of passionlessness.' And elsewhere, 'As I conceive it, sanctity is perfect pureness of mind, deeds, thoughts and words. In its last degree, it is sinlessness in dreams.' For: 'Abstinence from sins is not sufficient for perfection, unless a person also assumes the work of righteousness – activity in doing good'.[23] Nowhere in these early texts do we find any suggestion that perfection and holiness as Christian goals are primarily matters of particular types of private experiences. They are only too obviously matters of public behaviour. We find the same in a medieval thinker like Aquinas:

> [P]erfection [*sanctitas*] in Christian life consists primarily in the love of charity, and secondarily in the other virtues. . . . [It] consists essentially in charity: primarily in the love of God and secondarily in the love of our fellowmen as prescribed by the commandments of God's law. Perfection then consists essentially in obeying God's commands. But it also makes use of God's counsels as instruments of perfection.[24]

This communal and behavioural understanding of holiness and perfection should be contrasted with the post-Kantian subjectivism of Rudolf Otto (d. 1937). His concern in his book *The Idea of the Holy* is with an experience, a sense of 'the holy', of a *mysterium tremendum et fascinans*, found in all religions. This is a feeling of mystery, awe and fear which yet draws one on and in. The holy relates to humanity as a supernatural experience. We can see the same subjectivism at play in William James (d. 1910), who speaks of

> a sense of reality, a feeling of objective presence, a perception of what we may call 'something there', more deep and more general than any of the special and particular 'senses' by which the current psychology supposes existent realities to be originally revealed.[25]

The holy has become a cross-cultural, cross-religious category of experience. The essence of our meeting with and conformity to holiness has become private sensations, weird feelings, found across the religious spectrum. As worthwhile experiences their actual origins – God, meditation, breathing exercises, or drugs – become unimportant.

It seems to me this is, as such, nothing to do with the Christian call to perfection and holiness.

For Christian tradition, one who truly finds God is indeed transformed from sinfulness to virtue, although being human he or she has a tendency to fall back into sin again. Having found God, returning again and again to God in gratitude for forgiveness and worship, the transformation becomes deeper, the fall less and less. Eventually through God's grace one is fit for perfection, a perfection which expresses itself in *virtue*. The Christian view is that all this is indeed only through God's unmerited grace, to which one responds in gratitude. We don't have to bring about paranormal feelings. We don't have to have mystical experiences. This is, incidentally, something Shinran would very much have sympathised with.

Among the implications of all this is that the sort of strategies for mind-transformation that would be envisaged by the Christian are precisely the sort of strategies which, as a matter of fact, we find in Christian practice. They include the sacraments, especially attending Mass and the Sacrament of Reconciliation (confession), prayer, worship and so on. They may also include meditation and contemplation – as means of coming to know and love God and to follow His wishes all the more – but not necessarily. Thus once we see how the Christian is approaching these issues it simply does not follow that the Buddhist has more strategies for mind-transformation than the Christian. What is to count as a 'strategy for mind-transformation' – or for spiritual growth – depends upon the nature of the religion itself, and its vision of its goal.

Moreover it also does not follow that as a result of its many strategies Buddhism is more effective at 'mind-transformation' than Christianity. How effective strategies are will depend upon the goal of the strategies. Christians need to be very careful not to assimilate uncritically the presuppositions of Buddhist meditation, particularly as these presuppositions can often seem to coincide with the rather self-obsessed experiential orientation of much of contemporary culture.

Christians have traditionally thought of the ultimate goal not in terms of experiences as such, but in terms of a relationship of love between God and His people, and between His people themselves. This relationship is essentially dualistic. When erotic imagery is employed, as it is sometimes, the image used is that of the Church as the bride of Christ. This is a very early image in Christianity (see Ephesians 5:25, 27). Once we abandon the search for weird experiences we find God in *love* and *the Mass*. Love is not as such a sensation. All lovers know that such sensations are very short-lived. Rather, love is a way of being with an other, with others, in community. It is a way of dwelling together, each in the light of the other, a way of caring. That is where we find God. That *is* God. And thereby we live in the light of God.

Mother Teresa did not think that through love to those who were abandoned by others she would come to see God. She did not do good works with a goal in mind of seeing God, perhaps after death in heaven. Nor (as far as I know) did she go off after tending to a dying child and have mystical experiences of God. Tending to a dying child was neither a preparation for, nor an interruption in, her experiences of God. The experience of seeing God was not the ultimate goal of her compassion at all. Rather, her love towards the disadvantaged *was* her meeting with God, God under the aspect of the disadvantaged, and flowed from the fact that she had already found God. What other way of meeting God is there for us, except under some such aspect? As far as we are concerned that *is* the goal. And in the mode of *post mortem* existence, or perhaps in prayer, no doubt we can and shall meet God under another aspect.

Cardinal Hume, when asked what he had found after a lifetime as a monk, observed: 'I suppose a simpler faith. Deeper. Of course it isn't all a cloud of unknowing. God has revealed himself by becoming man.' And asked about prayer: 'Oh, I just keep plugging away. At its best, it's like being in a dark room with someone you love. You can't see them, but you know they're there.'[26] Peter O'Toole, in a film made sometime round about the 1960s, played a person who had decided he was God. Why? Because whenever he prayed he realised that he was speaking to himself (or should it be 'Himself'?).

Can we put our finger on how these two cases differ?

Inasmuch as liberation in Buddhism involves nonduality and nonconceptuality it cannot *in itself* involve any relationship of love, and inasmuch as it involves mental transformation its primary concern cannot be with the other (or indeed the Other, God). If we can speak here of a relationship of love, or use erotic imagery, it could only be love expressed finally in terms of personal experiences, the Great Bliss (*mahāsukha*) of perfect enlightenment spoken of particularly in Buddhist Tantricism. Love here must be reflexive. It turns back on itself

76

in the infinite play of consciousness, the infinite play of experiences.

I wonder if this primacy given to the reflexive play of experiences was what Cardinal Ratzinger (head of the Vatican Congregation for the Doctrine of the Faith) meant when, as I recall, he reportedly referred to Buddhism as 'spiritual auto-eroticism'? That did not go down at all well with Buddhists.

ON THE MORALITY OF THE
POPE'S CRAVING

The Pope, I gather, has a strong desire to see the Church into the new millennium. What is the problem with that?

A Buddhist, I suppose, would call this strong desire in a person who (as a Christian) clearly does not 'see things the way they really are', a craving (*tṛṣṇā*). Such craving is (for the Buddhist) paradigmatically wrong.

But what is so wrong about it?

Well, the Buddhist says, it can only lead eventually to suffering. But is that so obvious? Of course, such a strong desire *could* lead to suffering. It could lead to suffering through its unfulfilment. The Pope might become disappointed. The stronger the desire, the greater the disappointment. Even if that were true, however, would it follow that therefore the strong desire is wrong? All, or most, desires could be disappointed. Strong desires – cravings – could lead to deep disappointment. But to avoid a desire – even a craving – because it could lead to disappointment – even deep disappointment – would seem to be strange. These cravings might be wrong if 'right' and 'wrong' are defined in terms of whether or not they lead to enlightenment. But (apart from the question of our redefinition of 'right' and 'wrong') this would only be a convincing argument if we were first convinced of the paradigmatic rightness of enlightenment. And is it obvious that one's enlightenment is paradigmatically right, when attaining it involves the wrongness of all strong desires?

Perhaps the Pope's strong desire could lead to suffering because he would be inclined to subordinate all around him to fulfilling that desire. Others would become mere means to his all-consuming end. But again, does this follow? It seems to me that immoral exploitation of others in order to fulfil a strong desire is not an inevitable consequence of the strong desire itself. And a strong desire may have praiseworthy consequences. The Pope might take greater care of his health, for example, because of his wish to survive into the twenty-first century. All these consequences are contingent and do not follow from the strong desire, the craving, itself.

But cravings, the Buddhist tells us, nevertheless lead on to suffering because they project future rebirths, and future rebirths in such patently unenlightened people are always subject to *duḥkha* – pain, suffering, frustration and unfulfilment. Thus the Pope will nevertheless suffer for his craving in future lives one way or another.

The exact workings of *karman* – what follows in terms of future consequences from what Buddhists call 'skilful' (*kuśala*) and 'unskilful (*akuśala*) intentions – are said to be something only an omniscient mind, the mind of a Buddha, can comprehend. Only a Buddha knows that the Pope will surely suffer for his craving, if not in this life then in a future life, and how exactly this will come about. The rest must accept it on faith until they themselves see its truth when they too become Buddhas.

But to those of us who are unenlightened it does not seem obvious why this strong desire – this craving – to see the Church into the next millennium should *as such* 'project' (as it were) a future rebirth for the Pope. The craving will be fulfilled, I suppose, after twelve midnight on 24 December 1999 (the next millennium for the Catholic Church begins at the commemoration of Jesus' birth on Christmas Eve). Suppose the Pope's wish is unfulfilled. Suppose he dies at 11.55 p.m. on 24 December. Why should the failure to fulfil that craving lead to rebirth? If reborn, the Pope-rebirth could not then set about fulfilling his craving. If the Pope dies before the craving is fulfilled, that craving will almost certainly *never* be fulfilled for him. This would be the case even if the Pope-rebirth were the same person as the Pope, which for Buddhists is actually not true. Why, therefore, is it part of the nature of things that if an unenlightened person like the Pope dies with a craving which is unfulfilled, that craving as such would project a future rebirth for the Pope?

Well, we can keep asking 'Why?' But questions have to end somewhere. For Christians they end in God, as the answer to questions like 'Why is there something, rather than nothing?' and 'What is the final explanation, the final grounding, for why things are the way they are?' For Buddhists, that craving projects rebirth is nevertheless how it is. It is just the nature of things (*dharmatā*). Things just are ordered that way. And there is nothing wrong, as such, in declaring an end to the questioning at that point.

Desire, for the Buddhist, can easily lead in the unenlightened to craving. Craving leads to suffering, for craving is always going to be bound up with frustration, unfulfilment and impermanence. For the Christian, on the other hand, there is God, in whom all desires find their fulfilment. God is, of course, timeless. He is therefore not subject to impermanence. God is held to be perfect, supremely good, supremely beautiful, supremely merciful, supremely just, supremely loving and loveable. As such He is the very measure of all these qualities. All our desires are for what we consider to be good, or beautiful, or loveable, or whatever. God is the one who is really desired in all our desires, for if we desire good, beauty, love and so on, then it seems arguable that there would be no limit to how much of these we would (or should) desire, given the option. Thus we all really desire the perfection of good, the perfection of beauty, the perfection of love. That is God. He is their final fulfilment. It follows, therefore, that a strong desire for God is, from the Christian perspective, extremely laudable. Indeed a *craving* for God, if it is truly a craving for God and not something thought to be God, is in itself totally appropriate. And a craving for God, in finally achieving that which it craves, finds there complete satisfaction. In God there remains nothing that could separate us from Him. There is nothing remaining in this craving that could project future rebirth.

Here therefore, as so often, we find again that the Christian perspective is the exact opposite of that of the Buddhist. Which is correct? Which is most rational? Which is preferable? Is it obvious?

A BELIEF IN REINCARNATION IS NOT COMPATIBLE WITH BELIEF IN A GOOD AND JUST CREATOR

(A) Supposing there was a good and just Creator. Why should there be more than one life? To give everyone a fair chance? (Compare here one person who says to another, 'I don't like you – go away.' Or 'I hate you, go away.' Or even, 'I really hate you, from the bottom of my heart. Go away.' What would it take for the second person (God) finally to decide to take the first seriously and to acquiesce in the request?) In order to learn various lessons and attain to perfection? How many lives should be given? (i) If a finite number (n), then it would seem that the Creator is unjust in not allowing $n+1$, since the additional life could be the very life in which the lesson, or perfection, or fair chance, is attained. Moreover, the more lives, the more unjust it would seem not to allow $n+1$, since if $n = 10$, then $+1$ = + one tenth, while if $n = 100$, $+1$ = + only one hundredth. On this basis the Creator would thus be good and just to allow only one life, and less good and less just to allow more than one life. Alternatively, (ii) it would seem that the Creator should give a potentially infinite number of lives, i.e. however many lives are necessary in order to learn the lesson(s), to have a full and fair chance, and so on.

(B) But under this alternative, is it known in advance that each series will be actually finite (i.e. every being will eventually attain whatever goal the Creator has decided)? With a potentially infinite series of lives, any one life is potentially infinitely insignificant. Take the case of person X. X learns the lesson/attains the goal after 1000 lives. It must be granted that in each life one has the potential of failing to learn the lesson (any lesson at all). Inasmuch as a life is valuable only in order to learn the lesson etc., only the 1000th life is thus really significant. The other lives simply lack significance. But each life is the life of a *person* and, as different lives, each person is effectively different (even if connected in a causal series). Thus 999 persons lack significance. Alternatively, supposing one learns something soteriologically significant (i.e. relevant to the spiritual goal) in *each* life, it is only soteriologically significant if it is either the goal, or contributes to attaining the goal. Suppose that, in life (*a*), one learns something that means that the final goal is then attained. One needs to live only life (*a*). Suppose on the other hand that one learns in each life something that *contributes* to the attaining of the final goal. Then the person who attains the goal (at the end of the series) is a different person from the one who learns the lesson. Thus the person who learns the lesson is once more only significant in terms of his or her use to another (i.e. the one that finally attains the goal). This is unjust. Supposing the series of lives is infinite. If the series is infinite into the past, then each life with the exception of the one in which a soteriologically significant goal is attained is infinitely insignificant. Suppose that the series is infinite into the future, i.e. X never attains the goal. Then each life of X is finally infinitely insignificant. Thus in the case of X there are an infinite number of persons each infinitely insignificant.

It seems to me that the infinite insignificance of persons, or persons being significant only inasmuch as they contribute to the goal of another person, is not compatible with a good and just Creator.

There is another argument that might also be relevant here. Suppose a person does a very wicked deed. If the result has not occurred in accordance with *karman* by the time that person dies, then the very unpleasant result will almost invariably occur in a future life. Supposing it occurs in the very next life. We have seen already (and can see in more detail in Appendix 1) that the Buddhist position is that because of constant change the rebirth cannot be said to be the same person as the one who died. Thus it seems in fact that one person does the wicked deed and another person (albeit a person connected in some causal way with the first person) gets the unpleasant result. Buddhists do indeed hold that the person I am in this life undergoes experiences which are karmic results of deeds done in previous lives and therefore deeds done by persons that cannot be said to be the same as me. But if that is the case, then to what extent can I be said to be responsible for acts done by persons that are not me? Or suppose that I make a virtuous resolution in this life. Suppose I take the so-called 'bodhisattva vow' to follow the path to full Buddhahood throughout all my future lives for the benefit of all sentient beings. To what extent can one of 'my' future lives be bound by a vow taken by someone who cannot be said to be the same person?

It would seem to be unjust for someone to have unpleasant experiences as a result of something done by someone who cannot be said to be the same person as the one undergoing those experiences. And it would also be unjust for someone to be bound by a vow taken by someone who is not the same person. We do not hold in law that a person can be tried for an offence committed by someone who cannot be said to be the same person as the one undergoing the trial.

Now, as we have seen, 'moral order' is that good deeds produce happiness and bad deeds produce suffering. This is the so-called 'law of *karman*'. Thus, where this moral order involves reincarnation, moral order would seem to be unjust. If there is moral order it either involves injustice or it does not involve reincarnation. Therefore if there were a just God either moral order would be false or reincarnation (on anything like the Buddhist model) would have to be false.

Thus with a good and just God who has ordered things, either moral order, *karman*, would be false, or reincarnation would be false.

The alternative is to go with the Buddhist and argue that there simply is no good and just Creator God. But we have seen already that if we adopt this option we would have to hold that it just happens to be the case that moral order always prevails. We would also have to hold (as indeed the Buddhist does hold) that whether or not it is just, it just happens to be the case that moral order stretches over lifetimes. Thus we would have to argue for both a universal moral order and also a fundamental absence of justice being unexplainably 'the way things are'. This seems to me to be questionable as a satisfactory final explanation. Of course, we have here again reached a bedrock position. I have argued above that I prefer to argue from moral order to an Orderer. And if there were an Orderer who had taken the trouble to introduce moral order into His creation, it seems to me that such an Orderer would be unlikely to be unjust.

Therefore I can conclude again that reincarnation would appear to be incompatible with a good and just Creator.[27]

It seems to me patently obvious that if I am reincarnated (on *any* model of reincarnation) the person I am now in this life ceases to exist. This is blindingly obvious if I am reincarnated as a cockroach in South America. We could not say that I am the same person as a cockroach in South America. Could we any more say I would be the same person if my reincarnation involved a human embryo in Africa? Or in Bristol? And the standard Buddhist position explicitly denies that the reincarnation is the same person as the one who died. Thus reincarnation is incompatible with the infinite value of the person.

It follows from all this that reincarnation would be diametrically opposed to the whole direction of Christianity. If there is survival of death – and the faith of the Christian, originating in Christ's own resurrection, is based on that – it cannot be in terms of reincarnation. Reincarnation and the infinite value of the person are incompatible. This, among other things, is precisely what Jesus' salvific death and resurrection show. On that is based Christian morality. The Christian would say that finally the *only* basis for a coherent morality is the infinite value of the person, and the only basis for that is our origin in God. I am inclined to agree. Arguably, ideologies that undermine the significance of the person, and his or her uniqueness, finally provide a weak foundation for altruism and other forms of moral behaviour.[28]

For the Christian, what the resurrection of the body and the life everlasting means is that nothing of value relevant to our personhood will be lost. We have that promise and on that is based our hope. What this amounts to is up to philosophers and theologians to work out. One thing is clear: if reincarnation is true, our situation, inasmuch as it pertains to each one of us, is hopeless. I prefer hope.

DO WE KNOW WHERE WE ARE GOING?

Tina Quinn is a member of the wonderful RCIA team at Clifton Cathedral, in Bristol. The RCIA is the Rite of Christian Initiation of Adults. It is the programme by which adult enquirers interested in Catholicism are instructed in the faith. Although it is made clear that there is no commitment to becoming a Catholic simply in attending the meetings, it is very much a programme in catechetics. A Buddhist, for example, interested simply in finding out about Catholicism ('getting to know your Catholic neighbour') I suspect might feel very uncomfortable. But for me, when I finally started attending the RCIA meetings I was sure of what I intended to do.

Tina is my sponsor. Those enquirers who are seriously interested in becoming Catholics at some time in the future are given a sponsor. The sponsor is one's very own Friendly Face. She is someone to whom I can go with particular queries and observations, someone who will offer prayers in and for one's quest. The sponsor also has a particular ritual role to play, presenting the enquirer to the community at the Rite of Acceptance, which takes place at a Sunday Mass, when one formally declares one's intention eventually of becoming a Catholic and is accepted and offered support by the community. This particular stress on the communal dimension, the extended family of the Church, is very much a response to the changes introduced into the Catholic Church by Vatican II, the great Council in the 1960s that sought to modernise the Church and to which the Church is still responding. Vatican II is also responsible for the increasing – indeed central – role in the life of the local church played by the laity and by women. I very much like the feeling of being a member of a great visible and invisible family. The feeling of group support is very strong.

And unlike the Buddhism I am familiar with in this country, being a Catholic is not mainly an interest of a fluctuating group of the 'educated white middle class'. Once, I would have found this limited appeal understandable and a positive feature of Buddhism when compared with Christianity. Of course (I would have said) the final truth of things could not properly be appreciated by those without a good level of education, without a certain philosophical sensitivity. Few in this life really have that ability. Christianity is precisely a religion for the simple masses. As a Buddhist I thought that Christianity's main merit lay in its teaching of goodness, even though many Christians in history – missing the essence of their religion, I suppose – have, alas, been rather wicked. For the simple masses goodness will ensure that they gain favourable rebirths. In another life, when they are cleverer, they may well seek more deeply and more profoundly and come to Buddhism. There is no urgency.

This is why the Dalai Lama is so willing to encourage people to remain Christians. He repeatedly states that he has no interest in converting people from Christianity to Buddhism. This is why he is keen to stress the moral dimensions of Christianity (and other religions) that involve doing good, and why he is keen to downplay doctrinal differences with Buddhism as inessential and unimportant.

I remember many years ago my friend and former colleague, the Catholic philosopher Denys Turner, expressing his view of what heaven might be. It would be where we would all sit down in harmony and eat together. Even then I found that a wonderful image, redolent of the mass, of democracy, of love, of the community. But surely it must be just a metaphor for popular consumption? There is no great table in the sky. It is far from what Buddhists mean by *nirvāṇa*, or by Buddhahood. In India, where the structures of caste-dominated community are so strong, those who seek for final enlightenment tend to see it as the end of all rebirth, precisely, in the last analysis, the end of all communal involvement and (thereby?) all suffering. The seeker after enlightenment is usually one who renounces society and wanders forth 'from home to homelessness'. As I have argued, enlightenment is portrayed as involving finally not community but self-contained isolation. Final perfection lies in no dependence on others, no relationships.

Who is right? The inherent elitism of the Indian model worries me. But that does not make it false. Still, why shouldn't heaven be where we all sit down in harmony and eat together? Suppose it could be like that, with no suffering (such as indigestion or boredom with your fellow guests) ever involved. Would that be preferable to a timeless self-contained isolation, free of all pain?

Early in our six months of RCIA instruction we were discussing the lack of interest of many people (at least in the West) in much beyond this life. If we view life as a journey (the image we had been encouraged to use in our instruction), where are we going? Well, there is no reason why we should view life as a journey. To do so rather begs the question. Perhaps we are not going anywhere. But it is an image that is not unacceptable for a Buddhist. Buddhists often speak of 'wandering through the cycles of rebirth'. Where the Christian thinks of a journey from this life to eternity, the Buddhist uses the image of 'wandering'. The series of rebirths is infinite. It has no beginning, although it has a potential end in *nirvāṇa*, or in Buddhahood. In the infinite series of rebirths, known as *saṃsāra*, we *wander*.

Where, then, are we going?

Tina said confidently and with a smile that she knew where she was going.

Her assurance impressed me. I envied her. After more than twenty years as a Buddhist I had no idea where I was going, or even if it makes any sense to talk of 'going' at all. Part of the reason for that is doctrinal. The exact workings out of *karman* are complicated. They are said to be so complicated that only an omniscient Buddha understands them fully. It is perfectly possible, because of the complex causal patterns involved, for a person to be eminently virtuous in this life and to obtain a very unfavourable rebirth next time round. All we can be reasonably sure of is that the virtuous deeds will *eventually* produce happiness. But in that case, to whom will they produce happiness? It seems that as the series of rebirths gets further away, any even residual sense of the results happening to *me* recedes further and further. Thus, suppose I spend all my life being virtuous. Still, the person born in the next life cannot be said to be the same person as me, and may or may not be happy. All this is perfectly consistent with mainstream Buddhist doctrine.

Under such circumstances, do I know where I am going? It seems I am going nowhere.

But even on a more 'popular' reading of reincarnation, I cannot really say that I know where I am going. I do not know which of the causal factors will predominate at the time of

86

death, so I have no idea what type of rebirth I shall have next time round. I can hope, but I really have no grounds for assurance.

After my worries about the Buddhist idea of rebirth I have found little difficulty in embracing the Christian hope. Perhaps this too shows that I never really was a Buddhist. Deep down I was always a Christian. I am not sure whether I am entitled at this stage to say I know where I am going. But I have a much clearer idea of the possibilities. Wish fulfilment? I hope so.

TOGETHER FOREVER?

Sharon has raised another matter for concern. The Christian position is that husband and wife are united in 'one flesh'. What happens after death if one partner has chosen the offer of salvation and the other rejects it?

First thoughts

What can we say? Being of one flesh does not mean that husband and wife are literally of one mind (thank God!). Both have free will. One can freely choose salvation and the other reject it. That is all there is to it. Is that a tragedy?

But what are we to say of the love of the one partner for the other? Is it not the case that the eternal happiness of the partner who is saved would be blighted by the loss of his or her 'other half'? Surely this only appears to be the case because we have not fully appreciated what heaven is. We grow in greater and greater perfection, approximating more and more to what God requires of us. The partner who chooses to reject God's offer of love rejects also that growth. The two partners part, each for that which he or she has freely chosen, and really wants. The love of the one that loves God embraces his or her partner in the love of God, and in God finds all fulfilment. If the other freely chooses otherwise then the ecstasy of the embrace is rejected. But the embrace of God is not diminished thereby.

In some respects there is no difference here from Buddhism. For in the Buddhist case too, after death husband and wife are likely to be parted. The marriage bond is dissolved. Their love, in any real sense, cannot survive the trauma of death. That is why human love from a Buddhist point of view is ultimately *duḥkha*, suffering, frustration.

Of course, most people nowadays seem to think death is the end anyway. Then all relationships simply cease.

The Christian offers in Christ hope that husband and wife can be united for ever enfolded in God's love, in which there can be no loss but only perfect fulfilment.

In the bleak midwinter a star shows the way.

Second thoughts

Now, some time later, I am not so sure. I think in the original comments I was preoccupied with the significance of the free choice. I still am. But I have to admit that there are other ways of looking at it. Free choice is central, but so is love. And God is love.

If the two partners truly love each other, surely they will remain in love to the end, throughout all adversity that might split them apart. If they remain really in love even though one holds a very different vision of the world and his or her place in it from the other, then I feel (I hope) they shall not be parted. They will be together throughout all eternity. Love is itself eternity. The choice at marriage for those who truly love is a choice for eternity.

If something like that is correct, then what now can we say? If the one is saved the other must be saved also, not through their own choice but in spite of it, through the choice of their partner. The one has not made the choices that lead to salvation. The other has. And yet they truly love each other and have remained in love. If the one who has 'chosen life' (as the Bible puts it) is saved through the grace of God, and if the very being of the one who is saved is bound up with that of his or her partner, then it must follow that the partner is saved also. For the grace of God cannot be thwarted. Thus it follows that love triumphs over even the choice, the choice to follow the path of salvation or not. Finally, love is supreme. It is love that is truly redemptive.

And what of others with whom we have a real relationship of mutual love? Is it possible that through love we can perhaps redeem others too, not just our marriage partners? Maybe that is one aspect of the real significance of love.

I like this way of looking at it. I have no idea whether it is correct or not. But there is optimism about it that I associate with Christianity. It also means that my Catholicism should be approached with even greater seriousness, since I am practising for two (or perhaps more). I am happy to leave it at that, in the hands of a merciful and just God, who is Love Itself.

CAN WENSLEYDALE BE SAVED?

Little Lamb, who made thee?
Dost thou know who made thee?
Gave thee life, and bid thee feed
By the stream and o'er the mead;
Gave thee clothing of delight,
Softest clothing, woolly, bright;
Gave thee such a tender voice,
Making all the vales rejoice?
Little Lamb, who made thee?
Dost thou know who made thee?

(William Blake, 'The Lamb')

There are those who think that 'the Christian view' is that animals do not have souls. Thus animals cannot be saved and there will be no animals in heaven. This view is attributed to some form of human species chauvinism and traced back to the Bible where, it is alleged, animals were created *for* humans and thus subjected to them. Hence occur meat eating, animal experimentation, fox hunting and other forms of cruelty to animals.[29]

Tārā says she doesn't want to go to a heaven where there are no animals. She also says it is cruel to our cats, Wensleydale and Larry, who are very much a loved part of our family. Buddhism is much kinder to animals, since it at least offers them the chance of improving their condition through reincarnation and even finally becoming enlightened Buddhas.

I used to worry about this issue too sometimes. We are, after all, English.

But let us be clear. The Christian view is *not* that animals do not have souls. There is no one Christian view on the subject. Clearly, whether animals have souls or not depends on a prior understanding on what 'souls' are supposed to be. Christians have traditionally been vague on this, perhaps intentionally so. The Aristotelian view, which has been so influential on medieval thinking on the subject, holds that the 'soul' is simply the principle of life in living creatures. As such, a soul is something a human has – but also a plant or a cat – which a stone does not have. That is all. For Aristotle a cabbage is alive, but clearly it is different from a cat like Wensleydale (even when Wensleydale is asleep). Thus the principle of life in a cabbage is not the same as the principle of life in Wensleydale. A cabbage has what Aristotle called 'a vegetative soul'. Wensleydale has an 'animal soul'. Thus a cat *does* have a soul. In the same way a human, while also alive, has features such as (pre-eminently) imagination and a high degree of rationality that distinguish him or her from Wensleydale (even when awake) in much the same way as Wensleydale is distinguished from a cabbage. A human, therefore, has a 'human soul'.

A Christian Aristotelian like Aquinas – but not Aristotle himself – considered that certain souls, i.e. human souls, have something about them that enables them (through the will of God) to survive the death of the physical body. Aquinas does not think, however, that the survival of the soul after death is what we mean by 'the survival of the individual person', since the individual person is composed both of the physical body and the soul which gives it life. The *post mortem* survival of the soul means simply that with death the story is not yet over for the individual concerned. True survival of the individual person requires survival in some way both of the soul and of the body. Hence, eventually, the resurrection of the body.

Notice that there is no commitment here to what the soul actually *is*. It is simply the principle of life, which is capable of surviving the death of the body. It makes no sense to talk, as some books do, of Buddhism denying the existence of the soul. That all depends on what the soul is supposed to be. Buddhists certainly do not deny that something gives life to a living body. We are not really all dead matter. What Buddhism denies is the *Self*, understood broadly as one separate, unchanging referent for the word 'I'. One candidate for the soul is the mind or consciousness (and the mind too is not denied by Buddhists), but that is only *one* candidate. This option was adopted by Descartes. Descartes held that the mind is both the soul and the true Self. But this was not the view of Aquinas. Christian theology – even the forms of theology that follow Aquinas most closely – is not committed to the soul as the mind, nor (I think) to the soul as the Self, nor certainly to the soul as some sort of 'stuff' totally independent from the body. Indeed, it is not clear to me that Christian theology is committed to a soul as such at all. The only commitment here is to death not being the end of the story for the living person concerned, and (in Aquinas) to the reason for this having something to do with the *post mortem* survival of the essential principle that gives the body life.

Let me underline for my Buddhist friends what I am saying here, because I think this point is not always properly appreciated. It seems to me that Christian theology is not committed to *any* position on the existence or otherwise of the Self, as it is understood and specifically negated in Buddhism. It also seems to me that Christian theology is not committed as such to any position on the existence or otherwise of a specific metaphysical and intrinsically separable thing called a soul. As far as I know the New Testament make no mention either of the Self or the soul in any necessarily metaphysical sense. Where a term is used that is sometimes translated as 'soul',[30] it seems to me the concept employed is without specific metaphysical commitment. It usually means in this context little more than simply 'oneself'. At least, Christian theology does not need any metaphysical commitment in its use of the corresponding Greek and Hebrew terms.[31] What Christian theology is committed to is the supreme importance of the person, you and me, as embodied living beings created by God in His own image. This importance is such that even death cannot negate it. We are born for an eternal destiny, and this eternal destiny is bound up with our origins, as created in God's image, and our potential. Whether this necessarily entails a Self or a soul is still open. Historically the Christian tradition has been influenced in its treatment of these topics by certain Hellenistic and post-Hellenistic teachings concerning a soul, embedding the value of the person and survival after death in the existence of an identifiable something called a 'soul'. But there is no necessary connection between Christianity and these teachings (let alone any Buddhist notions of a 'Self'). One perfectly orthodox Christian view of the soul is that it is simply 'the spiritual element of a person's nature'.[32] As such, the soul could be a disposition or potential rather than a thing, the disposition or potential to act in certain ways, for example. If that were the case, of course, then the soul would be a property of persons, and totally dependent upon them for its existence. This too would be compatible with Aristotle and Aquinas, and also very compatible with the traditional Christian treatment of the soul. The Christian believes that through the triumph of Jesus over death in His own resurrection, death is not the end of the story for the person I am and you are. The Christian may choose to reject various views of a Self, or the soul, as incompatible with this orientation. And it also seems to me that the Buddhist denial of the *ātman* (the Self) tends to be interpreted in Buddhism in ways that cannot preserve personal identity, particularly through death. Thus the traditional Buddhist treatment is almost certainly incompatible with Christianity. But the Christian need not adopt any position on the existence of a soul or Self as such. These need not be the only ways of explaining the infinite value and spiritual potential of the person, and the fact that death is not the end of the story for the person we are.

Can Wensleydale go to heaven? Traditionally that would depend in part on whether (if we employ the Aristotelian terminology) animal souls, as well as human souls, survive death, and also what we mean by 'heaven'. Aquinas would say that *no* soul as such survives death. God wishes human souls to survive death because that is bound up with His intentions for His creation. Human souls and their survival have something to do with their origin, but this is significant mainly because of their potential. Humans, we are told in the Bible, are made in the image of God. This means that certain features of God, such as a higher degree of rationality, goodness, love and so on, are real possibilities for humans. Moreover, in Christ God became human, reconciling humanity to God. Because of this meeting point between God and humanity, humans have the oppor- tunity, by virtue of their rationality, free choice, capacity for love and morality and so on, for eternal life in a perfect loving relationship with God, who is a timeless Good. That is what heaven is. Heaven is not (except metaphorically) a place that might be boring because it has no cats.[33]

The features of capacity for a high degree of rationality, free choice, love and morality and so on are precisely the features that characterise a human soul. Animals do not appear to have them (or at least, not to the extent and in the ways required), and this lack is emphasised by Scripture. We do not find that God reconciled Himself to cats by becoming a cat. And Christ gave no teaching on the salvation of cats. To think that cats might be saved, therefore, would seem as far as we can tell to show a misunderstanding of what salvation is all about. Thus it would seem that animals cannot attain heaven. Even humans cannot attain heaven simply by virtue of having these capacities. They have to actualise the capacities in certain specified ways, responsive to the grace of God freely offered to all (humans).[34]

Poor Wensleydale. But then, she should not feel too upset. In the schools of the twelfth century, apparently, there was also some discussion as to whether *archdeacons* could be saved![35]

Of course, if animals *do* turn out to have the requisite capacities, then presumably animals would in theory have the option of doing what is necessary in order to be saved. There is nothing to stop God saving animals (or indeed non-human dwellers of Mars). But the way the biblical story of Creation is normally taken, and the Christian stress on the role of God becoming human, suggest that as far as we can tell He has not chosen to do so. If we accept that there *are* cats, i.e. not some other sort of creatures, but creatures with the features of *cats*, then we have to accept that cats cannot (as far as we can tell) attain heaven. Let us assume, as seems patently obvious, that Wensleydale does not have the capacity for a high degree of rationality, free choice, love and morality and so on (at least to the required degree), let alone the ability to act on those capacities in such as way as to attain heaven. Is all this monumentally unfair to Wensleydale? Is this species chauvinism? If it seems so, what are we actually saying here? Why should all creatures have equal treatment in all respects? If to be a cat is to be a creature with the features of e.g. Wensleydale, and if these features do not include capacity for rationality, free choice, love and morality and so on, then clearly this is really a question whether cats should exist at all. Is a world with cats better than a world that does not have cats? Should there be cats? Should Wensleydale exist at all? Notice here that one should not think of Wensleydale as in some sense pre-existing and ask whether it is fair that Wensleydale was made a cat rather than, say, a human. The question is whether Wensleydale should exist at all. Those who attack Christians for saying that animals cannot be saved, or animals will not exist in heaven, are apparently really saying that animals simply should not exist. A good God would have made a different world, in which all living creatures had the capacities for salvation. It would be better had animals never been created.

But that does not seem obvious to me. As we have seen, I am by no means convinced that a good God should be expected to behave differently from the way He does behave. I am by no means convinced that a good God should treat all sentient beings in all respects equally, or that He should have made a world with no cats (or any other animals), but perhaps more humans. Or that a good God is under some sort of moral obligation to make a world with no cats but perhaps with furry creatures with four legs, tails and pointed ears and all the spiritual capacities of humans. And would we really want creatures of *that* sort?

The Christian view is that all things that exist are good, as created by God. Thus the existence of Wensleydale as such is good. The good of Wensleydale's life is to be rejoiced in. It does not become less good because an additional possibility given to humans by God is (as far as we can tell) not a possibility for cats. It pleased God to create a world with cats in (as there are also flowers). I like cats. I for one am glad they exist. We cannot argue with it. When Wensleydale dies, I assume a good ceases. This is the case when each thing that exists ceases as such to exist. There is no reason why a good, *qua* good, should be eternal.[36]

Let me illustrate analogously what is meant by saying that existence as such is a good and that there is no moral obligation on God as such to supplement existence for all sentient beings with the possibility of salvation. Suppose I am given £20, totally freely, without any obligation or act on my part. Presumably I should be pleased. Suppose Archibald is given £10 under the same conditions. And suppose Fiona is given £30, again under the same conditions. Would it be reasonable for Archibald to complain that he has not been given the same as me, or the same as Fiona? Would it be reasonable for me to complain that Fiona has more? We might not know *why* one person has more than another. But we can scarcely say it is unreasonable, since we cannot detect any principle of distribution that we could claim is unfair. Presumably the only way we could do that is by appeal to a principle that all should be given equal amounts. But who said that that was the principle of distribution? And why should that principle be accepted, given that in every case one is being granted quite freely and with no obligation, something that one might not have had otherwise. Surely *any* financial gain under such circumstances is more than we could have expected and more than we were entitled to. Can I justifiably complain, having been given £20 without any merit on my part, that I should have been given £30?

Just so, the Christian wants to claim, with life. Life itself is a free gift. We cannot complain if some have more life, or some have additional benefits.[37] Granted, life seems to involve suffering. Suppose that, having been given the money, one was also taxed. Or robbed. Or beaten. Would that make the gratuitous gift of money in itself any less valuable, or generous, or worthy of gratitude? Why there is suffering in the world is logically a different issue from whether life in itself is a good or not.

Of course, if one does accept the principle that all should be given equal amounts, then there is something unjust in giving some people more than others. But why should God, in bestowing life, be subject to a moral principle that all should have equal amounts of life, or life in the same way? This doesn't seem obvious even in the analogy of money, let alone in the bestowal of life by God.

Now, supposing that some creatures are human, some cockroaches, some magpies, some cats, and one Wensleydale. Should they all be given the same length of life? Or all given life in the same way? And should they all also be given an extra thing, on top of life itself, namely the possibility of salvation? That is, should they all be given the possibility of infinite life? Particularly when that possibility requires features that they, as cockroaches, magpies, cats and definitely Wensleydale, cannot possibly possess? If God does not give them all this possibility of salvation, is God unfair? Is He immoral? It does not seem so to me, whatever our emotional response to the original problem might be. The fact that Christianity offers hope for only some creatures – humans – is no reason for rejecting that hope and that opportunity (as, I gather, an Anglican vicar threatened to do recently if there were no animals in heaven). And all this is no reason why Wensleydale should have been given additional features such as the capacity for rationality, free choice, love and morality and so on by God in order that Wensleydale too could have the opportunity of attaining heaven. Wensleydale's life is in itself a good, just as £20 freely given is in itself a good gift. Wensleydale cannot complain – nor is it unjust – if she has not been given £30.

No creature has the *right* to salvation, and no creatures have the right to the capacities that, if used correctly, can lead to salvation. Some creatures have these capacities and some, as far as we can tell, do not. This is simply because the world contains different types of creatures. Species pluralism is, arguably, also a good. We are often told so by environmentalists. Anyway, it is what God has chosen. We cannot say God was morally obliged to create an alternative world. Cats patently are not the same as humans. To think otherwise is sentimentality. When I say I like cats, I mean I like *cats*. I love Wensleydale – with a love appropriate to loving cats. And to think that cats might be saved as cats is to work with an idea of salvation and heaven that, as far as I know, is not that of traditional Christianity.

And I do not believe that an animal, because not saved, thereby goes to hell, at least if hell is understood as a state that is positively unpleasant. Hell too requires a high degree of rationality, free choice and so on. Is simply going out of existence (as the animal one is) so unfair? Many people believe that that is actually what happens to all of us anyway. The traditional Christian has nothing to lose in his or her hope for eternal life (for humans).[38]

There are those who will only believe in God if all things are arranged according to their idea of how things should be. But the reason for the existence of God (if it *is* a reason) – 'Why is there something rather than nothing?' – still stands. Whether or not Wensleydale is saved, that question still troubles us. Some would rather it were true that there were no God, with all that follows in loss of meaning, loss of charity and loss of hope, than that there would exist a God who might have given Wensleydale existence but not the chance of salvation. How strange! Better all are lost than some should have hope. Can we question equality? Christ rode on a donkey. Chesterton hymned the donkey. But no one before modern sentimentality said that the donkey should attain loving perfection in union with God. How could it? It is a *donkey*. If (as we are told by one Greek philosopher) horses might have religion, then no doubt donkeys too can have religion. But what is that to us?

ON HELL AND APOSTASY

Make no mistake about it. As far as Buddhists are concerned (at least doctrinally) I am almost certainly heading for the very lowest hell for a very long time. Of course, the Buddhist hells (of which there are many, all jolly unpleasant) are not literally permanent. After a hell birth one dies there and is eventually reborn somewhere else. But life in a hell is very long, and life in the lowest hell is very, very long indeed.[39]

I have been converted from Christianity to Buddhism, and from Buddhism back to a religion that very definitely holds what Buddhists call 'wrong views'. And wrong views are *wrong*. Although it is by no means a majority view in Buddhism, there is a tendency sometimes to see holding wrong views as itself entailing an unfavourable rebirth. Since wrong views paradigmatically exemplify 'ignorance' (or 'misconception'; *avidyā*), perhaps they entail, if not a hellish rebirth, nevertheless rebirth as a stupid animal. I am after all pig ignorant! And I am not just an apostate. I have abandoned a form of Tibetan Buddhism that involves commitments to regular (Tantric) ritual practice. The condition of initiation into these esoteric practices is that if commitments are broken the result is a very, very long sojourn in the lowest (Avīci) hell.

Perhaps my Buddhist friends hope I shall not find myself in hell. Perhaps they hope I shall return to my Buddhist practice and purify my misdeeds. It would be very difficult for me to purify *such* misdeeds. And I never was a good Buddhist practitioner. I was hopeless. My Buddhist friends have to face the fact that I am heading for hell. It is pretty certain. And they are not able to pray, putting my destiny in the hands of a loving and merciful God. I doubt that the Buddhas and bodhisattvas can intervene at the request of my friends to save me from the results of my actions. I have created my own destiny.

But then if I was such a hopeless Buddhist, I was no doubt heading for hell anyway. I could not attain enlightenment in this life even if it lasted a million years. *I* have had it. Shinran held that, as for himself, he was such an incapable practitioner (even though he had tried very hard) the result would surely be hell. He had nothing to lose. He abandoned himself to following what his teacher Hōnen taught, entrusting himself to the salvific power of Buddha Amitābha (Amida), who saves all who truly trust in his ability. He saves sinners, and even those most difficult to help – the arrogant and priggish goodies, the 'virtuous'. Shinran was relatively easy to save. He was a sinner. Shinran had nothing to lose.

Nor do I. It is ironic. Opponents often accuse Christians of sending to hell all those who do not agree with them, all those whose faith is other than their own particular branch of Christianity. But: 'The Roman Catholic Church has ... never defined that anyone, not even Adolf Hitler or Eichmann, has gone to hell. Some theologians ... believed that in the end everyone would go to heaven, even the devil himself'.[40] Moreover, the Catholic Church has also never said officially that anyone who is not a member of the visible Church, the Catholic Church as an institution in history, is thereby damned. The Christian can leave the issue of hell to the mercy and justice of God, trusting that many will indeed be saved.

I have nothing to lose. As a Christian I hope I shall be saved, which is infinitely more than I deserve. But if I am saved, I hope and trust I shall also see many Buddhists and many of my Buddhist friends in that wonderful place which exceeds all our imaginations.

DOES NO ONE CARE ABOUT SINNERS?

Ronald Knox (in *The Hidden Stream*) has suggested that in comparing religions one should compare what religions have to offer sinners as well as saints. What does Buddhism offer the one who has tried but honestly cannot make any progress? Among great Buddhist thinkers, Shinran alone, it seems to me, with his vivid awareness of his own tendency to egoism, really takes this on board. But at that level I feel better off with the historically-founded claims of Catholic Christianity, the religion for sinners, than with the legendary Buddha Amitābha whose historic existence is so problematic.

I have friends who consider that becoming a Catholic, of all things, indicates a feebleness of mind. The Catholic Church has, throughout history, been so jolly wicked. And yet, throughout history, it has survived. And it has produced Saints. An organisation that is fundamentally wicked is unlikely to survive, let alone produce Saints. But the Church was not set up for saints, the virtuous ones. It was set up for sinners (see Matthew 9:13). I am wicked. I am a sinner. It seems that I should feel very much at home in the Catholic Church. It is because the Church is so contaminated by sin that it is the place for me.

The Dalai Lama has said at one point that the problem for those who hold to the 'God-theory' is that 'there is the danger that the people will not appreciate the full greatness of the human potential'.[41] Here the Dalai Lama states his faith, a faith that it is possible for a human being through human agency alone to attain to the highest perfection. That is what Buddhism is, in the main, all about. But Shinran's view was that finally all one's own acts are necessarily egoistic and therefore fall far short of perfection. And from the Christian perspective, left to our own devices, short of the grace of God, we are still prone to do wrong. For we are tainted with the sinfulness of our fallen condition. Who is there we can point to then who has really actualised this 'full greatness of the human potential'?

I have just been sent a copy of a Sunday colour supplement concerning the case of the two Karma pas. The 16th Karma pa was the head of the Karma bKa' brgyud (pronounced: Kagyer) school of Tibetan Buddhism. He died early in the 1980s. This is one of the schools of Tibetan Buddhism that seeks for the child held to be the reincarnation of the previous hierarch. The child is then trained to readopt the position of his former incarnation. The two 'regents', high Tibetan monk teachers, charged with the job of finding the correct reincarnation, have each discovered a different boy. Each claims he has the correct reincarnation of the 16th Karma pa. Supporters of each faction, including many Western followers, accuse the other of fabrication. In India there have been battles between the two sides. People have died. Some have perhaps been murdered. The Dalai Lama himself favours one of the two candidates. And the faction fighting is perhaps set to get worse. The boy favoured by the Dalai Lama has recently escaped from Chinese-controlled Tibet. The other boy is also in the little country of Sikkim, south of the Himālayas. Followers of the two contenders are now in relatively close proximity to each other.

Actually, historically the institution of 'reincarnating lamas' in Tibet has always been subject to corruption due to the power, prestige and wealth involved. But it is all so sad and so depressing. Westerners, often so sensitive to the corrupt and bloody story of Christian history, had sought to find true spirituality in the gentle compassion and meditation of Buddhism. A natural response to what has happened here and in other cases of worldliness among modern spiritual teachers might well be complete cynicism about all religion and religious endeavour. Yet I do not think this has to be the response. Humans are humans. They are not gods. Religion involves ideals and aspirations. It also involves ultimate meaning. The perfection religious believers talk about concerns not what *is*, but what *ought* to be. The apparently inveterate tendency of humans to behave wrongly is what Christians mean by our sinful, fallen state. Actually, left to ourselves we are – *all* of us – not perfect. This is why we need redemption, and that saving redemption cannot come from other fallen humans. It flows from Perfection Itself. That is called grace. But receptiveness to grace requires first an awareness of one's own failings.

So from the point of view of Christian theology, it is not surprising that humans are prone to wickedness. The fault, if there is one, lies in those teachers who would allow their followers to think that they are or could be anything more than human beings, with all the failings of human beings. It seems to me that the fault here, and it is a great fault, is that of trying to be God. It is precisely because mainstream Christianity starts from a claim that we are all sinners in need of help that Christianity seems to me so attractive. It corresponds with what I find to be the case with human beings. So it seems to me that being a Catholic is very compatible with the historical corruption of Catholics.

'But this is absurd', I am told. Shouldn't a religion – if it is true – make its followers better? Is heaven full of the wicked? Well, heaven, I would imagine, is full of the ex-wicked. They have become, through the grace of God, perfect. If I were now perfect I would have no need of the Church. But I am not. The Church is the means by which I might be saved. For me it is the only means. How soon should one expect to see Saints in the Church? Should one expect to see Saints instantly? If not, then one should expect to see sinners in the Church. And some sinners are very great sinners. We all start from where we start. Since historically members of the Church were not Saints, it is not surprising that they sinned. They can also be forgiven. That, thank God, is the purpose of the Church. Even the really, really wicked can be forgiven. They can be forgiven if they truly, truly repent.

For me the Catholic Church shows very well the truth of Socrates' dictum, that the wisest people are those who know they are ignorant. The Church is full of those whose virtue lies in knowing that they are sinners, and the love and fellowship of those who are united in gratitude and hope. This is why Christians have often been so keen to proselytise, and why the move to conversion has been so resented and resisted by others. Christians have something wonderful to give people who do not realise they are even in need of it.

The measure of the Church, therefore, is not the presence of sinners. *That* is not surprising. It is the presence of forgiveness, the operation of grace through the sacraments, and the production (eventually) of Saints.

If God exists, and if the resurrection took place, then some sort of cataclysmic irruption of the sacred into our mundane world has taken place. This we call *redemption*. Only sinners need redemption. If that is true, then for the sinner the other claims of Christianity are well worth the leap of faith.

SELF-RIGHTEOUSNESS

It is the morning of the 1st January 2000. Later I shall go to Mass, which seems the appropriate way to begin a new millennium. Yesterday I drank no alcoholic drink. It was a Friday. A good Catholic should perform some penance on a Friday in memory of Our Saviour's crucifixion. I like wine, so renouncing it on Fridays would seem the proper thing to do. Unlike most people (it seems), on New Year's Eve I went to bed early. I was wakened only briefly by the sound of fireworks.

Today there is a mist. Smoke from the fireworks?

I fear I am beginning to feel smug and self-righteous! And I have not yet been fully received into the Catholic Church.

It is so difficult really to believe that we do not save ourselves. Perhaps it is more difficult for a former Buddhist, having spent so many years priding myself on the superiority of a religion that teaches reliance on one's own striving in e.g. meditation, rather than rituals, priests, or holy books. No wonder Buddhism has become so popular in countries like the USA, with a tradition of austere Protestant self-reliance and religion based on an individual's own direct relationship with, and experience of, God.[42]

Humility (the opposite of self-reliance?) and trust in an Other is so hard. Shinran contrasted his approach with that of his fellow Buddhists, those who practised the difficult and long path of morality, meditation and wisdom striving for enlightenment or Buddhahood – 'self-power' – what we traditionally think of as Buddhism. His alternative of relying on the 'other-power' of Buddha Amitābha was by contrast, he said, the easy way. But it is so very difficult really to take the easy way. Few truly believe that they cannot save themselves. Shinran's own followers sometimes thought mistakenly that they had finally found the way to save themselves: 'You save yourselves through abandoning self-power and relying on other-power'! The easy of the easy thereby is found to be the most difficult of the difficult. It is so difficult to let go of one's self-reliance, so difficult truly to let go of the self, to release egoity.

Not so many people nowadays seem to like the idea that we are really incorrigible sinners. As the Buddha said of what he had discovered, 'it goes against the grain'. It is not what people naturally expect. What would go against the grain, the Buddha thought, was his teaching of *anātman*, not-Self. In spite of what we are inclined to think, none of those psycho-physical things that make us up, or anything else, can be our 'Self', an unchanging referent for our use of the word 'I'. All is actually a changing flow, ourselves included. The role of 'not-Self' in Buddhism is played in Christianity by 'sinfulness'. Both go against the grain. Both require realisation in order to promote a certain sort of letting-go. Only then can we combine that realisation with a genuine morality based on humility and not self-righteousness.

WHY BAPTISM?

I happened to mention to Tārā how uncommon it seems to be nowadays (compared with my generation) for people to have been baptised at birth. She appeared surprised to learn that from a Christian point of view living a good life is not in itself sufficient for heaven. I suspect many people do not realise this, and think that so long as they are good, then *if* there is a God and heaven they will surely make it. The alternative, that being good is not enough – heaven is not some sort of reward for being good, like an investment policy – is seen as an example of Christian exclusiveness. Only those in our club will be helped and saved!

It is not surprising that Tārā might think this. She was brought up as a Buddhist. In Buddhism, other things being equal, what leads to a heavenly rebirth are good deeds. Why is this not the case in Christianity?

In Christianity the goal is specified using the term 'heaven'. Heaven for a Christian is often a fairly hazy concept, but one thing is clear. It is the highest possible perfection for a created being. We shall know God and be known by God as we truly are. The 'heavens' that Buddhists sometimes talk about, as impermanent states in the cycle of rebirth characterised by positive qualities like happiness and pleasure and inhabited by the 'gods' (*devas*), but quite different from the final goal of enlightenment or Buddhahood, should not be confused with the Christian notion of heaven. The role in the Christian system played by heaven is played in the Buddhist system not by 'heaven' (Sanskrit: *svarga*) but by liberation (*nirvāṇa*), or full Buddhahood (depending on the Buddhist tradition), the final goal itself.

For Shinran one cannot bring about the goal oneself, for one cannot do an action that is not pervaded with egoism and thus one cannot truly bring about that internalisation of not-Self necessary to liberation. He plays on the point that all my actions must be *mine*. Other Buddhists would be inclined to criticise Shinran's conflation of this obvious point here with the claim that all my actions must be *egoistic*. That simply does not follow. Even a Buddha's actions are his, but they are not egoistic. Nevertheless, psychologically, in the practicalities of everyday life, Shinran may well be right. Since Freud we all know that our actions often have many deep motivations largely hidden from our conscious awareness. How do we know that all our actions are not motivated by hidden springs of selfishness? Shinran was ruthlessly honest with himself. Others, he suggested, may be capable of actions that are not motivated by egoity. But as for himself, as far as he can see all his own actions are selfish. Even when he tried so very hard to practise the practices of Buddhism – meditation, study, making merit through positive actions and so on – he found he was really getting nowhere. All his actions were inevitably egoistic and were thus leading not to enlightenment but further into the cycle of suffering and rebirth (*saṃsāra*). Shinran was, we might say, a sinner and he knew it. Only by finally and deeply realising his own incapacity for enlightenment could he let go and thus allow the enlightenment which already existed and which he called 'Amitābha Buddha' to shine through, transforming and perfecting his very being.

Where Shinran talks of a complete inability to avoid egoity through his own power, the Christian speaks of an inability to avoid sin short of God's grace. Just as for Shinran we are by our very nature egoistic from the moment we are born (indeed before we are born), so for the Christian we are born with a tendency to sin. In both cases it means that all our actions, even where we try very hard to be good, fall short of what is required in order for the action to coincide with the religion's vision of the highest goal. Left to our own devices we always fall short.

Thus *of course* being good alone fails to coincide with what the Christian sees as heaven. How could our good actions, even our best actions, coincide with the goodness and perfection of Goodness and Perfection itself? Yet the Christian view is that this coinciding, this harmony, is what God intends for us. It is expressed beautifully as 'We are born for friendship with God.' Perfect friendship with God, and all that entails, is heaven. Real friendship with others – altruism – what we normally mean by 'being good', true morality, can only be grounded on God and therefore friendship with God. In this it again corresponds with Shinran's claim that real, true morality flows from Amitābha through the actions of the person who has really let go (has 'faith', Japanese: *shinjin*), and thus ceased to block Amitābha's activity in himself through egoity.

It follows from all of this that being good cannot in itself entail heaven. All 'being good' falls short of heaven. It is pervaded with 'sin', just as for Shinran it is pervaded with egoism. A fully articulated (unimpeded) friendship with God is necessary for heaven. And that friendship flows from God in grace, overcoming sin, just as for Shinran enlightenment must come from the Other-power, Amitābha. In Christianity the idea that we are born with a tendency to sin, left to our own devices, is expressed theologically as 'original sin'. 'Original sin' does not mean that we are born wicked. A new-born baby is not wicked. But left to its own devices it does have a tendency to sin. Similarly, for Shinran the fact that all actions springing from me are egoistic does not entail that I am now doing an egoistic act. It is a fact about our unenlightened condition. For the Christian we are also born with the potential for friendship with God. Every human being is born with the possibility, the potential, for heaven. Shinran would express the concept that plays the same positive and encouraging role in his system by saying that 'All sentient beings nevertheless possess the Buddha-nature.' Christians claim that baptism is the sacramental way set up by God for the activation of that potential. There is no necessary reason why activation of the potential has to be through baptism rather than, say, taking a sacramental bus ride. That is just the way it is.

Baptism removes something blocking a human being from receptivity to God's grace. Of course, God can bestow grace without baptism. There is no contradiction in that. Nevertheless the bestowal of grace is not the same thing as the reception of grace. And baptism provides the standard and optimal means laid down by God for expressing receptivity. We all have a tendency to sin, left to our own devices. Baptism marks the entering into God's devices and thus the possibility of overcoming the tendency to sin and thereby attaining the perfection of heaven. As far as we are concerned it is baptism that enables one who so chooses to grow in friendship with God. But one does have freely to *choose*. The self-conscious and free choice to strive in this is formalised in the sacrament of confirmation.

Baptism marks an entering into God's devices. But for a Catholic baptism is also much more than this. It is fundamentally anti-individualistic, for it marks an entry into a *community*, and the goal is seen very much in communitarian terms. 'God's devices' are essentially communal, they involve being with others in a perfect relationship with the Other that is God. The Christian community involves a whole vision of the world, and a set of duties and obligations to others, within which the concept of 'heaven' gains its place and meaning. There is no sense of 'heaven' as understood by the Christian outside this vision, and thus no sense of heaven outside its intrinsic involvement with the community, the extended family. Just as one is born into a family, so one is baptised into a family. Heaven is the family living in harmony and perfection. Just as one can certainly do good to those who are not members of one's own family, so doing good is not itself sufficient for heaven.

So one is good because that is what God wants. In order to grow in friendship with someone, one does not keep disappointing them. But heaven, the perfection of that friendship, does not as such come simply from being good.

Hence we remove the block to our potential and undergo baptism. Then with the blocks removed, through reception of God's grace, we strive to create true friendship with God harmoniously within the community that God has established for that purpose. Perfected, that is heaven.

WHAT DIFFERENCE DOES IT MAKE?

If Christianity is true, *everything* changes. If there is a God, if God vindicated the claims of Jesus in the resurrection (unbelievable?), even more so if Jesus was truly God as well as truly man, nothing can be the same again. For this really to be thought to be true – to be believed in the fullest sense of the word – must *itself* be what Buddhists call the *āśrayaparāvṛtti*, the complete revolution of one's very being in the world. It is the spiritual equivalent of the Copernican revolution. Unlike Kant's epistemological version of this revolution, the revolution here is ultimately the revolution from self to Other, and that Other is God. It is *conversion*; it is literally *ecstasy*.

Imagine what it must be like to see the world this way. It is astonishing. Nothing looks the same as it did before; nothing looks the same as it does for those without faith. For them this is madness. The one who sees Christianity as true goes *de facto* out of his head. Is Christianity true? Something that, if it is true, would have such radical implications *cannot* be allowed to rest. It must be examined. It must worry, and be worried, like a puppy with a slipper. Perhaps this worrying is the most important thing in life.

Before Christianity is dismissed, or left, are we as sure as we can be that there is nothing in it?

MUSING ON RELICS: A THEOLOGICAL REFLECTION ON THE TURIN SHROUD AND FAITH

Before we say anything about the Turin Shroud we need to be clear about the following. Whether or not the Shroud is authentic does not in the least bit affect the truth either of the Christian message or of Catholicism. Moreover, if the Shroud is found not to be genuine it should not affect one jot the prestige (or otherwise) of the Catholic Church. There have been doubts expressed about its authenticity from medieval times, and acceptance of it is *not* a requirement for Catholics.

The Shroud preserved in Turin purports to be the burial cloth of Jesus. But what is so astonishing about the Shroud is that it seems to show a complete and detailed image of a body when photographed in negative. This body demonstrates remarkably accurate evidence of scourging, a crown of thorns and crucifixion. If, as many suspect, it is a medieval forgery, then extensive research has failed to show with complete conviction how such a forger could have done it. Indeed, the evidence for it *not* being a forgery, from examination of what is portrayed by the Shroud and other material remains, is impressive. One might be prepared to argue (as I shall for the resurrection itself) that the burden of proof has now shifted to those who would maintain its inauthenticity. One might, but for one reason. Three independent laboratories have carbon-dated the linen of the Shroud to somewhere between 1260 and 1390. That would seem to settle the issue.

I have been looking at Ian Wilson's book, *The Blood and the Shroud*. Wilson is a well-known supporter of the authenticity of the Shroud. But in spite of the lurid title and appearance of this book, which looks like another sensationalist attempt to make money out of the Christian religion, Ian Wilson is a reputable writer in the field. He is also scrupulously fair-minded and he writes well. I wanted to see how anyone could still support the authenticity of the Shroud after the carbon dating. I also wanted to examine a full-length photograph of the Shroud myself. I had read that among the unexpected features of this image is that it shows clearly that the crucifixion nails passed through the *wrist*, not the palm of the hands. This is in keeping with recent research into methods of crucifixion, but appears to have been unknown in the Middle Ages (although it was suggested as a possibility in the sixteenth century). All medieval paintings (as far as I know) show nails passing through the palms of the hands. It is the sort of feature one can be reasonably sure a medieval forger would not have thought to question.

The Shroud image does indeed seem to show wrist impalement, along with other astonishingly detailed anatomical features of crucifixion. Wilson's book makes grim reading. But when all is considered it looks to me as if once again we have evidence that is compelling – I would say evenly balanced – on both sides, for and against authenticity. As for me, if it were not for the carbon dating I would have no hesitation in placing my faith on balance in the authenticity of the Turin Shroud.[43] But even if the Turin Shroud were the genuine burial shroud of Jesus, it could be argued that what it shows is open to dispute. It may be just an intriguing survival from Jesus' life. It certainly could not in itself imply the truth of any of the claims of Christianity, from the existence of God to the resurrection, let alone that Jesus was God incarnate.

I want to approach the Turin Shroud from a different angle, a theological angle. The evidence for its authenticity is, perhaps, evenly balanced. We do not have proof. It is rather like the evidence for the existence of God. If one accepts the authenticity of the Shroud there remains a mystery (the carbon dating). This mystery is not necessarily insoluble. Wilson gives what looks like strong arguments to doubt the validity of the carbon dating too. And recently 39 scientists have testified that the image on the Shroud could not be the result of painting. It must have been caused by oxidation or by the dehydration of a human body (*The Catholic Times*, 2 April 2000). But I am no expert. As with philosophical reasoning, experts can perhaps argue backwards and forwards interminably. But at some point one makes a choice. If one denies its authenticity, there remains a mystery too (the astonishing image). Thus whichever option one takes involves some sort of leap that is at the moment beyond the evidence. One could of course remain agnostic, but that is to make some sort of decision, a decision that a leap beyond the evidence would be unwarranted. Nevertheless it is not obvious to me that a leap beyond the evidence in either direction would be *irrational*.

Let us assume for a moment, for our present theological purposes, that we are Christians and the Shroud *is* authentic. The image on the Shroud is clearly seen and its amazing nature understood only in photographic negative. Thus the importance of the image had to wait until the advent of photography to be appreciated. What might this tell us about God's intentions? Whatever His intentions, they were not for earlier centuries. Thus God might be thought to be saying something to 'modern humanity'. But whatever He is saying, He cannot intend to give scientific *proof* of the claims of Christianity. Otherwise, since we are assuming for the purposes of argument here that the Shroud is genuine, the problem of the carbon dating would not have occurred.

Could it be that God does not want scientific proof of theological claims? Could it be that God actually wants the evidence to be fairly evenly balanced? Under such circumstances the leap of faith is as rational as denying faith, but it is still a leap. It is not a leap *in spite of* the evidence, but it is still a leap into the dark, a leap *beyond* the evidence. If something like this were correct, what would it tell us about God and His plans for us?

We are like children standing on a high rock. Our Father asks us to jump, trusting that He will catch us. As in some forms of Buddhism (particularly Madhyamaka), we are asked finally to let go completely. In thus finally letting go we find we are caught up in the divine life. That freely given trust may be precisely what it is all about.

I wonder what happens to the person who lets go of letting go?

'Underneath are the everlasting arms' (Deuteronomy 33:27; King James version). The one who lets go of letting-go finds himself in the everlasting arms. Or should that be 'The Everlasting Arms'?

WHY DID JESUS HAVE TO DIE ON THE CROSS?

The issue of why God seems to have required Jesus to die such a horrible death has puzzled Christian theologians from earliest times. Buddhists, in common with non-Christians everywhere (when they consider the matter at all), tend to consider that the image that Jesus' death gives us of God is of a vengeful bully who will not hold back from slaughtering His own son if it fulfils His warped sense of law and the debt owed to Him by sinning humanity

Yet I very much doubt that this is what the doctrine of the atonement really means. It is not the unanimous view of Christian theologians. Let me see if I can suggest an approach that may be (for me) more satisfying.

The idea of atonement for the misdeeds of God's holy community, His nation, is central to the religious law said to have been received directly from God by Moses (see, for example, Leviticus 4:13–21). But much of the Jewish law concerning sacrifices was in fact developed over some centuries and taken from common Near Eastern legal traditions. This is not surprising, and theologically it makes perfect sense for God to seek to tame His 'obstinate people' with the sort of severe restrictions and ritual behaviour that they would expect and understand. The whole story of the Bible shows God gradually refining His message to His people and its implications. It starts very primitively indeed, in the blood of lambs and bulls.

At the time of Jesus the blood still flowed. Yet, for the Christian, God was still not satisfied – though not because insufficient blood had been spilt (see Isaiah 1:11: '"What are your endless sacrifices to me?" says Yahweh ... "I take no pleasure in the blood of bulls and lambs and goats"'). God has no need of the spilling of blood and there is no absolute value in such sacrifices – even the sacrifice of the cross. Rather (as we know from so many of Jesus' parables), God was not satisfied because of His love. There is indeed absolute value in love.

The relationship between God and His people was still radically awry. Jesus was to be the sacrificial lamb. Jesus Himself died for God's people. But I do not believe that Jesus died because God required His death as a legal atonement for the sins of the community. Clearly God has no need of such things. Rather, God was responding to a community that still thought in terms of blood sacrifice as atonement for sin. We know from the crucial parable of the 'prodigal' son (Luke 15:11–32) that the Father is more than willing to welcome back His repentant children. He does not demand murder. But for a people that still thinks of blood sacrifice as atonement for the sins of the community, God is saying:

> Look! Can you not see? *I* fulfil the requirements you think you need. I myself make the sacrifice. I sacrifice my very own Son for you, my people. And my Son is *Me*. What more can I do to show you how much I love you? No more is needed. Come back to Me, my people – please.

Out of His love for His people all the sacrifice that is needed is made by God Himself. It is finished. The actual blood sacrifice

– that *this* was the way God sought to bring His people back to Himself, rather than any other way – was a response to the particular religious history of the particular people God had chosen. Its universality springs from the universality of the redemptive message arising from their very particular religious history.

God had no need of His Son's death. But He is a God of history. There, and then, love did.

A PRAYER ON CHRISTMAS EVE: PRELUDE
TO THE MYSTERY OF THE BECOMING
OF GOD

O most Perfect One,
You who alone Are what you Are –
Though my faith is now but the slightest spark in Your winter hearth
Blow on it the breath of Your love,
That faith may flare into a welcoming fire,
Stoked by the fuel of my ego,
Melting the hoar-frost of my heart,
Cheering the ox and the ass.

O Being, the Emptiness,
Who is beyond our nothingness –
Within it and without it –
Becoming one of us –

Redeeming nothing –

No longer what we are
May we become what we always were,

Be what you would have us be,
And – O Breath of our breath –
Do what you would have us do.

What is Becoming but the ecstasy of Being?
When I was a Buddhist we would celebrate holy days by

taking vows of austerity. We would temporarily enter a state something like that of monks or nuns. Thus we would vow for, say, twenty-four hours to eat only one meal – and that before midday – and not to wear perfumes, garlands, or other showy fripperies.

Now it is Christmas Eve. I am going to a celebratory party. Tārā is coming with me. I bathe, put on deodorants, talcum powder and after shave. I dress in clean clothes. I try to look smart. It is the proper thing to do, out of respect to the host and the guest of honour. One does not go to a party wearing grime and sweat. I don't suppose anyone does. And certainly not *this* party, a party for this very special baby. Born tonight.

I am not much of a guest. I am not very good at looking smart. My trousers are *always* baggy at the knees. And I do not really know the host, or the guest of honour. Not yet. I want to, so very much. Soon. I must be patient. We have not been introduced properly. Not only the English stand on ceremony! But I shall not be turned away.

When I was involved with Buddhism we used to celebrate holy days by austerity, by extra-special seriousness. Soon, soon (we thought) the period of mourning will be over and we shall be liberated, enlightened, for ever.

At the cathedral the tears we cry are tears of joy.

Tomorrow we feast. And I shall drink wine.

MORE ON DRINKING WINE

I have always liked the story of the miracle of the wedding feast at Cana, in which Jesus at the request of His Mother turned jars of water into wine for a couple who had the great misfortune of having miscalculated the demand for alcohol at their wedding.

It is a strange story. It is supposed to have been Jesus' very first miracle, occurring, according to Jesus Himself, a little before the proper time for miracles had come. One is tempted to dismiss it as later legend, intended to glorify the Master. Yet if so, why such an apparently trivial story? One could imagine a much more impressive entry into the Lord's earthly ministry.

The very triviality of the story suggests to me that here we have truth. Had the story been fabricated, perhaps with the purpose of teaching some doctrine or another, Jesus' first miracle would have been made much more spectacular. Only the actual truth of the story kept it alive.

Turning water into wine at a wedding is very much a miracle concerning everyday life and everyday embarrassment. It has little relevance to those not directly involved. But the poor couple. In cosmic terms their discomfort was not much, and yet for them – ordinary people with ordinary feelings – it was intensely distressing. Not enough wine. What a way to start married life.

This is the God for me. This is a God who *really* cares. He turns water into wine for good people to prevent their embarrassment at a party. And he makes *lots* of wine. Good wine. He matures (quickly) the very best. Israeli wine had never been so good.

What is going on here? The seventeenth-century Catholic poet Richard Crashaw composed a Latin line to commemorate the occasion: 'Vidit et erubuit conscia lympha Deum.' That is, 'The sensitive water saw God and blushed'! At the wedding, while the bridal couple fussed about *their* awkwardness, the water saw God approaching. She knew it was God. And she not only saw God. She was in her turn seen by God. When we are seen by God we are all naked. God could see right through her. In her embarrassment she blushed. A wonderful, intoxicating blush.

The wine of God intoxicates. He takes us out of ourselves. We let go. We lose ourselves; we lose self-control altogether. We too can blush.

ON READING THE GOSPELS: DON'T MIND THE TRUTH, FEEL THE ALLEGORY?

I am no expert on the Bible, to say the least. But sometimes I wonder whether being such an expert is always an advantage in understanding Christian thought. I notice that at a recent conference on the resurrection a marked difference occurred between the approaches of biblical scholars and philosophers.[44] Maybe that explains the annoyance I felt at some of the implications of a talk on the miracle of the wedding feast at Cana, just given, as chance would have it, to our RCIA group.

The apparent triviality of the story, which I take as indicating that it is very possibly true, seems to have embarrassed theologians from quite early on. But there is, I gather, an alternative way of understanding the miracle of the wedding feast. That is to read the whole thing as an allegory. It seems that in the allegorical reading, which goes back at least as far as St Augustine (and presumably through him to Origen), the 'Mother' is the Church. The good wine that is given last is the wine of Christ and His new dispensation, the water that is turned to wine is the water of Jewish ritual observations, and so on.

Now I have nothing against allegorical interpretations, except that they can turn a beautiful but simple story into an esoteric code. Still, it seems to me that a story is capable of literal understanding, and whatever meaning can be derived from a literal understanding, *as well as* an allegorical interpretation where that may also be helpful. I cannot resist some feeling of concern when the allegorical interpretation is given (as it seemed to me) as the *whole* meaning and point of the story. Did the miracle of the wedding feast actually occur, as a historical event? Or was it inserted by the author of John's Gospel simply as an allegory? Well, the author – let us call him 'John' – does not state it is an allegory. Would his mixed audience of Jews and Hellenistic Gentiles have understood it as an allegory? I doubt it. Or at least, I doubt that they would have understood it *solely* as an allegory, and certainly not in the detailed, codified way we find in later interpretations like that of Augustine.

So I have my doubts as to whether John intended the story as an allegory. And I am sure he thought it was a literally true story. Why should it not be? It is not enough to say (as I was told in the RCIA class) that we have no way of knowing whether any of these stories were literally true or not. *Therefore* we should treat them as allegories. It is not a question of knowing something is literally true versus allegorical interpretation. Do we know that the story is factually *false*? I don't think so (unless we flatly deny the possibility of miracles altogether). In that case, why not take it as true, on the level of believing it until such time as it is shown to be false? Most 'simple' believers do, and it seems to me they are right to do so. I too think it is true. This is the God for me! If we believe the story is true, its significance then becomes susceptible to the sort of interpretation I have given above. Or another interpretation. The story gains in flexibility and richness. We can then also add, 'Oh, and there is the following allegorical interpretation as well.' We might even give some historical notes on the context in which this and other allegorical interpretations were taught.

If we were to treat a story as allegorical because we do not know for certain whether or not it is historically true, we would have to treat the whole story of Jesus as an allegory. Are we to say that John's Gospel, for example, is no different from C. S. Lewis's Narnia stories? When C. S. Lewis tells us of the great lion Aslan who died to save a naughty but mistaken schoolboy and then came back to life to defeat the wicked witch and her hench-creatures, is this no different from the story of the Gospels? Lewis's fable is wonderful and moving, but it is just an allegory of the Christian story. If John's Gospel is not like that, shouldn't this be made clear?

I have no objection to allegorical interpretations. But I do worry when a lovely story like that of the wedding feast is treated without comment as though it were *only* capable of being an allegory, and this approach is justified with the claim that we cannot know for certain whether any of these stories are factually true. Can I put my finger on what particularly worries me? I think it is that the question of the factual truth of the story seems to be an embarrassment. I see here an unwarranted move away from factual truth, a too easy abandonment of truth, Being, for symbols. We brush aside factual truth as quite unimportant. It is not. 'Symbolic truth' has, of course, its own kind of truth, but we need to be careful before throwing over literal, cognitive truth. Why not say the stories of the resurrection, or the virgin birth, are simply allegories? Of course, some theologians do, but they are not normally Catholics. How can one justify recourse to allegorical interpretation in the one case and not in the other? Perhaps they are all just 'edifying stories' intended to give the central message of the

Church. It seems to me that down that path of nonrealism (or perhaps even antirealism) lies subjectivism and relativism. In adopting a cavalier attitude to truth we eventually lose Truth altogether.

Perhaps what especially concerns me theologically in the move towards allegorical interpretation, particularly any implication (even if unintended) of exclusively allegorical interpretation, is its tendency (it seems to me) to minimise the significance of the incarnation. In the incarnation God became Man. In Jesus we see God involved in the day-to-day little things of life. The concern of Jesus for the embarrassment of the bridal pair is not incidental, unimportant, or merely the vehicle for an allegory of the relationship between the Church and its teachings and the previous Jewish dispensation.

I like the story of Jesus changing water into wine for a feast, so that bride and groom do not start off their married life embarrassed. This is the sort of love and care one might expect from the Lord. And joyousness and affirmation of community, fun and the body. In comparison our being able to break the code of an allegory is thoroughly *boring*. I wonder if it also shows a subconscious antipathy towards fun and the body, perhaps a subconscious (Manichaean) unease with the sheer goodness of things? If this allegorical interpretation originated with Augustine (or indeed Origen) that would not be surprising. One detects an embarrassment about the physical body, and thus about God as Man. But brushing aside the literal truth of the story in favour of an allegory that we have no reason to think was in John's mind anyway, but which suited the later development of Church doctrine, might be fine for theologians like Augustine. I am sure it was of crucial importance in the clarification and development of proper dogmatic understanding. I would be the last to underrate its importance. However, if I understand it correctly Christianity offers more. Stories like that of the miracle of the wedding feast at Cana are not just of importance in the history of Christian dogma. Indeed (dare I say it), perhaps this is not the most significant aspect of the story at all. Crucially, the events of Jesus' life speak to our present everyday concerns as well. Christianity offers 'abundant life', an abundant life seen in God's becoming not just Man but a man.

HOW MUCH CAN ONE TAKE OF ONE'S FELLOW HUMAN BEINGS?

I am worried. I have just been to the post-Christmas sales at the shopping centre in Bristol. After a few days of Christmas food, drink and new possessions, the sales seem to be nothing more than an excuse for further greed. So many people pushing and shoving with one thought in mind – to get more things (even things they do not really want and have no space for) as cheaply as possible.

I, of course, am not like this. I bought a needed new pair of shoes (saved £20), a few other bits and pieces, and came home with contempt for others.

This attitude of mine no doubt reflects my own character. Sharon is always accusing me of being a snob and an elitist. A Brahmin in an Indian village I worked at briefly many years ago commented on how everyone considers his own group to be superior to other groups. Even among Brahmins each sub-caste will hold that 'I am superior, and purest of all.' Buddhist sources often speak with thinly veiled scorn of the *bālapṛthagjana*, the foolish, alienated common folk. One does not ask cow-herders about Truth, as one renowned Buddhist philosopher put it. Everyone is ranked in a spiritual hierarchy. The best most people can hope for is a favourable rebirth through their virtuous deeds. If one chooses to remain a lay person then particularly important among virtuous deeds is giving to monks and nuns, helping them to follow seriously the path to enlightenment.

All this is not necessarily false, or even wrong. A society based on a rigidly hierarchical social structure is not in itself going to be any less congenial than one based on ideals of equality. Yet I would look around at others and think what a shame it was that all these people are undoubtedly heading for unfavourable rebirths. Still, what can one expect, given the way they behave? The chances of a human rebirth, one is taught, are extremely low indeed. We have now attained that rare achievement. Looking at the behaviour of most people, one could see that they were unlikely to achieve it again for a very long time. What a pity. Yet what is to be done? Greed, hatred and delusion just lead to suffering. That is the way it is. One can point it out, but most people are incorrigible sinners.[45] No one can save other people, can they?

I remember Denys Turner once accusing me of what G. K. Chesterton (following Aristotle) called 'priggishness', a sort of conceitedness springing from a feeling of moral superiority. In Christian terms this priggishness reflects a failure to recognise one's own sinfulness in common with others, and a tendency to think that one can attain a quite superhuman perfection through one's own acts. Turner was right, although at the time I did not realise it. I don't think I was boringly self-righteous. I just felt that I was morally and spiritually superior to others, and most others had little hope of improvement. Chesterton associated this attitude very much with the Manichaeism opposed by St Augustine, and what he saw as similar tendencies among the medieval Cathars. He traced it to an attitude that the world is fundamentally evil. People can be ranked hierarchically in accordance with the extent to which they have managed to release themselves from the bonds of evil matter. Most people in this life cannot progress very far on the path of release. But the believing masses can at least gain merit through the virtue of supporting the austere and morally upright elite, the *Perfecti*, who are much closer to release or have maybe actually attained it. Perhaps others, through their devotion to the *Perfecti* in this life, will be able to do better in future lives. For the Cathars also held to reincarnation.

Why did I come home from the sales worried? I think I was worried about a growing awareness of my own moral elitism, a moral elitism that leads to my dislike of my fellow human beings at the post-Christmas spending orgy. Sharon has often commented on my tendency to begrudge the happiness of others when that happiness comes from something harmless but to which I have a (priggish) moral objection. Why shouldn't people go to the sales? Why shouldn't they seek happiness and bargains, and happiness through bargains? I do not know what their individual situations are. Perhaps the sales are important to them and their families (that too sounds patronising!).

In particular, on this day, the day after the Feast of the Holy Family, I should simply enjoy seeing families out together and enjoying themselves.

Where'r the Catholic sun does shine
There's music and laughter and good red wine
At least I've found it so,
Benedicamus Domino.

(Hilaire Belloc)[46]

Families going to the post-Christmas sales are a modern tradition of the Christmas holidays.

Dear Lord Jesus, you who chose to be born in an ordinary family, we are all equal in your sight. You love us all with a much greater love than we can ever imagine, and perhaps you rejoice to see us happy at the shops without harming others. Please forgive my conceitedness, my sense of superiority, my tendency to dismiss my fellow human beings. Help me to join in with others, and help me to gain wonderful bargains at the sales. Amen.

2

ON THE RESURRECTION

> But take courage, O Lady: for when God wills, strange wonders are
> easily accomplished.
>   (Orthodox Liturgy for Feast of the Annunciation)[1]

Did the resurrection actually take place, as a historical event? If
there is a God, and a God who cares about the world, then
miracles (if the resurrection *is* theologically a miracle) must
always be possible. But can we ever show that one has
occurred? One could argue, with David Hume, that the onus is
always on the other side to prove that a miracle has taken place.

But is that reasonable? Isn't it always logically possible that
a plausible case could be constructed for the occurrence of a
miracle, such that the onus of proof moves to the other side to
show that the miracle did *not* occur? In any common case of
asking for a proof this is always an accepted possibility. If it is
ruled out in the case of miracles, it looks very much as if the
opponent wishes to subject miracles to a test for proof which is
much stricter than ordinary tests for proof. In fact, if it is *never*
accepted that the onus of proof moves to the other side in the
case of miracles, then it looks as if no ordinary plausible case
for the occurrence of a miracle could ever be constructed. Thus
the opponent can always deny that we have a plausible case
for the occurrence of a miracle. But this is unreasonable. What
the opponent is doing in fact is stating that he or she will accept
no evidence for the occurrence of a miracle. This point is irres-
pective of whether as a matter of fact there *are* any such cases.

It seems to me, therefore, that we could reach the stage where
the onus of proof is on the other side to construct a more
convincing and plausible case of what did happen instead of the
resurrection. Until we have such a more convincing and
plausible case, belief in the resurrection is reasonable and may
even be *more* rational than denial. Whether we have now

reached that stage is up to each enquirer to judge for him- or herself. Note here that the issue is one of the rationality of acceptance – or, if you like, the rationality of belief – not one of *proof*.

I do not have much of any originality to say on evidence for the resurrection. But there may be some value in mentioning briefly the grounds for claiming that it is rational to believe that the resurrection took place, since many people interested in Buddhism are unfamiliar with the arguments and therefore with their strength. I was myself. I had never really thought very much about it, but inasmuch as I had, I was sure there must be some rational explanation for the claimed resurrection. Anyway, I could never imagine this aspect counting in convincing me to become a Christian. My interest was in philosophical argument, not reports of magic.

But anyone involved in Tibetan Buddhism soon becomes quite familiar with reports of 'magic' and with those who accept them without question. Belief in bodily resurrection ought not in principle to be more difficult for one involved in practising Tibetan Buddhism than many of the other things he or she believes in. But material on the arguments for the resurrection is easier to come by, and has been subjected to much more critical examination, than material on the arguments for, say, Nāgārjuna living for 500 years. Not to mention arguments supporting Padmasambhava flying through the air on a horse and Tantric *siddhas* bringing fish back to life, or whatever. And it is the arguments that should be of interest to us here.

I shall not examine the case for the resurrection being false on the grounds that Jesus simply never existed. There are still some who think that, but I don't and I shall not deal with such fringe views. Also, there have historically been those who held that Jesus existed but was not actually crucified. Perhaps someone else was crucified in Jesus' place, as was thought by at least one of the early Gnostic teachers. But as no evidence has ever been offered for this contention, I shall not take it seriously.

So given that Jesus existed and was crucified, He was certainly *considered* to have died and all the evidence suggests He was placed in a tomb. It is at this point that the issue of resurrection comes into play. On the third day Jesus is held by

Christians to have emerged from His tomb alive, resurrected by God from the dead. The grounds for this lie in the earliest Christian tradition, including purported eyewitness accounts of those who claimed to have seen Him after His death. Those who do not accept resurrection as the most economical explanation must have an alternative. So what are the options?

Jesus' tomb was either not empty after the purported resurrection and still contained His body, or it was empty and did not contain His body.

THE OCCUPIED TOMB

If Jesus' tomb had not been empty and had contained His body, then there would have been no problem. All would have pointed to His body, and the resurrection stories would never have been taken seriously. But in spite of many having an interest in disproving the story, as far as we know absolutely no one in ancient times adopted this strategy. Opponents said the disciples must have stolen the body, but no one said the body was still in the tomb and showed it still there (see Matthew 28:12–13).

Of course, there would still have been a question about why stories became current that Jesus had resurrected. A number of alternatives have been suggested by those who still want to hold that Jesus was not literally bodily resurrected:

(a) Those who said the tomb was empty had, perhaps, in their grief gone to the wrong tomb. This seems to me very unlikely and could soon have been corrected.
(b) The disciples pretended that Jesus had resurrected. But as far as we know, and understandably, the disciples were dispirited, defeated and terrified. They were ordinary men and women (actually not very bright) whose leader had been horribly killed. Moreover a number of these disciples were later martyred for their belief in a resurrected Christ. They had become extremely brave. Why? And what motive could they have for such a conspiracy? No one, even under torture, confessed it was all a plot and the body was still in the tomb. If they had, and if the

body had been there, their opponents would certainly have made the fact known. Moreover, for a conspiracy it was completely inept. Why base a conspiracy on the initial testimony of *women*, whose testimony was not admissible in Jewish law? Why centre a conspiracy on resurrection from the dead, which would have cut no ice with Jews? They were not expecting and could not accept a Messiah whom God had allowed to die 'on a tree' (and was thus declared in Jewish law to be 'cursed of God' – see Deuteronomy 21:22–23). Jewish expectation was for a Messiah who would save them from their worldly enemies. Jesus' very mode of death conclusively showed for orthodox Jews that He could not have been the Messiah. A plot based on resurrection and ascension would have made no difference. It was pointless. But the early disciples – and our earliest material for these events dates to within a few years of the crucifixion and to people who knew Jesus and claimed to have seen His resurrected body – clearly believed that He had genuinely come back from the dead. Everything indicates that they had not concocted a conspiracy. Otherwise Christianity would soon have collapsed. The same point could be made about the idea that the resurrection of Jesus was a legend developed by the disciples and the early Church.

(c) Those who claimed to have seen the resurrected Jesus were subject to hallucinations. John Hick, for example,[2] has argued that what we now know of the function of the mind suggests that the post-resurrection experiences of the disciples might indeed be based on psychogenic origins. In other words, we have to take seriously the suggestion that they were hallucinations, perhaps brought on by grief, exhaustion and expectancy. This seems to me highly unlikely. No one expected a resurrection of the Messiah to occur immediately after crucifixion. Indeed, no one expected the Messiah to be crucified at all. For Jews it was a totally repulsive idea, a sign of abandonment by God. So this could not have been a case of wish-fulfilment. We are told that Jesus appeared a number of times, sometimes to very large groups. And then the resurrection appearances ceased after forty days. This does not seem to fit with the way hallucinations are said to occur. In order for Hick's suggestion to be plausible, he has to give at least a reasonably believable account of how a hallucination of what was culturally totally unexpected and theologically pointless might have occurred to a number of large and separate groups of uneducated, ordinary people during a fixed period, before ceasing. It is not just enough to state 'a hallucination'. This was a hallucination that was radically life-transforming and that fitted with no religious or social structure which could obviously give it meaning. But even if Hick could give such a plausible account (and as far as I know he does not), he would still have to explain not only why so many people were subject to an unexpected hallucination but also why no one subsequently produced the body. All agree on that.

(d) Some modern writers have argued that while Jesus' body was indeed still in the tomb, the 'resurrection' is a way of speaking about how the early Church came to understand the spiritual meaning of it all. Jesus was, as it were, 'resurrected' – His mission continued in spite of His death. I find this very unconvincing. If He had died and was still in the tomb His mission precisely would not have continued. In terms of messianic expectations He was finished. There was no spiritual meaning to it all, certainly no spiritual meaning believable to first-century Jews. Had the resurrection not taken place it is difficult to consider that the terrified disciples would have thought otherwise. They would have kept their heads down and fled, probably home. They would not have drawn attention to themselves, especially with the body still in the tomb. Crucifixion was a very nasty death and they had no wish to invite it on themselves. What would be the point? The martyr and very elderly Polycarp of Smyrna, writing no later than the early years of the second century CE, states, against those ancient and many modern theologians who would deny a literal resurrection: 'to pervert the Lord's words to suit our own wishes, by asserting that there are no such things as resurrection or judgement, is to be a first-begotten son of Satan'.[3] Polycarp's views were certainly moulded by the first generation of Christian evangelists, within decades of the resurrection itself. And as the early Church knew, what is *post mortem* resurrection for us is the result of the first resurrection undergone by Christ Himself.

(e) There is a view that those who saw Jesus saw not His physical body – the one that was mouldering in the tomb – but saw something else, perhaps a 'spiritual body'. This is not, however, the evidence of the earliest sources, which speak of Jesus after His resurrection eating and drinking and able to be touched. The martyr Ignatius of Antioch, an older contemporary and friend of Polycarp, states against those who would deny it that 'For my own part, I know and believe that He was in actual human flesh, even after His resurrection'.[4] He wrote this as early as 107 CE, but he was expressing a view that he had clearly been taught and held since before he became a bishop in 69 CE. Jesus certainly did some strange things after His resurrection, like appearing and disappearing. But the accounts are careful to show that nevertheless this was to all intents and purposes a physical body, albeit amazingly transformed. Anyway, there is no suggestion that the resurrected Jesus was a different body altogether from the one that was still in the tomb. The Romans and the Jews did not proceed to produce the body.

There may be other alternative suggestions compatible with the body still being in the tomb, but I doubt they could be more plausible.

THE EMPTY TOMB

Supposing Jesus' tomb was empty and did not contain His body. Either He was not resurrected, or He was.

If Jesus had not been resurrected, what happened to His body? Various possibilities have been suggested:

(a) The possibility most widely mooted by the authorities at the time was that the disciples had stolen the body. The problem with this suggestion is that it collapses into the conspiracy theory (see (b) above). Moreover, none of the disciples was ever arrested and charged with stealing the body. Presumably, at the very least, there was no plausible evidence that they *had* stolen the body. And one might expect that eventually some news of the whereabouts of Jesus' body would have leaked out. Even in a culture where the burial places of great spiritual leaders were revered, no news of the actual site of His burial ever leaked out. No one gave it away, not even children or those early converts who might have discovered the awful truth.

(b) But perhaps someone else had stolen the body. Who? There would only really be the Romans or the Jews. But we are told that the Jews and the Romans had a guard placed on the tomb. Roman guards at this time of the empire were not likely to be slack in their duty. There is no reason why Romans or Jews would have wanted to steal the body, let alone then fail to produce it when challenged with stories of a resurrection, or even state that actually it was they who had taken the body away. Christianity could so easily have been stifled at birth. It was not. Moreover, if Romans or Jews had stolen the body this would not tell us why the disciples then concocted stories of a resurrection. That too falls within the problems associated with a conspiracy. And, as we have seen, since Jesus had *died* on the cross, a resurrection would not in any case have been enough to convince Jews that He was the Messiah. Remember, Jews were not looking for a Messiah who had been killed in what was for Jews an abhorrent way. The disciples would not themselves have expected it and would have had nothing to gain by fabricating such a story.

(c) There is one other possibility that is sometimes thought to be quite possible: that Jesus did not actually die on the cross at all. He merely swooned and revived in the tomb. Initially this suggestion looks quite plausible. It could entail theologically that God actually saved Jesus from His death and that He had not died 'on a tree'. Therefore He might well be taken by Jews as the Messiah. But to be honest I find the suggestion of swoon and revival naïve in the extreme. First, the Romans knew well enough how to kill a man. We have little understanding of how crucifixion was carried out, but it would have been pretty effective. Jesus is supposed to have had a spear thrust through His side by a Roman sentry, precisely for the purpose of making sure He was dead. Roman sentries also knew well how to kill with a spear. And supposing Jesus had swooned and revived in the tomb. He would have been very severely injured, quite unable to walk, in a state of considerable shock. He would have been unable to get out of the tomb. And even if He had, He would surely have left a distinctive trail which would have been obvious to everyone. He would not have been moving around, eating, teaching and speaking gently and consolingly to His followers. He would not Himself have been setting up a fraudulent case of resurrection, either by himself or with others. In actual fact He would no doubt have died from His injuries. And some tradition of His burial place, or what had happened to His body, would eventually have leaked out. If He had not soon died, He would have tried to escape. No one caught Him. No one ever claimed to have seen Him alive again, after the forty days of post-resurrection appearances. Or, stretching imagination to the limit, Jesus might have appeared in the public square and announced that He had survived crucifixion. God had saved Him, as He was supposed to do for the Messiah in Jewish expectations. But He did none of these things. There is another point that strikes me. We have no other account of anyone in ancient times being crucified, swooning and recovering. It is unlikely that anyone else had ever heard of it happening, or they would have said so. What an amazing coincidence it would have been if this had just happened to occur to a teacher who claimed to be the Son of God.

THE NON-EXISTENT TOMB

There is one other possibility that has been put to me by a Buddhist friend, which strangely enough is not really considered by other books. This is that the tomb was empty because *there never was a tomb*. Actually, the body of Jesus was discarded for wild animals to devour. It was suggested to me that this would have been a common way of disposing of the bodies of executed criminals.

Initially this looks a very plausible explanation. But I am still not convinced:

(a) No evidence has been given that this was the usual way of disposing of the bodies of those executed by crucifixion. I rather doubt it. If this were a common way of disposing of the bodies of crucifixion victims, then it would be very unlikely that anyone would have been impressed with the Christian claim that Jesus had risen from the dead. The authorities would just have pointed out that Jesus had not been buried in a tomb, and anyway bodies were regularly discarded. They might have been able to produce a half-devoured skeleton – or *any* half-devoured skeleton – and few would have been likely to believe the Christian story. Under those circumstances, one could not imagine the authorities being so embarrassed that they claimed the disciples had *stolen* the body. What body? Didn't they know bodies were thrown to birds and animals?

(b) I very much doubt that the Jewish authorities, with their strict rules on ritual purity, would have been happy to leave bodies, even those of criminals, lying around. It would strictly contradict God's own injunction at Deuteronomy 21:22–23. After a few bad experiences the Romans were fairly careful not to offend against Jewish ritual rules. Moreover, John's Gospel (19:31) states that the Romans broke the legs of the two criminals who were executed with Jesus at the request of the Jews in order to make sure that they were dead well before the beginning of the Sabbath. This was in order that executed bodies would not defile the Sabbath. Jesus had by that time already died. It is inconceivable under such circumstances that the bodies, particularly the bodies of Jews, would then be taken down and just left lying around for wild animals. It is also inconceivable that the Jews would have been content for the Romans to take such bodies away, knowing that they would be left for animals. It would be far too inflammatory in a political and religious situation that was already very tense.

(c) We know from an eyewitness account of the martyrdom of Polycarp of Smyrna, who was executed sometime in the middle of the second century CE in what is now Turkey, that after his death his cremated bones were collected by his followers. Indeed, there was an attempt to prevent the actual body being taken away in case (it was thought) the Christians might start to worship him instead of Jesus.[5] This shows very clearly that Jesus' body had indeed been removed from the place of crucifixion by His followers after His death. That was thought by the opponents of Christianity to be one reason why His followers could suggest, without risk of contradiction from the authorities showing the body, that He had returned from the dead. Collecting the bodies of executed Christians was clearly normal. As is well known, the body of St Peter was buried in Rome, and knowledge of where his body was buried was preserved down the centuries. Thus Constantine was able to build a church over the body of St Peter. According to tradition Peter was executed by crucifixion, and this could not have been very many years later than Jesus' own execution. Therefore it does not seem to have been normal for the Romans to throw the remains of those executed to wild animals even in Rome, let alone in Jerusalem where the horror of ritual pollution would have been so much greater. Bodies could be collected by friends and relatives. And why not?

(d) If the body of Jesus had been thrown to birds and wild animals and was thus unavailable, it would follow that the account of the resurrection was the result of a conspiracy, or hallucination, or both. I have argued above that these theories seem highly unlikely. Jesus' early followers seem to have had no problem with the claim that His body was collected by His followers and placed in a tomb. If there had been a conspiracy, and it was normal for bodies of executed criminals to be thrown to animals and birds, then it would have been pointless to say that Jesus' body had been placed in a tomb and had then walked out!

When all is said and done it would be astonishing if a religion could survive, let alone spread so rapidly, based on a carpenter who wrote nothing, taught for very few years and was executed in a manner reserved for the lowest criminals. Such an execution was so horrible that few Roman sources would talk about it. Yet we find an example of mocking graffiti on the wall of a palace *in Rome*, possibly dating from as early as the Emperor Nero's time (54–68 CE), showing someone worshipping a person who has been crucified. The crucified has an ass's or horse's head. An inscription reads 'Alexamenos worships his god'.[6] It would be astonishing if this remarkable religion was actually fabricated by a determined group of Jewish fishermen who claimed that their leader had come back from the dead and were willing to die for it! It would be astonishing if someone in Rome were to follow, within twenty years or so of the death of Jesus, a religion that must have seemed not just bizarre but utterly disgusting, if that religion were the result simply of a conspiracy of fishermen. For it would be a conspiracy based on someone coming back from the dead when everyone knew bodies of executed criminals were missing simply because they were thrown to wild animals.

All these alternatives just seem too implausible. Even supposing there was a conspiracy whereby Jesus swooned and the disciples removed the body, perhaps with the connivance of some of the authorities, it still seems just too unlikely. Why such a conspiracy? What did anyone have to gain by it? The 'Christian story' would never have convinced the Jews. Jesus had nothing to gain through any of it. Where did He finally go? And why were the disciples willing to die for a fraud? How, under such circumstances, did Christianity – a religion based, totally against all expectations, on a horribly tortured and crucified God – ever survive at all, let alone rapidly expand across the Mediterranean and survive times of vigorous persecution?

We find an absence of the body, accepted by all sides. There is the total surprise of a resurrection in terms of cultural expectations. There is the universal acceptance among early Christians within at the very most twenty years or so of the crucifixion that resurrection had actually occurred (see 1 Thessalonians 4:14, dated by most authorities to about 50 CE and no doubt based on what Paul heard from Jesus' disciples in Jerusalem). There is the radical transformation of the disciples from a defeated group of ordinary people to a self-confident band of proselytisers, and their willingness to die for their acceptance of Jesus and his resurrection. There are also the many claimed witnesses to the risen Christ, who could be pointed out by St Paul soon after as still living. With all of this we have to remember that in terms of the comparative History of Religions our sources are very early, within a few years of the death of Jesus in some cases.

There is no doubt a distinction to be made between *resurrection* and *resuscitation*. Jesus was resurrected. Lazarus was resuscitated. At least, as far as I know the Church has never considered that Jesus' resurrection was literally anticipated in the resurrection of Lazarus. Jesus had triumphed over death and subsequently ascended into heaven. Lazarus, presumably, was resuscitated and lived out a normal lifespan (whatever that was; see John 12:10) before dying. But it seems to me that the distinction between resurrection and resuscitation here is a theological one. I leave it to theologians to argue over what exactly the distinction is. It does not follow that because there is a distinction between resurrection and resuscitation that this distinction lies in the issue of physicality. Thus I see no reason to deny that Jesus' resurrection was a literal bodily resurrection, just because that corporeal quality also applied to Lazarus' resuscitation.

There are also those who would argue that Jesus' resurrection cannot have been a literal physical resurrection, since clearly His body did not behave like an ordinary body. It kept appearing and disappearing and finally it simply ascended into the sky. Unless we hold that heaven is literally a physical place in the sky (as they did in the Middle Ages) it is difficult to see how Jesus' physical body can simply have disappeared beyond the clouds.

I am not sure if all this disproves a physical resurrection or not. It certainly makes the issue complicated, but I am happy that whatever happened it is only impossible for God if it involves a logical contradiction (if one finds this arbitrary, I can only assume one has a very limited idea of God's capabilities). Thus the fact that Jesus' body in some respects did not behave like an ordinary physical body would only entail that it was not an ordinary physical body if there was a logical contradiction between its being a physical body in the ordinary sense, and the way it behaved. Is there a logical contradiction in an ordinary physical body appearing and disappearing, or ascending into the sky and then passing beyond anyone's ken? Unless we define 'ordinary' as meaning not doing these things, it does not seem obvious to me that there is. A contradiction has yet to be shown. An ordinary physical body could behave under certain circumstances in an extraordinary way without it ceasing to be an ordinary physical body. Whether it can or not depends on what the ultimate nature of matter turns out to be. Do we know that yet? We do not say that a boat *qua* metal is not an ordinary metallic object just because it floats.

I am not claiming that we can prove the resurrection. But it seems to me that the onus of proof has indeed passed to the other side, not just to suggest an alternative scenario, but an alternative scenario that is more convincing. Not to do so (it seems to me) would only be more acceptable if one was also convinced prior to any consideration that *no* evidence could account for such a miracle. That, I have suggested, is unreasonable.

There are events, and there are the meanings of events. It seems to me that the overwhelming balance of possibility is that the resurrection occurred. It is (for me) an event. But what does the resurrection *mean*? Perhaps the resurrection simply occurred, with no meaning beyond itself. A man, a religious teacher – Jesus of Nazareth – was brutally executed. He died and came back to life on the third day. It is all finally meaningless, perhaps some sort of coincidence. This seems to me neither satisfactory nor likely. So let us suppose it does indeed have meaning. What meaning? Does resurrection from the dead as the most plausible explanation of what happened make Christianity true? Does it vindicate Jesus' teaching? Not necessarily. There are Jews who accept the resurrection but do not accept Christianity. If Jesus had been the Messiah, God would not have allowed Him to die on a cross. Or Buddhism could be true, and Jesus might just have been a powerful bodhisattva. His resurrection may have been due to His great magical power of *siddhi*, and nothing to do with God. Or Jesus might have been resurrected from the dead in enough time for God to tell Him He had got it all wrong and then cause Him to go out of existence. Or after the resurrection Jesus may have tripped and fallen in the Dead Sea and drowned. Or gone to Egypt and fallen in love with a priestess of Isis, as I seem to recall D. H. Lawrence suggesting in his short story, *The Man Who Died*.

It is indeed quite possible that the meaning of the resurrection is utterly different from what Christian tradition has said it is. Christianity may have had the meaning of its central event wrong for two thousand years. But that too seems unconvincing. If the resurrection happened to Jesus, and He was a religious teacher – a teacher of meaning – then the chances are that the meaning of the resurrection is something like the one He Himself gave it. And is it really very likely that Jesus could come back from the dead, explain what it all meant, and yet the Christian tradition that follows Him proceeded to get it all hideously wrong? If Jesus can come back from the dead, the odds are He knew what He was doing. Anyone who can do *that* can also ensure that its meaning is preserved. And what would that meaning be but precisely what Christians have always said it is? Where would that meaning be preserved but in a Church, *the* Church that can demonstrate its institutional and doctrinal continuity back to earliest times?

And it does not seem to me that any other religion or spiritual teaching has anything so dramatic or convincing as resurrection from the dead – a resurrection that still seems plausible two thousand years later – to support its claims. Buddhists (and others) sometimes talk about the wonders their spiritual heroes and heroines have done and can do. But nowhere is there a case so clearly and plausibly demonstrated as the resurrection. That, it seems to me, is a fact.

Jesus' followers expected something to happen. They did not expect Jesus to die His horrible death. His words on the cross referred to his abandonment by God. If Jesus rose from the dead then it seems to me something quite extraordinary really *did* happen. Unless one holds that there is no God at all, it is reasonable to accept Christianity's own self-understanding. Jesus asked why God had forsaken Him. He rose from the dead. Ergo God had not forsaken Him.

If that is not a vindication of Jesus' teaching I do not know what would be.

One has to be willing to make a commitment eventually to what seems most likely to be the best explanation, on the evidence available at the time. Such a plausible case of resurrection from the dead by a great spiritual teacher – the only such case – when combined with the historical survival of Christianity and the palpable goodness and wisdom of many Christians, is enough for me at least to take the leap and accept Christianity.

Faith, as I have argued, is an act of will, a willingness to assert e.g. the *credo*. That declaration, in public, I am very willing and happy to make.

3

CATHOLICISM

TELL ME WHAT TO THINK!

There are those who object to Catholicism because they do not want to be told what to think. It doesn't bother me.

Any religion teaches things that go way beyond the ability of one's present unaided understanding to fathom. The Buddhist tradition I am most familiar with distinguishes between things that can be known directly, things that are hidden, and things that are very hidden. The first category covers what is obvious to the senses. The second are those things that can be known only by inference, such as the ultimate way of things (the *dharmatā*). An example of this would be that there is no such thing as an unchanging Self, the immutable referent for the word 'I'. Another example would be the (claimed) fact held by some important Buddhist traditions that absolutely all things are ultimately empty (*śūnya*) of their own intrinsic existence, and exist only in dependence upon mental imputation, conceptual construction. Or that there is no such thing as the God held to exist by theistic traditions like Christianity. All these things, it is claimed, can be demonstrated by independent reasoning. If one can think honestly, clearly and accurately enough, then on these issues all discussion can be brought to an end in agreement. The last category, however, covers things of such a nature that they can be known only by an omniscient mind. In other words, they can be known directly only by Buddhas. An example would be the exact details of the workings of the moral law. How exactly does this wicked deed lead to a particular unpleasant result? The rest of us have to accept those things on faith, based on the reliability of the teaching of the Buddhas as regards other issues that we can verify, until such time as we too have become Buddhas and can see them directly.

All religions teach the truth of assertions whose verification or falsification goes beyond the ability of our senses or our inference. Moreover, I have come to feel more and more the limitations of my own powers of reasoning. A terribly clever person may argue something. I may agree. Or I may disagree and argue back. I may think I get the better of the argument. I may base my life on what I have discovered by our intellectual sparring. At the end of my days someone even cleverer may come along and I may fail this time to win the day. Or I may succeed. None of this shows the inadequacy of reasoning as such. But it should lead to humility as regards certainty concerning our own reasoning. And what about elsewhere, and after my death? In Tibet Tsong kha pa (fourteenth/fifteenth centuries) was terribly clever. But then in Europe Aquinas was terribly clever too. Do we know who would have won, if they had met in debate? Perhaps Tsong kha pa would have become a Christian. If you say that is impossible, what are you saying?

Can I base my life on the results of *my* reasoning? Well – to a certain extent I must! In these meditations I am doing just that. Even if I decide to rely on the reasoning of others, I still have to be able to argue that the reasoning of those whom I choose to rely on is (other things being equal) likely to be worthy of credence. Or if I rely on some revelation for my access to truth, I still have to be able to argue that *this* revelation is worth relying on, rather than *that*. There is no escaping using one's brain.

Christianity simply is not – or need not be – a matter of 'blind faith'. To say otherwise is to betray simple ignorance of at least the Catholic tradition. Aquinas (like my Tibetans) argues that there is a great deal we can know by reasoning, although not *all* that is necessary to our salvation or to living a virtuous life can be so demonstrated. But Aquinas and Tsong kha pa disagree very much on what those things are. And Aquinas also adds that revelation is necessary even of those things that we *can* know by reasoning, since not everyone has the time and training to work it out by his or her intellect alone. Christ came to save all and save them *now*, not in some future life, for all (even the simple) are infinitely valuable. Thus (Aquinas thinks) we can indeed show by reasoning that God exists. But for one reason or another not everyone is capable of the demonstrative argument. Fortunately, revelation also tells us all we need to know for our eternal salvation and, fortunately, some people who lack time and ability to reason are born into families that already have faith.

Any religious system includes claims to the truth of statements that cannot be known by reasoning. And all religious systems include many statements accepted as true by their adherents that those adherents have not themselves shown to be true through valid reasoning. This seems to be how things are with the great religious systems which seek to explain so much, and on which people stake their lives and deaths.

Thus in adopting a religion I should expect de facto to be told what to think on at least some important topics. How can I possibly know their truth otherwise? And if their truth is important to the very meaning of things, and to the eternal life of myself and others, then all I can say is, please tell them to me. I want to be told these things. One is reminded here of the famous and wonderful Anglo-Saxon simile applied to the teaching of Christ by one of King Edwin's councillors and given in Bede's *A History of the English Church and People*:[1]

> Your Majesty, when we compare the present life of man on earth with that time of which we have no knowledge, it seems to me like the swift flight of a single sparrow through the banqueting-hall where you are sitting at dinner on a winter's day with your thanes and counsellors. In the midst there is a comforting fire to warm the hall; outside, the storms of winter rain or snow are raging. This sparrow flies swiftly in through one door of the hall, and out through another. While he is inside, he is safe from the winter storms; but after a few moments of comfort, he vanishes from sight into the wintry world from which he came. Even so, man appears on earth for a little while; but of what went before this life or of what follows, we know nothing. Therefore, if this new teaching has brought any more certain knowledge, it seems only right that we should follow it.

Are we really sure in our cleverness that things have changed that much? On what grounds should one rely on Buddhism rather than Christianity? On what grounds should one rely on Buddhism rather than relying on Catholicism? Or Catholicism rather than Buddhism? Are you sure? Faced with the need once and for all to make a choice, will you stake your eternal life on it?

The person who does not want to be told what to think is the person who will never think very much of deepest interest and importance.

OPTION FOR CATHOLICISM

Suppose that one accepts that God exists and that He has vindicated Jesus' teaching in raising Him from the dead. What does it all mean? How could one answer a question like this? Through reasoning, or through revelation? No doubt some types of reasoning are appropriate (e.g. theological reasoning), but here reasoning also reaches its limits. Perhaps, then, one could answer a question like this through revelation? But what sort of revelation? Scripture? But Scripture is not a neutral factor. What is to count as Scripture, and how to interpret Scripture, is given by the system within which one is carrying out the investigation. Personal religious experience? But again, the same applies. What is to count as revelatory personal experience (as distinguished from fantasy, or lunacy)? How is religious experience validated? What is to count as a valid experience is again given, one way or another, by the system.

And yet it is clear that if God exists and intervened in the world in some inexplicable way in raising Jesus from the dead, He would not leave us adrift as regards discovering what it all means. It would appear, however, that either we *are* adrift in incomprehensible subjectivity, or meaning is given by the system. What it all means, this astonishing reorientation which comes from the teachings of Jesus validated in the resurrection, cannot be a matter of incomprehensible subjectivity, my own personal guesswork. Thus in understanding fully what it all means, once again we needs must have recourse to the system.

But what could 'the system' be if not another name for the Church? It seems to me it is God's will, a will that coincides with the imperative of rationality, that there be a Church which explains the meaning. Since the very Scriptures themselves, and personal religious experience, must be subordinate to the

Church, the Church itself (as, we are told, guided by God – the Holy Spirit) must be the final authority. And since the earliest documents and events of the Christian story need the bestowal of meaning, God not only intended a Church but also intended the Church to be such that it *can* – gradually or otherwise – reveal meaning.

In support of this last point, the Church as a means of revelation, we should note that Scripture is often obscure. No one actually holds to a literal fundamentalism. Scripture always needs some sort of interpretation (even the interpretation that says that here no interpretation is needed), and all translation involves interpretation. 'Fundamentalists' who claim to follow the Bible literally and then quote e.g. the King James Authorised Version for what the Bible 'literally' says, are ridiculous. But on what grounds do we interpret 'God's word'? There is clearly no reason why God's revelation should be limited to Scripture. To think otherwise seems to me ludicrously restrictive on God's power. And how to interpret Scripture cannot logically be derived from Scripture itself. Thus there must be a basis for authoritative interpretation, and also for an ongoing revelation to suit different circumstances. I cannot see what this could be (if we are to avoid rampant subjectivism) if not an authoritative Church.

There must be a Church with the authority to reveal meaning. Which? With the exception of the Eastern Orthodox Churches, all Churches viable for me exist as derivatives from or in opposition to the Roman Catholic Church. They all gain their distinctive features from their relationship to Rome. The Eastern Orthodox Churches and Catholicism are for our purposes here more or less the same. In spite of cultural differences in, for example, robes and details of liturgy, the Eastern Churches are very similar to Catholicism. The recent *Catechism of the Catholic Church* says of the Eastern Orthodox Churches that 'this communion is so profound "that it lacks little to attain the fullness that would permit a common celebration of the Lord's Eucharist"' (para. 838). That is, uniquely, the Eastern Orthodox Churches are very nearly almost (Roman) Catholicism. The main difference lies in the employment of the *filioque* clause in the creed – the Catholic assertion, made, according to Eastern Orthodoxy, without a general Church

Council to settle the issue, that the Holy Spirit proceeds from the Father *and the Son* (Latin: *filioque*) rather than from the Father alone. The other major issue is that of the supreme and final primacy over Christians of the Bishop of Rome, the Pope. As regards the *filioque* clause I have nothing to say. That is a matter for theologians. As regards the final primacy of Rome, the traditional Orthodox view is that this is a matter of power politics. The different bishops of the main sees, such as both Rome and Constantinople, enjoy equal status as bishops and in terms of their individual authority over fundamental teachings on faith and morals. Infallible authority lies not in the Bishop of Rome – the Pope – as such but in the Church as a whole, through its Councils of bishops. The Catholic claim is that Rome has always enjoyed pre-eminence, based on the pre-eminent status originally given to the disciple Peter. This pre-eminence of the Bishop of Rome is granted by the Eastern Orthodox Churches. It was granted at least as early as the Council of Nicaea, in 325 CE, the first of the great Church Councils. It is quite explicit at the following Council of Constantinople in 381, when the Bishop of Constantinople himself replaced the Bishop of Alexandria explicitly as second in eminence after the Bishop of Rome. This reflects the growing importance of Constantinople, which was not founded as a capital of the empire until 324. A second place for Constantinople was not accepted by Rome until the Lateran Council in 1215 (when Constantinople was under crusader occupation), but the first place for Rome, based on its being the site of the martyrdoms of St Peter and St Paul, was granted by all. What was not granted, and is still not granted by the Eastern Orthodox Churches, is the supreme – indeed now infallible – status of the Papacy on issues of faith and morals. A follower of Orthodoxy would consider the claims of the Papacy sheer arrogance and presumption. A Catholic would argue that actually the point is theological. In the last analysis the Church has to have an earthly leader (as in secular politics the earthly leader is traditionally the emperor), and Christ intended it to be this way. He would not have thought, nor does He intend, otherwise. The Church is a theocracy, and finally Truth cannot be discerned through Councils, voting, discussion and even prayer. History show that what then determines 'Truth' is bribery and factions. A panel of equal authorities is in the last analysis a recipe for disaster, not for survival. This applies particularly at times of political and cultural collapse, periods only too familiar in the history of both Western and Eastern Christianity, although initially a much more serious problem for the West.

Finally there has to be one arbiter of orthodoxy, and this is what Christ intended in his declaration in the Gospels that upon Peter the Church would be founded. The alternative would be endless problems in establishing Church unity. It is noticeable, a Catholic would say, that when Christ stated to Peter at Matthew 16:18 that 'on this rock I will build my community', He added '[a]nd the gates of the underworld can never overpower it'. Of the ancient pre-eminent sees of Rome, Constantinople, Alexandria, Antioch and Jerusalem, only that of Rome has flourished throughout the ages and is still flourishing as leader of a worldwide Christian movement, the largest in existence. 'And how many divisions has the Pope?' Stalin is reported to have asked. Divisions or not, it was the impact of a visit of a Polish Pope to Poland in 1979, followed as a direct consequence by the formation of the independent trade union Solidarity in 1980, that was the spark that led eventually to the collapse of Communism in Eastern Europe.[2] There are enormous theological problems in seeing this as the action of divine providence. I doubt it. But what it does show is the continuing immense importance of the (Catholic) Church two thousand years after its foundation by a young teacher who was horribly executed after preaching for just three years, mainly to a few distressed poor under foreign occupation. Reports of Catholicism's imminent demise have been greatly exaggerated. The Roman Empire still survives. Stalin's divisions do not appear to have overpowered it.

Orthodoxy or Roman Catholicism? I can see arguments either way. But for someone in the modern world these issues seem fairly esoteric, and I would still argue that for someone in Western Europe who does not him- or herself come from an Eastern Orthodox background I strongly suspect that a good argument is needed *not* to join the Catholic Church.

But what of Protestantism? Why not remain an Anglican? It seems to me that all the Protestant traditions show greater or lesser degrees of spiritual (and psychological) impoverishment when compared with Catholicism. I was brought up an Anglican. That is really the only Protestant tradition that might tempt me. I have never felt any attraction to low-church beliefs or practice. I could not see myself becoming a Methodist, or a Baptist. In what follows, although I talk mainly about Anglicanism and the English situation, I would want to say broadly the same thing about (other) Protestant traditions.[3]

Was Protestantism so necessary to God? Can one really hold that, although the story is not very edifying nevertheless the Henrician Reformation in England was guided by the Holy Spirit?[4] Can one really hold that the Elizabethan 'middle way' – carefully crafted to harmonise both moderate Protestant and Catholic wings of the Church in England (out of communion with the Pope and the Christian mainstream), and known only in Britain – was nearer the historical intentions of Christ and Christianity? Were they really closer to spiritual and dogmatic truth than mainstream European Christianity? We now know that the late medieval pre-Reformation Church in England was flourishing and widely popular.[5] There was very little demand for reformation. Reformation had to be imposed by the state, and in the process enriched the king (Henry VIII, but also his successors) and his supporters. Was it really worth over two hundred years of religious wars and persecutions? So worthwhile that we can see the action of the Holy Spirit? Was the mainstream Church of Europe, centred on the Pope, so wrong?

If the great Saints of pre-Reformation Christianity returned to England today, what would they think? In seeing the many denominations it seems to me inconceivable that Saints like Augustine of Hippo, Gregory the Great, Augustine of Canterbury, Anselm, Thomas Aquinas, or Thomas à Becket, would not request guidance from the Pope in Rome on what to do. And they would certainly take his advice. Could we really imagine that these Saints would look at the contemporary Christian world, study the history of the Reformation and decide that the reformers were right, breaking communion with Rome themselves? And how could I now follow a denomination that would be rejected by the Saints of the Church?

I am not convinced that God could have wanted the Protestant Reformation, in the sense that the Protestant Reformation was all part of His project for His creation. There certainly were corruptions at times in the pre-Reformation Church, the corruptions of any large and rich human organisation under the same circumstances. But there was also great sanctity. With fallen humanity one might expect corruption. One should judge the presence of the Holy Spirit by the sanctity, not by the corruptions. A Church that produced St Thomas More, by the standards of his day a good and indeed saintly man martyred for refusing to accept Henry VIII as head of the Church in England, could scarcely have been *that* decadent and unpopular.

I was brought up an Anglican. I was a baptised and confirmed member of the Church of England. Earlier converts like Newman spent a long time in agonised and minute theological argument with themselves before (in Newman's case) finally opting for the Church of Rome. Perhaps that reflected an age when the social risk of conversion for a member of the Church of England was so much greater and there was so much more sophistication and understanding of the details of theological debate and disagreement. Anyway, Newman was a professional theologian. But for me the argument works the other way. What reason is there to be an Anglican rather than a Catholic?

Perhaps I am unfair, but I suspect that many people in this country remain Anglican simply because that is how they were brought up. I have been a Buddhist for over twenty years, so that in itself would not be enough to persuade me of Anglicanism. I have great respect for the Anglican liturgy, and they have some of the most beautiful buildings in the country.[6] But apart from that there is for me only a deep feeling of nostalgia about an Anglican church service.

Or perhaps some people favour Anglicanism because it is, as they say, 'a broad church'. Anglicanism is widely tolerant, and there are some who feel that Anglicanism suits them precisely because it is not intellectually restricting. The journalist and broadcaster Jeremy Paxman tells the following story:[7]

> I once asked the Bishop of Oxford what you needed to believe to be a member of his [Anglican] Church. A look of slight bafflement crossed his face. 'An intriguing question', he answered, as if it had not occurred to him before.

THE UNEXPECTED WAY

In religion I incline towards the exact opposite. Historically the Christian Church has not been particularly tolerant of divergent views. Indeed, G. K. Chesterton sees the intolerance of the Church in the very open and tolerant religious atmosphere of the late Roman Empire as responsible for the survival of Western civilisation when the Western Empire collapsed. Civilisation, he observes, once very nearly perished of tolerance.[8] Although it is a presupposition of an awful lot of contemporary (woolly) thinking on religion, it seems to me that tolerance – while generally highly laudable – is not in itself a virtue.[9]

It seems to me that any Church which is to claim continuity with Christian tradition – particularly early Church tradition – should be reasonably clear what it teaches and not at all 'a broad church'. With that clarity there should be definite and clearly stated limits to tolerance. The Church is a theocracy, not a democracy. I can understand those who prefer the intellectual freedom of Anglicanism, but it would not suit me. I have argued that in religion I *want* to be told what to think.

Perhaps there are those who incline towards something like Anglicanism (or another form of Protestantism) because they consider that with doctrines like the Virgin Birth, or transubstantiation, the Catholic Church is simply incredibly bizarre. I am not one of those. Granted that if something is logically possible God can do it, I would not be at all surprised if religious truth were quite unexpected, indeed quite bizarre, to the non-believer. The more unexpected – the more bizarre – the greater the miracle. The greater the miracle, the more the mystery. The more the mystery, the greater the wonder. The greater the wonder, the more the joy and the life-transforming impact of finding it *true*. The demise of the unexpected, indeed the non-rational (counter-intuitive), in religion is the demise of the religion. But how do we know of competing non-rational claims which are true? Here we need to refer to our faith that the Church is guided by the Holy Spirit. In other words, revealed tradition will show us which claims (such as a virgin birth, or changing water into wine) are true. The non-rational needs a Church which is confident of its authority, and a Church which is confident of its authority would not be, I suggest, a broad Church.

In religion the non-rational is not (like contradictions such as nonconceptual experiences) irrational. A religion that is embarrassed about, or minimises, its non-rational aspect is of no use to me. I want a religion which glories in the non-rational and is confident about which non-rational doctrines are true.

Question: 'How many bizarre but non-contradictory things can you believe are actually true before breakfast?'

Answer: 'As many as God requires of me.'

Question: 'How many is that?'

Answer: 'As many as the Church declares.'

I still do not understand why I should be anything other than a Catholic.

The presupposition of so many in countries where forms of Protestantism have been dominant in recent centuries is that authentic Christianity can be based only on what Jesus taught during His earthly ministry, or on what the Scriptures teach. Thus if something is found in the Catholic tradition that is not part of the faith of, say, the New Testament or the very earliest Church, its inauthenticity is taken for granted. Or at least it is seen to be problematic as a genuine part of Christianity. It is in the name of some sort of principle like this that Protestants attacked relics, the cults of Saints, purgatory and the cult of the Blessed Virgin Mary.

But this presupposition is not only debatable, it is actually paradoxical. The presupposition is debatable because it assumes that all that is true and relevant (perhaps even central) to the Christian life must have been taught by Jesus during His earthly ministry and can be found explicitly stated in the Scriptures. Thus there can be no ongoing revelation, gradual revealing of truth, or appropriate clarification to suit changing circumstances and new challenges. This whole idea is based on a lack of confidence in the Church and thus demonstrates its historical and contextual origins in the anti-Church reaction of the Reformation. But a lack of confidence in the Church must surely be a lack of confidence in the heritage of Christ for posterity. It is also a lack of confidence in God and His continuing care for us. One wonders what is left for the Holy Spirit to do. And much more important for our purposes, the presupposition is paradoxical. As far as I know, nowhere is the presupposition itself stated in the Holy Scriptures. Nowhere is it stated in the New Testament, for example, that all that is true and relevant (perhaps even central) to the Christian life must have been taught by Jesus during His earthly ministry and be found explicitly stated in the Scriptures. Thus appeal to the very principle upon which a great deal of the criticism of the Catholic tradition is based actually contradicts itself.

If one is to avoid contradiction one has to accept the possibility of teachings and practices true and relevant to the Christian life outside the Scriptures and even the practices of the early Church. But how is one to validate as authentic such innovative teachings and practices? It can only be through a visible Church that can speak with complete authority (*magisterium*), the authority of God. Such a Church could be no democracy. It would see itself as a theocracy. And it needs *must* speak with confidence.

I have been enormously impressed by reading some of the early Church Fathers, particularly Ignatius of Antioch. He is important to me because he was martyred in 107 CE, by which time he had served as Bishop of Antioch for some 40 years. Shortly before his death he wrote a series of letters of advice to other churches. We can reasonably assume that the ideas Ignatius expresses were current by 69 CE, and very likely much earlier, and were taught directly by Jesus' disciples. What we find in these letters, it seems to me, are most of the essential elements of the Christian faith as preserved in Roman Catholicism. We find a very clear idea of the identity, unity and authority of the Church. We also find clearly expressed the Trinity of God the Father, God the Son and the Holy Spirit. In the following, which is separated out from the prose epistle as a verse bearing the hallmarks of an early creed, we see Jesus Christ, the Son, identified as God Incarnate:[10]

Very Flesh, yet Spirit too;
    Uncreated, and yet born;
God-and-Man in One agreed,
Very-Life-in-Death indeed,
Fruit of God and Mary's seed;
    At once impassible and torn

By pain and suffering here below:
Jesus Christ, whom as our Lord we know.

(Staniforth 1968: 77–8)

Elsewhere in Ignatius's epistles, when referring to certain heretics, we find clearly expressed the dogma of the real presence of Christ's body in the Mass (transubstantiation):[11]

> They even absent themselves from the Eucharist and the public prayers, because they will not admit that the Eucharist is the self-same body of our Saviour Jesus Christ which suffered for our sins, and which the Father in His goodness afterwards raised up again.

This is of crucial importance because, of course, the doctrine of the real presence of Christ's body in the bread and wine at the Mass was a central issue at dispute in the Protestant Reformation. It seems from this quite clear to me that the real presence must have been a teaching of the very earliest Church. That at least is the obvious way to take Ignatius's statement.

Ignatius mentions the virgin birth ('truly born of a Virgin'). One has to admit that there is some unclarity here, however, since he also states that Jesus was truly of David's line 'in His manhood'[12] and elsewhere speaks of Him as being 'the seed of David according to the flesh'.[13] The problem is that, according to the genealogy at the beginning of Matthew's Gospel, Jesus was of the line of David through Joseph who was the husband of Mary, Jesus' mother (cf. Luke 3:23). That has been something for the Church to sort out. Ignatius repeatedly refers to the resurrection. He it is who tells us that Christians celebrate Sunday as the Lord's Day rather than the Jewish Sabbath in memory of the day of the resurrection.[14] There is repeated mention of resurrection of the body for true believers, but little or no mention of an expected imminent Second Coming of Christ. Ignatius even seems to me to imply some sort of pre-eminence in the Church for the Christians in Rome and therefore for the Bishop of Rome (see the preface to his *Epistle to the Romans*, and its whole tenor), although that is a matter of interpretation and would be disputed.

But in the last analysis the Catholic Church is the only viable Christian Church for me that has the backing of continuity (lineage), history, spiritual and philosophical profundity, experience, tradition and – above all – clear authority. It is the only Christian Church that speaks as if it had the Truth (Chesterton). It is the Church that asks for straightforward obedience. It may not always look like it, but if there *is* a meaning-bestowing Church this must be it. *That* is the voice of God.

Everything I meet with in Catholic doctrine, practice and conduct, when greeted with openness, encountered as part of the living tradition of belief and practice and not through intellectual isolation or romantic distance, feels like coming home. It is all *right*. Lived in the context of the whole, everything falls into place. This is what I really sought, for all those years, in all those places, so far from home. This is what I sometimes glimpsed in the distance, through shadows and hazy sunlight, glimpsed behind trees, on the mountain tops, in the waves. This is what I sought in ruins and in incense, in bookshops, in philosophy and in meditation. Through all He saw me clearly. He has not found me, for He never lost me. He would not let me go, even when I tried to run in denial and fright.

'Do not be afraid. I am with you. I have called you by your name. You are mine.'

I am so *very* grateful.

GREAT CATHEDRALS

I remember hearing Denys Turner talk about the way that the great British cathedrals were stripped of their 'Catholic' paintings and trappings at the Reformation. The wonderful medieval wall paintings were hacked out, or whitewashed over. In doing this Protestants were expressing bodily their theology of direct access to God, without the intermediaries of created means like artistic representations and priestly ritual.

The Protestant reformers were thereby stating two things. First, access to God was through the Scriptures as read by oneself in one's own language and illumined by God in one's own heart. Second, other traditional means of access to God were really idolatry, to be stripped away in order to leave room for the full scope of this inner illumination. Thus the very fabric of medieval cathedrals and churches in Great Britain shows forth a sort of *via negativa*, the way to God through stripping-away. By contrast, therefore, the richly elaborated art, music, liturgy and sacramental life of the pre-Reformation Church and post-Reformation Catholicism show a sort of *via positiva*.

And yet the *via negativa* is very difficult as a means of access to God. It throws everything back onto an unmediated experience. It places experiences to the fore and cuts away communal mediation from under the experience. In doing this it undermines the role of the Church, but also it undermines the very framework which can put religious experience in its place. Unmediated religious experiences are, I would suggest, meaningless experiences. Inasmuch as they have to be given meaning, and it can be done now only by the person who has undergone the experiences, that person lacks all basis for meaning apart from private hunch or subjective speculation. Private hunch, subjective speculation, are all too often essentially egoistic. Of course, in Protestantism the principal means of attempted escape here was the role played by the Scriptures. Religious life transcends pure subjectivity by scriptural validation. But in the last analysis the Protestant reformers had problems justifying their failure to extend their primacy of personal experience of God to individual, subjective interpretation of the Scriptures themselves. Thus to the extent to which they stressed unmediated experience, the Protestant reformers locked their followers into a 'sensational circle'. That is, they were locked into a circle of experiences validated by experiences validated by further experiences, from which it was very difficult to escape. Under such circumstances it becomes very difficult (I would suggest) to gain access to the real world of the Other – God – or indeed the other – such as the objective existence of tables, chairs, trees and monkeys, or fellow human beings and their welfare. All becomes, to use a Buddhist image, a 'play of experiences', a 'play of representations', a 'play of consciousness'. As Pope John Paul II says in a similar context,[15]

The interpretation of this word [of God] cannot merely keep referring us to one interpretation after another, without ever leading us to a statement which is simply true; otherwise there would be no Revelation of God, but only the expression of human notions about God and about what God presumably thinks of us.

Scripture must at some point transcend the interpretive spiral. Since all personal reading of Scripture is necessarily, *qua* personal, implicated in subjectivity, interpretation of Scripture must at some point transcend the personal – whether of individuals or human groups – in order to gain access to objective truth. That is, the understanding and use of Scripture cannot be based purely on the individual's own reading of it, or on a group of individuals as such. It is difficult to see what transcendence of subjectivity and access to objective truth can be if it is not through something that is not itself subjective. That is, access to truth here must be through God (cf. the philosopher's notion of pure objectivity as the God's eye view of the world). But access to God cannot itself be through subjective experience or interpretation, or we are locked back into subjectivity again. Thus, for the leap to objectivity, at some point one has to appeal to a body that cannot be subjective. In Christianity this has always been seen as a theocratic Church, and as a body that cannot be subjective it has to be a Church which is clear about its unarguable authority, the authority of the Holy Spirit. That is what we mean by saying that in the last analysis, on crucial matters of faith and morals, the Church has to be infallible.

The grounding of created things on uncreated necessary Being, the grounding of subjective assessments, individual taste and choice in religion on objective truth, and the grounding of moral behaviour on objective right and wrong rather than on subjective factors (like sensations of pleasure and pain, or the interests of society, class, or some other group) appear to be all part and parcel of the same broad opposition. This is the opposition between subjectivity and objectivity. As the Pope puts it:[16]

> It is there [in the Bible] that we learn that what we experience is not absolute: it is neither uncreated nor self-generating. God alone is the Absolute. From the Bible there emerges also a vision of man as *imago Dei*. This vision offers indications regarding man's life, his freedom and the immortality of the human spirit. Since the created

world is not self-sufficient, every illusion of autonomy which would deny the essential dependence on God of every creature – the human being included – leads to dramatic situations which subvert the rational search for the harmony and the meaning of human life.

Pope John Paul would want to argue that finally, if one is to be consistent, one has a choice between a subjectivity that collapses into relativism or an objectivity that can only be based on God and an authoritative Church. To the extent to which all forms of Buddhism see the everyday world of common experience as existing in dependence upon the mind, and liberation as lying in mind-transformation, it seems to me that all forms of Buddhism give priority to subjectivity. The move towards basing religion as such on sensations, experiences, and so on – as we find in the last analysis in Buddhism, or in some ways of interpreting mysticism – must be a move towards subjectivity. In making that move, Pope John Paul would want to say, one is likely to lose an ability to ground objective religious truth and thus to ground moral behaviour and finally God Himself. God and the authoritative Church stand or fall together.

The tension between a purely subjective individualism in religion and a (I think largely unsuccessful) attempt to claw back a role for the wider Church and thus to that extent deny individual interpretation, marks much of the history of Protestantism. Yet having broken with Rome and the absolutist claims of the Papacy, what grounds could be given for any assured role for a lesser body, such as national or local Churches? How, for example, could the Church of England claim access to truth? Voting will not suffice, for a majority, even after debate, persuasion and (dare I say it) prayer, can be wrong.

It is not surprising, perhaps, that philosophies which emphasised the primacy of direct sensation ('perceptions') developed in post-medieval Europe primarily in nations influenced by Protestantism. And with someone like the Scottish atheist philosopher David Hume, for example, we find that in a consistent primacy given to sensations we eventually lose God altogether. That makes sense. For, as we have seen all along, in the move towards experiences we reach the point where God becomes experiences. And if God is experiences then, *qua* experiences, we can no longer validate them as God. Experiences are mundane aspects of psychology and as such nothing to do with God. But if experiences have primacy, what grounds do we have for claiming God at all?

Nevertheless it seems to me that this is quite the wrong approach to Christianity and the Christian tradition. Even as regards understanding the Bible, to quote from Pope John Paul again,[17]

> A radically phenomenalist [based on sensations, and hence subjective] or relativist philosophy would be ill-adapted to help in the deeper exploration of the riches found in the word of God. Sacred Scripture always assumes that the individual, even if guilty of duplicity and mendacity, can know and grasp the clear and simple truth. The Bible, and the New Testament in particular, contains texts and statements which have a genuinely ontological content. The inspired authors intended to formulate true statements, capable, that is, of expressing objective reality. It cannot be said that the Catholic tradition erred when it took certain texts of Saint John and Saint Paul to be statements about the very being of Christ. In seeking to understand and explain these statements, theology needs therefore the contribution of a philosophy which does not disavow the possibility of a knowledge which is objectively true, even if not perfect. This applies equally to the judgements of moral conscience, which Sacred Scripture considers capable of being objectively true.

When we look inside a great medieval British cathedral we are often deeply moved. But what moves us? Is it the absence of paintings on the stone walls, or the absence of statues of the Blessed Virgin Mary, or stained glass smashed during the Reformation? Is it the absence of the great shrines? This absence might make us sad. It might even move us to tears for the loss. But if we are moved *religiously*, I doubt it could be due to these absences as such. What moves us religiously is what is left, not because it is all that is left but because what is left is often so supremely beautiful in itself and (as was intended) moves the mind to the contemplation of the greatness, perfection, beauty and peace of God. In other words, inasmuch as it is beautiful and performs its function, we are spiritually moved by what is *present* in a great cathedral.

This is no *via negativa*. It is the old *via positiva*. If the original paintings on the stone walls, or statues of the Blessed Virgin Mary, or stained glass windows, had been beautiful and performed their function, they too would have moved us spiritually. Surely, inasmuch as we do speak of religious experiences, one central dimension is to be moved spiritually to contemplation of the greatness, perfection, beauty and peace of the objective Living God. Thus it would be better if those paintings and statues were still present. It would be better if we still had a fully-fledged *via positiva*.

And that, it seems to me, is Catholicism.

CAN ONE FIND GOD IN SHIT?

I have heard it said, by young people in particular, that God is in everything. Thus surely, since God can be found anywhere, there is no reason why one should go to church in order to find God. Indeed, why bother to follow any denomination at all? This view more often than not appears to be underpinned by a vague sort of pantheism. Since God is everywhere and in anything, why is going to church so special?

I am not sure I ever thought this myself, mainly because pantheism – the idea that God is identical with the totality of things – never really attracted me. It is not as such a Buddhist view, although of course in Buddhism it is said that the way things ultimately are can be found through properly understanding any particular thing. Pantheism easily collapses into no-theism. The pantheistic sort of God is no God at all. It is itself a form of very confused and woolly atheism. If God is identical with the totality of things (or even, indeed, if God includes all things but also exceeds them), then each thing must be a part of God. If so, this is certainly not the God I have defended. It is not the God of Christian orthodoxy, a necessary being, the answer to the question, 'Why is there something rather than nothing?', a being that is good, just and merciful, a being that is all-powerful, a being who is love, a being that can be expressed in Trinitarian terms. My desk is not part of such a being. My left kneecap is not part of such a being, and what sense can I make of my mind, or the number two, being part of such a being? When I eat toast and marmalade I cannot in any meaningful sense say I am eating part of God. Suppose it were true: would toast and marmalade be anything other than, actually, well – toast and marmalade? If it were true, where would God have gone? If all these things can be said to be part of God then we are clearly not talking about *God*. We are just using a fancy way of talking about *things*. Perhaps it is a new way of looking at things. But that has nothing to do with God as such. Things are in constant change. God is not. Things are in time. God is not. Things could have not existed. God could not. God is not the sort of being that can have parts. If that is the God that atheists deny, then so do orthodox Christians.

Modern pantheists sometimes like to shock by adopting an expression perhaps derived from Japanese Zen. God, they say, can be found as much in a lump of shit as in church. But what can this mean? God is not *in* anything. God cannot be identical with a lump of shit. A lump of shit cannot be a part of God. And God is not behind a lump of shit. God cannot be the stuff of a lump of shit. All they can mean (if they are Christians at all) is that all things – including a lump of shit – are created by God and are, as such, good. What this entails is that any thing, including a lump of shit, would go out of existence quicker than instantly if God withdrew His will for its existence. Thus all things – including a lump of shit – are capable of being used as a way of suggesting their Creator. All things sing of God. If we can hear and understand the song, we shall come to know and love God more fully. And that is true. But in that case, logically, we can find God in church as much as in a lump of shit.

Moreover the issue is not one of whether or not God created the lump of shit, such that it can suggest God. Of course God created it, inasmuch as it absolutely depends for its existence on the will of God. It would be a strange world where everything depended absolutely on God except a lump of shit. The issue, then, is one not of the objective status of lumps of shit. Rather, it is an issue of the subject, us, and also perhaps an issue of the nature of God. Humans are so constituted, or at least the humans I am familiar with in my society are so constituted, that beauty is more likely than lumps of shit (other things being equal) to raise the mind to God. One would prefer a beautiful church service to contemplating a lump of shit for an hour. And that preference is not just self-indulgence, for God is not just the source of all things. God is also, in an analogous way to the beauty with which we are familiar, supremely beautiful. Thus, when properly experienced, the beautiful sacraments of the Church are more likely to raise the mind to God than the activities of a cesspit. Indeed, Catholics believe that the sacraments have been so ordained, under the influence of the Holy Spirit, to be potent means of raising the mind to God. Shit has not. This is not to say that shit could not have been so ordained, if God had wished. And it is also not to say that, in individual specific cases, contemplating a lump of shit may not also raise the mind to God. Or attending a sacrament may, in certain circumstances, not raise the mind to God. Who is to say? One can indeed imagine a Christian teacher in a particular context, wishing to draw attention to the fact that all things inasmuch as they exist are created by God and are, as such, good, stating that 'God can be found in a lump of shit'. But that is all. It is not so dramatic, not really so terribly profound.

And none of this means that one could or should contemplate a lump of shit as much as go to church. Not only have the sacraments been ordained by God and tradition as the most potent means of access to Him, but the God in whom Christians believe is a God of community. One cannot be a Christian and not be a member of the community. This is the case right from baptism, through confirmation and Eucharist, to death and beyond. The Christian community does not meet together in sewage farms. It meets in churches. Christ ordained the Eucharist and is indeed literally present in the Eucharist. Catholics believe that the communion wafer and the wine at the Mass are literally transformed through a particular grace into the substance of His body and blood. Thus God can indeed be found truly and easily in attending Mass. Christ does not do all this for lumps of shit. I am not sure *why* one would want to find God through contemplating a lump of shit.

The person who says God can be found anywhere is right, if

by this is meant that anything can potentially be used as means of raising the mind to God as its Creator. But as a reason for not attending church it is, for Christians, deeply confused. God has so ordained it that He is particularly available in church. He has so ordained it that He is essentially found in community. One who is a member of that community and attends church has found God. One who contemplates shit or any other created thing instead, has probably not. The promised state of perfection is expressed in terms of community, participation and beauty. Swimming in shit is a traditional image of hell.

It is a sunny Sunday. It feels as if spring is in the air, although it is still early February. The Catholic newspapers are full of leaks that the new Cardinal Archbishop of Westminster, in succession to Basil Hume, will be Bishop Cormac Murphy-O'Connor. I do not know if it has been confirmed yet. If so, it is very welcome. Apparently Cormac Murphy-O'Connor 'rivals Cardinal Hume for sheer niceness and has a way of putting a human face on even the thorniest of Church teachings'.[18] Cardinal Hume apparently convinced the Vatican before he died that the United Kingdom requires special treatment, a sensitive and congenial moderate at the top. In apparently heeding his advice the Pope is showing how much Hume was trusted and loved by all shades of opinion in the Church, and how much the Vatican shares our loss. And surely Cardinal Hume himself is well able still to care for the Catholic Church in the United Kingdom. I am very happy. It is funny how quickly I have come to identify with the interests of the Catholic family.

While walking back from Mass I was thinking about Christianity and Neoplatonism. Alas, it can be terribly boring, so unless you are interested in this sort of thing I would go on to the next section if I were you.

Neoplatonic philosophy is associated with the pagan Hellenic philosophers Plotinus (205–269/70 CE) and Porphyry (234–c.305 CE), although it was also extremely influential on certain of the early Christian Fathers including Augustine. As it is normally represented, Neoplatonism is a monistic philosophy. Ultimately only one thing exists, the One. This One is the final source of all things, incorporeal, free and perfectly good. The One projects itself out into lower levels of being, and each level is weaker than the one that precedes it. Thus things 'emanate', as it were, from the One, and to the One they all return. As things get further and further from the One, the influences of Its own characteristics get less and less. Eventually things become so far from the perfect Good that we come to call them 'bad'.

Taken at face value, it is difficult to see how this is compatible with Christianity. It is the thought of Athens, not of Jerusalem. Christianity, it seems to me, is essentially dualistic. The Neoplatonic model would seem to be very similar to the pantheism treated above. It is akin to what I sometimes call the 'bubblegum theory'. All things are blown out by the One, out of itself, like bubblegum blown into a bubble. Our lump of shit would be an emanation – admittedly a remote emanation – from the One, God. If the One is finally all that really exists, then all things, including the lump of shit, would appear to be in some sense 'made' of the One. The One is their stuff, their substance. The lump of shit is a remote effluence from the bubblegum.

We find similar views expressed in some forms of Indian philosophy, but apart from metaphor I have always been unable to make much sense of them.

It struck me that possibly, however, there is a way of reading the Neoplatonist perspective that is quite compatible with Christianity, even the Christian Aristotelianism of someone like Aquinas. This involves understanding the emanationist model in terms of greater or lesser proximity to God, without taking 'proximity' in any spatial sense or in any sense of material 'emanation', emanation of any stuff, any cosmic bubblegum.

Take the case of a beautiful work of art. We can indeed say that since the work of art is beautiful it is close to God. What we mean by 'close' here is that (i) the work of art exists and is therefore created by God in the way that all things that exist are created by God. And (ii) inasmuch as God is perfect Beauty God also bears an analogous relationship to the beautiful work of art. That is, just as with the quality of goodness, we can say that God is truly beautiful and beautiful to a supreme degree, although we cannot know in the case of God, from God's own side as it were, what it means to say that God is beautiful. Now, take the case of a lump of shit. Inasmuch as the lump of shit exists, it is indeed created by God. But God is not in any way analogous to a lump of shit. Apart from existence itself, there is no additional quality like beauty in a lump of shit that we can say God also possesses to a supreme degree.[19] Thus we can say that a lump of shit is further from God than, say, a beautiful piece of music. In terms of properties like 'being created by God' and 'bearing an analogous relationship to God', a lump of shit has fewer of them than a beautiful work of art. Take now the case of the wickedness of Hitler. As we have seen, the wickedness of Hitler lay in Hitler's falling short of how a human being should behave. Therefore Hitler's wickedness, as a 'falling short', is a negative thing. Negative things do not, as such, exist. Thus Hitler's wickedness does not possess even the property of 'being created by God'. We can say therefore that negative things are even further from God than existent things.

This Christian way of drawing on the Neoplatonic model of 'emanation' from God is indeed ontological, for it does concern levels of existence. In my three levels introduced here there are:

(A) The level of existing and thus created by God, as well as having qualities that God also has to a supreme degree but analogously.

(B) The level of existing and thus created by God, but not having additional qualities that God also has to a supreme degree but analogously.

(C) The level of being a negative thing. Therefore, as such, this is a level of things not created by God at all.

Thus there is a sense in which the level of negative things is a level of the absence of God. This is particularly so in the case of evil, sin and wickedness. That is precisely why they are evil. That level of absence of God, as an environment in response to wickedness, is by definition what we call 'hell'. Hell is simply where God is not. This, perhaps, is why supremely evil people gravitate towards hell. They flow into it, as their natural place. They do not have to be *sent* there. God would much rather they came to Him. But they cannot. They cannot be where God is. It is antithetical to their nature. They have acted in such a way that, implicitly or explicitly, they do not *want* God. They have *chosen* denial of God. And denial of God is what they get. And yet, using our Neoplatonic model, God is all there is. There thus can be no level – there is nowhere – without God. God, as it were, 'fills' all things. He is the very fullness of all things, for they are created by Him. This is what is usually thought of as the 'emanationist' model of Neoplatonism, and this is why Neoplatonism is read as saying that evil is to be explained in terms of remoteness from the Source. In what sense, therefore, can there be any absence of God? As the Psalmist has it (Psalm 139:7–8):

> Where shall I go to escape your spirit?
> Where shall I flee from your presence?
> If I scale the heavens you are there,
> If I lie flat in Sheol ['hell'], there you are.

But how can evil involve both the presence and absence of God? The answer, surely, lies in the nature of negative things. They are parasitic upon things that exist. The level of being a negative thing is as such one that is not dependent on the creative function of God. Thus God is not responsible for the wicked acts of Hitler, for those wicked acts are a failure on Hitler's part to be what he could have been. But these negative things require the existence of all kinds of created things. They can occur only because of created things. The failures of Hitler required the existence of Hitler. Hitler himself, for example, was not a negative thing. As such Hitler was created by God, and as such Hitler was created in God's image and was good. Thus, wherever the failure is, there is also one who is failing. God is present as Creator wherever there is a creation. Wherever there is the level of negative things, it exists in direct dependence upon the levels of creation. Therefore where there is wickedness God is still present. Where there is hell, there also is God. In this sense, using our Neoplatonic model, wickedness is a level of remoteness from God, but not *other* than God. There is nothing other than God.

We can indeed speak of each of these three levels as successively further from God, participating less and less in God. But as far as I can see, nothing of this way of understanding Neoplatonism involves monism, pantheism, or indeed anything incompatible with Aquinas.

There – I said it was all terribly boring. I said I should go on
to the next section if I were you. But I am writing these meditations for myself. I *am* you. I wonder what I did?

ON DOING THEOLOGY BY NUMBERS

The BBC has commissioned a special end of year poll of leading
British figures on attitudes to traditional Christian beliefs. It
should come as no surprise to find that the modern media
thinks theology can be done by a questionnaire, and truth can
indeed be settled by voting.[20] This sort of thing provides just the
material for the post-Christmas (not to mention post-Christian,
postmodern) news, when because of the holidays nothing much
else has been happening. And it is ideal for the beginning of a
new millennium. That requires at least some token reference to
Jesus. Any existential doubts felt by people can at least
temporarily be put to one side by the amusement of hearing
churchmen on radio or television struggling to reduce beliefs to
coherent soundbites.

The great discovery of this survey, it seems, is that very few
churchmen (and, I assume, churchwomen) believe that the
world was literally created in six days. This seems to be taken
to entail some reservations concerning the creative activity of
God. Perhaps it even implies some unease about the very
existence of God, at least as literally understood, by some
churchmen. And the other discovery is of considerable doubt
about the literal truth of the virgin birth. I am glad to say that
only one of the Catholic churchmen who replied to the survey
expressed any doubt on the latter score.

It seems more likely that one would find belief in the literal
truth of the biblical account of creation of the world in six days
among certain groups of Protestants than among Catholics.
The Bible is held by Catholics to be the inspired word of God,
but as far as I understand it the literal truth of the biblical
account of creation has never been an explicit item of faith for
Catholics. One of the roles of the Church – a role rejected by
many Protestant reformers – has been precisely to explain to the
faithful how to understand the accounts of biblical revelation.[21]

And we know from the New Testament description of the risen Christ's teaching on the road to Emmaus (Luke 24:13ff.) that Christ Himself engaged in interpreting the accounts in what Christians call the 'Old Testament' in the light of later revelation and understanding. None of the creeds makes explicit mention of adherence to the literal truth of Genesis. While I think it is quite possible for God to create the world in six days – in fact He could create infinite worlds instantly – overwhelming scientific evidence seems to be that He did not do so. I have no problem with that. Nor, as far as I know, does the Church (nowadays) or most other Catholics. None of this has anything to do with the issue of the existence of God, and the absolutely literal complete and utter dependence of the existence of things on God. As we have seen, God would exist as the Creator of all even if there were no beginning, let alone a beginning as described in a literal interpretation of Genesis. And Aquinas would agree.

As regards the virgin birth the situation is quite different. Belief in the virgin birth is (as I understand it) an item to which a Catholic is required to offer assent. It is mentioned in the creeds and has long been an item of Christian belief. There is nothing impossible for God in a virgin birth for His son. The idea that God can create the entire world and all that is in it yet cannot create an eensy-weensy sperm in the womb of Mary without needing a male human intermediary (if that is what He did) seems incredible. Presumably those who would deny the virgin birth are not saying that God cannot bring it about. Rather, they are saying that God would not, or did not, do so. But how could they possibly know that? How could they know what God would or would not do? On the issue of what God has or has not done, the verdict of Scripture and the Church, inspired by the Holy Spirit, is likely to be more reliable than one's own hunch or suspicion. Thus those who would deny the virgin birth must deny either the power of God, or the inspiration and reliability of Scripture and the Church. Of course, they can deny those things. But it is difficult to see how one can deny these things and be a Christian, at least in anything like the orthodox or historic sense.

Perhaps those who deny the virgin birth do so on the basis that a virgin birth is just not very likely. But why should our understanding of God's actions, or the incarnation of Christ, be based on what is likely? One might expect the exact opposite. It is indeed not very likely that what God would do is what is most likely, what would be most expected. The Christian message is indeed one of God behaving in the most unexpected way. Denial of the virgin birth on these grounds would suggest doubt as regards the whole message of Christianity. What are we to make of Jesus as the Son of God if we reject the virgin birth? Are we saying that the Blessed Virgin Mary was not a virgin at the time of Jesus' birth, although nevertheless a male partner was not required for Jesus' conception? What a strange idea! And what grounds are there scripturally or in tradition for *that*? Or are we to say that Jesus did indeed have a human father? Then in what sense was He the Son of God? Let alone God incarnate. Jesus for orthodox Christianity was not, repeat *not*, simply a good human being, that was perhaps adopted by God because of His goodness and their closeness (the heresy of Adoptionism). He was always God, including from the very moment of His conception. Rejecting the virgin birth would seem to entail rejecting orthodox Christianity altogether.

I have no difficulty whatsoever in believing the doctrines of the virgin birth and indeed the immaculate conception and the assumption of the Blessed Virgin Mary bodily into heaven. Spiritually these truths seem so wonderful. It is just what we *should* expect if God were to become man, and if the Blessed Virgin Mary were to be the very prototype of redeemed humanity, free of all sin. Inasmuch as, for example, the doctrines of the virgin birth and the assumption concern the Blessed Virgin Mary I think we can know in some sense what they mean – or at least, what they are denying. If God became man through the Blessed Virgin Mary the doctrine of the virgin birth declares that Mary conceived and gave birth to Jesus through the Holy Spirit, while remaining an intact virgin. What else should we expect with the Mother of the Son of God? And the doctrine of the assumption declares that the Blessed Virgin Mary, who as the vessel for the Son of God was from birth completely free of all sin (immaculate conception), was bodily taken up into heaven as we all shall be when we are finally freed of all sin. Catholic Christianity is not a dualism, it does not hate the body and it sees the final achievement in bodily terms. As persons we are body and soul, and the final achievement we shall be is what creation and we were always intended to be. The Blessed Virgin Mary, as free of all sin, has to have achieved that goal already. Her bodily assumption, again, is just what we should expect.

So these doctrines, inasmuch as they are about the Blessed Virgin Mary, are perfectly comprehensible. And inasmuch as they are about the actions of God they are perfectly possible. They are not contradictory. But inasmuch as they are about God Himself we can say no more. We know what we can indeed say truthfully about God, but we do not know what we are saying when we say it. These are mysteries. We know that God became man and we know that the Blessed Virgin Mary, as free of all sin, was taken bodily into Heaven, as we all shall be at the end. But we do not know what we are saying about God in Himself when we say these things.

Wonderful mysteries! It seems to me that spiritual richness is enhanced by mystery, mystery within a framework of rationality. Such doctrines as the virgin birth and the assumption, along with the immaculate conception and the whole role of the Blessed Virgin Mary, only make Catholicism more compelling to me. But I could never have known of all this without the Church. Credo ut intelligam.[22]

Of course, virgin births are not very common! But then, neither is the incarnation of God, nor the resurrection. Interestingly, there was in the poll overwhelming support among churchmen for the resurrection (although one would dearly like to know what some of them understand by 'the resurrection'!). This suggests that in at least some cases churchmen tend to apportion their belief (as David Hume might say) to the evidence. The evidence for the resurrection is (it seems to me) overwhelming. As far as I know, apart from church teaching, there is no independent evidence for the virgin birth.

But is that the right way round in religious faith? Why should church teaching on such issues not itself be overwhelming evidence? If a teaching is the teaching of a Church of which one has chosen to be a member (or which for other reasons one intends to join), isn't it correct to hold a belief as true until there is compelling evidence against it? (Interestingly enough, the Dalai Lama has said the same about adhering to Buddhist beliefs in the light of scientific counter-evidence.) If God can do something (i.e. it is not contradictory), and the Church which one intends to join and tradition say He has done it, then I have absolutely no problem in believing the literal truth of that providing there is no overwhelmingly compelling evidence against it. I am astonished that others in the Churches seem to have problems with this.

Funnily enough, it may be just this attitude of churchmen tending to apportion their belief to the evidence that is responsible for the alienation of many young people from the Churches. To abandon the miraculous in religion in favour of what seems scientifically warranted may be not only theologically and philosophically suspect. It may also be insensitive to the yearning for magic and mystery among so many young people, and an extremely unwise evangelical strategy. If one looks at the New Age movement, or at the beliefs of, say, those who flock to the spiritual centres of Glastonbury or California, what one finds are beliefs easily as extraordinary as the virgin birth. When I was a Buddhist in one of the Tibetan traditions and people asked what I was trying to believe, I often used to reply that 'You wouldn't believe what I believe!' St Augustine has put it very well:[23]

> From now on I began to prefer the Catholic teaching. The Church demanded that certain things should be believed even though they could not be proved, for if they could be proved, not all men could understand the proof, and some could not be proved at all. I thought that the Church was entirely honest in this and far less pretentious than the Manichees [Manichaeans, whom Augustine had previously followed], who laughed at people who took things on faith, made rash promises of scientific knowledge, and then put forward a whole system of preposterous inventions which they expected their followers to believe on trust because they could not be proved. Then, O Lord, you laid your most gentle, most merciful finger on my heart and set my thoughts in order ...

New Age bookstores are full of books apparently believed by many, detailing much more astonishing things than a virgin birth. The churchmen who abandon traditional beliefs in favour of what seems more scientifically warranted not only make a mockery of traditional Christianity and the very nature of religious belief, but also deny precisely the spirituality and sense of mystery for which people are searching. Of course if religion is true it is extraordinary. Of course it is deep, deep mystery. The current vogue in some circles for a cult of 'the Goddess' should be very sympathetic and responsive to the magic and miracle of the Blessed Virgin Mary.

It is a shame that some churchmen are moving in exactly the wrong direction. Even their philosophy, their reasoning, is wrong. More mystery, more miracle, when it is seen as perfectly rational mystery and miracle, is (I suggest) the way to attract back to the Christian faith so many of the young people currently searching in the New Age and Buddhist bookstores.

AN ARGUMENT TO PROVE HELL
AND PURGATORY

This is an issue that came up at one of the RCIA meetings.

I am told that there is a biblical reference that in Christ one is *totally separated* from one's sins. If so, then why can't even Hitler, for example, be saved?

(A) Supposing Hitler = H, and Hitler's sins = s. Then Hitler+sins = Hs. Hitler minus sins = H − s. Archibald+sins = As, and so on.

(B) In Christ As is turned to A − s. But Hitler's sins included ideologies and deeds that, it could be argued, became part of the very identity of Hitler. Thus H − s would be so far removed from Hitler as to be no longer Hitler. Therefore if Hitler were separated from his sins we would no longer have Hitler. It would be for Hitler to be eliminated. The remaining being, 'quasi-Hitler' with no sins at all, would be a new creation that could have no justification for existing. Thus there would be no quasi-Hitler. Therefore either (a) Hitler retains his sins, or (b) he is eliminated. If (a), then since sin is incompatible with God, and an absence of God is hell, Hitler must be in hell. If (b), elimination would seem to be incompatible with justice. For someone as wicked as Hitler (or whatever example you wish to use), simply to cease to exist, it could be argued, would be unjust. Hitler presumably did not really believe in God. He probably expected cessation at death all along. He cannot have expected an Aryan heaven (surely). It seems to follow from this that hell must exist for those who have become so identified with their sins that separation is not logically possible with continuing identity of the person involved.

Damnation creeps up on us. It is made of the little but regular denials of God which we make in our everyday lives. We hardly notice them because they do not seem important. But they are nevertheless our free choices. Buddhists too, I think, would agree with that. Christianity requires (to use an expression applied by Richard Gombrich to Buddhism) 'total responsibility in theory and practice'. We freely opt for hell. We choose damnation. No one else sends us. Where the Buddhists and the Christians differ is particularly in the significance of only this life. How many chances do you (as the person you are) want? Hell is absence of God, freely chosen by those who would prefer to be without God – those who would prefer to be without perfect Goodness, the source of all good and happiness. How many chances can a particular person have? And when that person is dead? Then how many more chances *should* they have?

Until the end Christ stands welcoming us (us, you and me) with His outstretched arms. As St Catharine of Genoa says, the one 'destined' for hell leaps into hell voluntarily. No one *sends* them to hell. God does not want anyone so to deny Him, the source of all happiness, nor would He ever wish them to find themselves in such a state. For we all gravitate towards the place we have chosen for ourselves, as the natural place for us. One of my Buddhist friends has expressed astonishment at this. Surely no one would want to go to hell? But hell is by definition where there is no God. Those who hate God so much (and there are ways of hating God without always realising it) want to be where God is absent. They want hell. They *want* to be where their natures draw them.[24]

We do not know for certain who will find themselves in hell. But we do know that they will have chosen it themselves. Hell, Jean-Paul Sartre says, is other people. He is wrong. Hell is absence of God. In God, Love is other people.

(C) But what is it like to have become so identified with sin that separation and continuing identity of the person involved are not logically possible? How many sins have to occur for this stage to have been reached? It could be argued that this is not a question of either/or. Rather, it is a continuum. As one sins more and more, or in certain ways, without repentance and turning to God for forgiveness, so gradually one becomes identified with one's sins until, failing repentance and forgiveness at the last, identification reaches the stage where its reversal is no longer logically compatible with personal identity. At that stage there is hell. But for one that has not reached that stage, separation of the person from the sins is still possible. What is left? The person without his or her sins could have become so lacking in content by this stage that the perfection of heaven – where all is good – is impossible. They are a mere wraith. We have lost so much, if not yet the person. The person needs trans-formation, needs rebuilding. The person needs a course of spiritual exercise and vitamins, even if the exercise is not much fun and the vitamins taste ghastly. Thus there needs must be a stage of development between heaven and hell.

Hence purgatory.

IS SATAN REALLY WICKED?

It has been suggested that I read Milton's *Paradise Lost*. Actually, I think I did many years ago. There Satan, the Devil, is sometimes seen as a sort of anti-hero, heroically standing up against God. Occasionally people feel sorry for Satan. He was created by God who must have known all along he would oppose God and precipitate the Fall. Why did God make him that way, knowing what would happen? Satan was after all only being true to his created nature.

I have no idea. But I imagine one would have to be clear what the theological ground-rules are for this debate. In spite of common perception, Satan is not some sort of anti-God, a being corresponding on the negative scale to God on the positive scale. Some such a view may be that of dualisms like Manichaeism or some forms of Zoroastrianism. But it is not the Christian view. Nor could it be compatible with God as the answer to the question 'Why is there something rather than nothing?' God is the very condition for there being anything at all. There is no rival to that. There could not be a competition between two alternative candidates. Thus God is not just a being who is very, very powerful, and very, very good, fighting with Satan as a being who is very, very powerful (though perhaps not as powerful as God) and very, very bad.

It seems to me that the Devil was *not* being true to his created nature. As with all things, the created nature of the Devil was good. According to the myth, Satan desired to usurp the position of God. That is absurd. It is even a logical absurdity. No created thing could usurp the position of the Creator. It is, to use an expression of the philosopher Gilbert Ryle, a cosmic 'category mistake'. Creator and created are totally different orders of being. They are not on a continuum. How could anything usurp the answer to the question, 'Why is there something rather than nothing'? The reason why the Devil is the very prototype of evil, and his fall the very prototype of the Fall, is that one way or another all wickedness eventually reduces to hubris, the pride that would place some created being on the throne of God. The wickedness of the Devil lies in trying to be what he cannot possibly be. All wickedness is thus based on absurdity. And Satan cannot possibly have been true to his created nature in his pride. Quite the reverse. The fall of Satan lay in *not* being true to his nature. Satan is a created being who made his choice, a choice for absurdity.

As in Dante's *Inferno*, Satan has fallen as far from God as it is possible to fall. To be as far from perfect Goodness as one can be is to be very, very wicked. He is very, very wicked not just because of his original choice but because of his continuing activity. Meeting Satan would not be much fun. Everything that we know that is most immoral, most wrong, most fearful, most disturbing, most alien to most of us, is but a slight participation in the nature of the Devil, a participation in that primordial Absurdity, that primordial Pride.

He is no hero who thus stands up against God. He is absurd, ridiculous.

Of course, in one sense one might feel sorry for the Devil. It may even be a good thing to do so. But it will not help. Feeling sorry for those who are suffering – and as the epitome of Absurdity certainly the Devil must suffer – is itself virtuous. But virtue is of the nature of God. It is the very antithesis of the Devil. The sorrow of Milton's readers for Lucifer would burn the Devil more than all the fires of hell. The very presence of Goodness there is absolutely unbearable. The Devil does not want your sorrow.

ON CONTRACEPTION

If the Church says contraception is intrinsically wrong, and I say, 'Well, I don't know, I could imagine a situation in which contraception would seem to be the right thing to do', what am I actually saying? There are some cases where one can know by one's own unaided reason that certain things are right or wrong (intrinsically right, intrinsically wrong – even if not everyone sees it). But does this apply to all intrinsically right or wrong things? I very much doubt it.

In choosing to follow a Church, one is also choosing to follow it in its declarations of intrinsic rightness or wrongness in cases where one cannot know this by one's own unaided reason.

Since many people in the Church consider contraception (and homosexuality, for that matter) to be particularly problematic areas for Catholicism, it should be obvious that these issues cannot as such be deciding factors for church membership. What am I to do? I have argued for Christianity, and I have said that I need a good argument not to join the Catholic Church. Is the Church's attitude to contraception and homosexuality that good argument? For me, no. Even if I was quite convinced that the Catholic Church was simply wrong on these issues, it would not overrule the other factors which have convinced me to become a Catholic.

But I am not convinced the Catholic Church is wrong in its view that contraception and homosexuality are sinful. These are difficult areas for the Church because they are so out of step with the direction of modern ideas. That in itself, of course, would cause no problems for the Church. But what it should do is alert us to the way in which the Catholic Church often approaches issues with very different presuppositions to those of non-Catholics. Writing in the late eighteenth century, the philosopher David Hume expressed the presupposition under-lying much modern discussion in moral philosophy when he stated that 'You cannot get an "ought" from an "is"'. That is, the fact that things *are* a certain way does not in itself entail any prescriptions about how they *should* be. The implications of this are wide-ranging. It means that issues of, say, physics, chemistry, biology, or the nature and structure of the universe – which concern how it *is* – simply cannot in themselves entail moral conclusions – how things *should* be, or how we should behave. It was only a short step from this for some philosophers to conclude that moral issues are a matter of personal ideology, personal preference, or (dare I say it) private sensations, feelings. But issues concerning how things are relate to the publicly observable arena of science. The one is private. The other is public. And never the twain shall meet. Morality is a private matter. Sexual morality relates to what goes on in private. It is thus a matter of personal preferences, sensations, our private consciences. And our consciences, so many hold nowadays, should be free of religious interference.

Hume may well be right. But his view is very different from that of, say, the Greeks or medieval thinkers. And it is quite different from the very orientation of the Catholic Church, which draws on classical and medieval intellectual models. Here we find it commonly taken for granted that the world – all that, as created being, is – is *teleological*. That is, the world is not just a matter of neutral data. The very existence of the world and all that is within it is polarised towards a goal, the attainment of which is its good. Or, in other words, the world has a purpose. The world is a creation of a good God and, in the light of that, all that is moves towards a goal which is that of God, and is therefore by definition good. So how things are and how things ought to be are inextricably bound together. Morality is, of course, a dimension of 'ought'. Thus from this perspective morality is inextricably bound up with the public, with the very nature of the universe itself. It is not a matter of one's own private sensations, or conscience understood as a totally personal affair. It is not subjective. There is an objective right and wrong. Right and wrong spring from a divine origin, because they relate to God's purposes, the very purpose of creation. And, as we have seen with religious dogma, an objective right and wrong cannot be known by each through private experience. In the last analysis it comes from an authoritative Church. It is not a matter of private conscience at all. And it is not a matter of being responsible for one's own behaviour, or what one gets up to in private being one's own affair.

It can be seen here, I think, that the very way in which the Catholic Church approaches these issues is quite out of step with the modern world. For obvious reasons it can cut no ice with the Church to say that in this it is wrong, that it *should* be in step with the modern world. And it simply begs the question for someone to object that still, in the last analysis, whether to follow the Church is a private matter and therefore the Church has no right to legislate on sexual morality. As far as the Church is concerned creation has a purpose, and the Church's purpose is to make this and what follows from it for our behaviour, or duties, known. The Church would be failing in its purpose precisely if it did *not* legislate on sexual morality.

All this means that in asking about the morality of something it is in place to ask also what its purpose is in the light of God's ultimate purpose. How does this apply to sexual morality? As far as the Church has always been concerned, it seems clear that the purpose of sexual activity is first and foremost the reproduction of the species, as well as the enriching of the love and mutual support of the two partners. It is worth noting that in this the Catholics are in perfect harmony with Buddhists. The Dalai Lama reportedly annoyed a group of homosexuals who visited him by beginning with a reference to the purpose of sex, which he did not think to question was that of reproduction.

For Catholics this purpose is in order that God's wishes for beings to know and love Him, and live for ever in unity with Him, can be fulfilled. It is what creation is all about. Reproduction should occur within the social unit that would supply, if ordered correctly, the optimum setting for God's purpose to be fulfilled. That is the family, in a state of marriage according to God's stated model, where any children are brought up to know and accept God's model as revealed in Catholic teaching and thus to enjoy the sacramental structure of the Church. The family is a little society within which caring for others, tolerance, understanding and forgiveness – in other words, love – can be nurtured. Thus the Catholic view is that marriage rightly ordered is itself a sacrament within which the partners can find God, for God is the very nature of Love and the community of the faithful under God is definitive of what Christianity is all about.

Clearly within this framework there is simply no place for sex outside marriage, homosexuality, or indeed sexual activity that is carried out with another goal as its primary aim. The fact that sex is also pleasurable and bonding does not entail that it would be right to engage in sex purely for fun. We repeatedly find that Catholicism does not give the primacy to sensations, experiences, as such. Marriage is a sacrament with a divine purpose. Thus contraception is wrong because it is based on presuppositions which are not those of the teleology of creation. Sex has a purpose and sexual morality occurs within that framework.

I am not saying here that the Church is right in all of this (although as a Catholic I think it is). I am simply outlining the presuppositions on which the Church is operating and why, therefore, it draws the conclusions it does.

The Church has said that contraception and homosexuality are wrong. Some Catholics favour so-called 'natural' means of contraception, working with the times in the menstrual cycle when a woman is naturally infertile. Recently the Church has expressed theological caution here. Intercourse at times of natural infertility is fine, but it begins to become morally problematic if it is based on a 'contraceptive mentality'. That is, if intercourse is engaged in only when the woman is infertile, with avoiding having children as its primary intention, then this begins to look very much like sexual intercourse completely divorced from the purpose of sexual intercourse.

What am I to say to all this? As a philosopher I can, of course, try and think up cases where the Church might have to accept contraception as the lesser of two evils (although this is not so easy with homosexuality). These are precisely the sort of topics discussed in classes on moral philosophy. The Church is quite aware of them. But for my present, practical, context it seems to me that all I can say is that as long as the Church's ruling on the matter stands, then individual cases of moral dilemma which result are a matter of pastoral care between the believer and his or her priest. Priests are trained to be sympathetic and helpful. I still think that I would indeed be out of my head if I decided not to be a Catholic on these issues alone.[25]

There is one other point to be made as regards issues like contraception. Non-Christians often presuppose that Christians spend much of their time trying to be 'holier than thou' or racked with guilt because of their moral failings. No doubt some do. But the Church is a Church of sinners, sinners who have before them an ideal of sanctity that they know is impossible to attain short of the grace of God, and is highly unlikely to be attained in this life. Perfect people do not need the Church. In my experience we are all subject to moral failure. And we resolve to try again. We fail again too. As we are, sin appears to be our natural state. Thus if contraception is wrong, and yet couples do still use contraception, they are no more sinful than the rest of us. But it seems clear that, as the Church's teaching stands, they are still sinful. The mercy of God cannot be received if one will not accept doing wrong. Where the whole issue becomes much more problematic is when the couple considers that they are *not* sinful because contraception (or other matters of sexual morality) is a matter of individual conscience.

Catholicism is a holistic religion. Things are interrelated. And the polarisation of the whole is towards God and away from personal feeling. All flows from the Other, not from the self. As we have seen, to portray these issues as matters of subjective conscience, and therefore individual private experience, would be to go against the whole Catholic orientation in these matters. Catholics do indeed talk about the conscience and, indeed, the centrality of conscience. But 'conscience' in Catholic theology has a very different meaning from the way it is used in common discourse and the way I have been using it here. For Catholics, our consciences relate to the God-given faculties that enable us to discern objective moral truth and apply it in particular instances. One of the documents of the Second Vatican Council puts it this way:[26]

> In the depths of his conscience man detects a law which he does not impose on himself, but which holds him to obedience. Always summoning him to love good and avoid evil, the voice of conscience can when necessary speak to his heart more specifically: 'do this, shun that'. For man has in his heart a law written by God. To obey it is the very dignity of man; according to it he will be judged (cf. Rom 2:14–16).

Conscience is thus not a private, subjective matter. We know in our hearts what is objectively right and wrong. Since the Church too, through the guidance of the Holy Spirit, declares objective morality, our consciences should not differ from the moral teaching of the Church. Where difference occurs, either we have misinterpreted (as is quite possible) what our conscience is telling us, or the Church has misinterpreted the guidance of the Holy Spirit. The latter is (for a Catholic) unlikely. Thus the Church is there to help the Catholic discern what his or her conscience is saying.[27] In objective truth our hearts, our consciences and the Church coincide. As Pope John Paul II says:[28]

> The judgment of conscience does not establish the law; rather it bears witness to the authority of the natural law ... The truth about moral good, as that truth is declared in the law of reason, is practically and concretely recognized by the judgment of conscience, which leads one to take responsibility for the good or the evil one has done. If man does evil, the just judgment of his conscience remains within him as a witness to the universal truth of the good, as well as to the malice of his particular choice. But the verdict of conscience remains in him as a pledge of hope and mercy: while bearing witness to the evil he has done, it also reminds him of his need, with the help of God's grace, to ask forgiveness, to do good and to cultivate virtue constantly.

Thus it is not that Catholics hold the same views as other people, but happen also to hold that there is a God, happen to hold teachings concerning Jesus Christ, and among other things happen not to approve of contraception. All the elements that make up the Catholic teachings and life are interrelated. This means that Catholics see the world in quite a different way from non-Catholics. To claim to see the world that way and yet to treat issues like contraception as a matter of private and individual conscience, one's individual sense of morality, is to create an incoherence, an inconsistency, in a carefully balanced holism. It would be to adopt an orientation which is fundamentally at variance with that of Catholicism, because it relies on fundamentally divergent presuppositions.

In the case of a Catholic couple who employ contraception it seems to me that surely this again is a matter for the pastoral care of their priest. It is possible to be absolutely and fully compassionate and supportive within a framework of objective right and wrong. It is also possible to be absolutely and fully forgiving when repentance is expressed. Again and again. God does it all the time.

Do I wish that the Catholic treatment of contraception were different, more liberal? It would certainly make life much easier. But then, there is no reason why life should be easier. Do I hope it will change? Only if that is what God wants. How do we know what God wants? The Church tells us. Does God change His mind? No. Does the Church sometimes come to discern more clearly God's intentions? Yes. Is the Church likely at some time in the future to discern God's intentions on these issues in a way that would permit contraception under certain circumstances (say in a stable married relationship and using only 'natural' methods)? Possibly. If so, when might that be?

God knows!

ON CHRIST'S CORPOREAL PRESENCE IN THE MASS

It seems so obvious that when Jesus said, 'Do this in memory of me', He was not asking that his followers engage in some sort of play-acting, regularly reminding themselves of something that happened a long time ago, and to someone long gone. What, theologically, would be the point of that? To remember someone dead and gone, like some sort of anniversary? In a wonderful, magical, image, the American Catholic sociologist Andrew Greely tells us that at the Eucharist 'God is among us at a family meal'.[29] I really believe this is true. And there is a world of difference between God being among us, and remembering when God *was* among us (or among our ancestors). A whole world of difference. Even those who do not believe in the True Presence must surely wish they could. For someone who believes that God is there at the banquet – and that God *is* the banquet – everything looks very, very different. The whole world is magically transformed. The wonder, the holy, is among us. History is now. Isn't this the mystery and magic – rendered palpably, believably present – that we were yearning for?

And the 'memory' of the Last Supper must surely be taken with its salvific sequel. Christ rose bodily from the dead. The victorious Christ who was bodily risen from the dead told His followers that He remained with them, even to the end of the world. Any recollection of Jesus must involve an awareness that He is present even now, most fully present, and present (in some inexplicable way) bodily. Otherwise the resurrection is marginalised and its meaning eroded.

Thus if the bread and the wine in the Mass are to remind us of Jesus, they must remind us of the Jesus who is living *now*. His living now is bodily and Christianity redeems the body. The bread and wine do indeed remind us of the crucifixion and all that it means, but the crucifixion as issuing in resurrection. There is no point in being reminded of the crucifixion without the resurrection. The remembrance of the Eucharist is a remembrance of a present living body. But how can what is done in the Eucharist lead to a remembrance of a present living body? Is it a matter of inference and intimation? Is one supposed to recollect Christ's passion and then go on to recollect that He also rose from the dead and is present bodily (somewhere, somehow) even now? If this is what we are supposed to do, then why did Jesus not explain it for us? Why did the early Church not clarify it? Remembrance of Jesus without the resurrection and His living bodily presence would miss the whole point.

Coherence and economy of explanatory chains suggest that the Eucharist itself, the very sacramental presence of the bread and wine, is the remembrance of the bodily presence of the living Christ. It is a reminder that Christ is even now bodily present for us, as He said He would be. But *where* in the Eucharist is He bodily present for us? Why did Jesus say of the bread (etc.) 'This *is* my body', and 'This *is* my blood', if He did not mean what He said? Where else is His body and blood supposed to be present *now*, when and where the Eucharist is taking place in accordance with His bidding, if not sacramentally present in the bread and wine themselves? That is, after all, the focus of the whole event. In what way they are present it is up to the Church to tell us, inasmuch as such mysteries can be expressed and we can understand them.

We can compare here John 6:48–58:

> I am the living bread
>> which has come down from heaven.
> Anyone who eats this bread
>> will live for ever;
> and the bread that I shall give
> is my flesh, for the life of the world.

> (Verses 48–51)

Here Jesus first claims that He is the bread; second, that one must eat that bread; and third, that the bread is His flesh. If the bread that one eats is only a symbol of Jesus' flesh, then clearly one cannot be said to be eating His flesh. One would be eating only a symbol of His flesh. Perhaps it is for reasons like this that the Church has been clear from very early days (see Ignatius of Antioch above, p. 149) that the bread in the Mass is literally the flesh of Christ. Nowhere in John 6:48–58 does Jesus explain to the scandalised Jews and followers who were beginning to doubt His sanity that what He means is simply bread as a *symbol* of His flesh. Who would question the sanity of that?

Christ's corporeal presence in the Mass is not contradictory, and is thus possible. It is also most satisfactory hermeneutically, theologically, spiritually, mystically and aesthetically. To believe it is thus perfectly compatible with reason. This has also been the view of most Christians – saints and sinners – throughout history. Christ's body is literally present in the Mass. The remembrance is thus a re-enactment. The salvific past is for ever present. Why would anyone want to deny that such wonderful things could be true – *are* true? The humdrum everyday world is made new.

The magic returns. *This* magic is not just coherent but it seems to me convincing.

GILT-EDGED GUILT

Sharon and I were driving along a road in Bristol. A boy, perhaps two years old, out walking with his father, escaped and jumped with sheer innocent joy into a great puddle. Myrddin used to do that. Boys do, Sharon tells me. She thinks it is something to do with adrenaline. It is no use smacking them. That makes jumping into great puddles even more exciting. Punishment won't work. The only thing that will help, Sharon reckons – if it can be done – is a good dose of guilt.

Sharon should know. She works with some of the most difficult children. All too often their problem is that they do not think that what they are doing is actually wrong. They have no sense of guilt. Guilt is a corollary of morality. It is how we respond when we know we have done what we ought not to have done, or failed to do what we know we should have done. Guilt is a response to 'ought'. Where there is no genuine moral sense of 'ought' and 'ought not' it is difficult for there to be a sense of guilt.

Morality is a problem for cultures based on the primacy of the individual and individual sensations. Guilt occurs when we know we have fallen short of moral standards. It is uncomfortable. The proper response to guilt is confession, apology, a plea for forgiveness and a resolution to try and do better next time. In other words, the discomfort of guilt is eased by acknowledgement, learning and an aspiration to improvement. But when all one's own discomfort is seen as someone else's fault, and when one can never admit to falling short in standards over which one has no personal control, standards that are not one's own personal feelings – that is, falling short in objective moral standards – guilt is seen as a totally unacceptable discomfort. It is to be avoided at all costs not by morality but by morality's denial.

Catholicism, we are told, makes one guilty. Well, in itself this does not seem to me to be a fault. All it says is that Catholicism teaches objective moral standards and we, being what we are, fall short. If there are objective moral standards, if moral subjectivity and self-indulgence can be transcended, then it is good we should learn how. Let us have more sense of guilt. We should be quite clear: guilt (as Sharon has found with the children at her school) is a healthy thing. It is a response to moral standards and an honest awareness of moral failure. What is not healthy is wallowing in guilt, with no way out. Wallowing in guilt is obsessively self-indulgent and unhealthy. It too is giving the primacy to personal sensations. It can lead to despair, and despair is the very antithesis of the hope that is in Christ. That is why Catholicism teaches confession and forgiveness. Objective moral standards, guilt at failure, repentance, confession and the joy of forgiveness all go together.

It is not practising Catholics who wallow in guilt. Catholics are free of guilt because they acknowledge it and are forgiven. Perhaps it is in Protestant traditions that have closed down the confessionals that we find people troubled by overwhelming guilt. And perhaps also those who accuse Catholicism of piling on the guilt are those who are not practising Catholicism. It is not Catholics who talk about the guilt experienced by Catholics. It is the lapsed Catholics.

I agree with Sharon. If we bring up children with objective moral standards we shall also bring them up with a heightened facility for guilt. Good! Little monsters that jump in puddles should feel guilty. That way they won't burn the school down.

CONFESSION?

My brother Pete has more than once objected that with the sacrament of reconciliation – confession – a sinner can receive absolution, repeat the sin, confess and receive absolution again and again. It all seems too easy and rather hypocritical.

I have not yet been fully received into the Catholic Church. As such I do not have any experience of confession. But G. K. Chesterton points out in his *Autobiography* that after repentance, confession and absolution one feels completely remade by God. This, Chesterton says, is the first reason why he became a Catholic:[30]

> For there is no other religious system that does *really* profess to get rid of people's sins. It is confirmed by the logic, which to many seems startling, by which the Church deduces that sin confessed and adequately repented is actually abolished; and that the sinner does really begin again as if he had never sinned.

I yearn for absolution as one who has fallen into a cesspit must yearn for a bath! As I understand it, absolution is given conditional upon repentance and a firm decision with God's grace to strive to desist from repeating the sin. But, Pete would say, isn't it hypocritical to receive absolution knowing that as a matter of fact one will repeat the sin (perhaps it is a horrible habit) anyway?

Well, first, I am not sure of the logic here. Supposing in the past I have committed horrible sin X. I genuinely repent of the sin and confess it. I resolve not to repeat that horrible sin, receive absolution and perform the appropriate penance. Call a subsequent repetition of that sin Y. At the time of my confession and absolution Y has not occurred. Why should I not receive absolution at that time? Presumably one cannot be censured, let alone punished, for a sin one has not yet committed and expressed every intention of not committing. But to deny one absolution would indeed be a grievous punishment. Of course, if my repentance and firm decision are not genuine, then my absolution would have been obtained under false pretence. In a case like that, in reality it would be unlikely that I would bother to go to confession. But it seems to me to be perfectly possible psychologically for repentance and decision to be genuine, and we have to take it here that my repentance for X and firm decision at that time not to do Y are indeed genuine. Confession is for genuine penitents, not those who would cheat.

But, Pete might urge, supposing X is an action of a type I frequently do. I confess and each time resolve not to do the action again. After a time the very repetition of the action suggests that my repentance and resolution were unrealistic, if not self-deception. When I confess X now, I know that as a matter of fact I will do Y. Under such circumstances, it could be urged, the confession might have made me feel better, but really I have no right to feel better and no right to absolution. However does this follow? Does it follow that if I repent X and vow not to do an action of that type again, when I frequently repent actions of type X and then repeat them, that my present repentance and vow are not genuine, or are the result of self-deception? In terms of the sheer logic of the situation, Y is a new, different action from X. We simply cannot argue from the repetition of actions of type X in the past that therefore Y will as a matter of fact occur. We simply cannot, as a matter of logic, claim at that time to know that Y will occur. It might not. For this reason a genuine penitent is also entitled psychologically to resolve firmly at that time that Y will not occur. Each situation is new. In terms of sheer logic he or she is entitled psychologically to resolve repeatedly and genuinely that actions of that sort will not be performed. The fact that such actions have reoccurred in the past does not entail an inference to a new situation in the future.

I have argued (using, incidentally, a version of Hume's critique of induction) that in terms of sheer logic a future situation is a new one, and therefore a penitent is warranted in vowing that the sin will not be repeated. But Hume would argue that on the basis of past experience we would be inclined *psychologically* to assume that we would be prone to repeat the sin. Pete might urge that therefore nevertheless the repentance and vow are a sham. Morally, if not logically, the repentant is a hypocrite. I do not agree. Hume would be the first to hold that our psychological tendency is not warranted by the logic of the situation. It seems to me perfectly reasonable to expect that this psychological tendency could be overcome by the religious context, the context of hope and trust in God's grace. Thus the genuine penitent, even though he or she may have repeated acts of type X hundreds of times, is entitled in logic to take Y as a new event. He or she is entitled to resolve not to engage in Y.

He or she is entitled psychologically (and therefore, I would argue, morally) as a Christian to hope that they will not repeat the act. And they are entitled to trust in God's grace in helping to avoid repetition. He or she is also entitled to expect miracles! To think otherwise would be a sin. It would be the sin of despair.

I have heard it said that just before the Reformation it was possible to drop money into a collection box on the way to a brothel and receive there and then absolution for the act one was about to commit. It may be true. If so, that is quite obviously a corruption and an aberration. In terms of logic one cannot repent and vow not to repeat an action not yet committed. And in terms of psychology one can only buy 'absolution' in advance if one intends to or suspects one will commit the sin anyway. But if one intends to commit the sin anyway then there cannot be any regret and intention not to do the act. But regret and intention not to repeat the deed must be associated with repentance and the vow.

The healthy psychology of confession is wonderfully expressed in an earlier medieval source, the confessions of an abbot, Guibert of Nogent (1055–c.1125):[31]

> You know that I do not sin because I see you as merciful; rather I proclaim you merciful with full confidence because you are available to all who implore your forgiveness. Every time I succumb to the compulsion to sin I do not abuse your mercy; but I would abuse it sacrilegiously, if assuming that nothing is easier than turning back to you after sinning, I were to delight in sinning even more. I do sin, of course, but when I recover my senses it pains me to have given in to my heart's inclinations. It is entirely in spite of itself that my spirit beds itself into baskets full of manure.

The fact that at one time the system of confession may have become corrupted does not mean that confession as such is corrupt, a cop-out, or a licence for hypocrisy. If anything, confession, the sacrament of reconciliation, seems to me to be a licence for sanity. Confession, repentance and the vow are the antidote to despair. All this seems to me to provide a perfectly good spiritual foundation for the repeated solace of confession. And why shouldn't it make life easier?

I agree with Chesterton. Confession and forgiveness provide a powerful argument for becoming a Catholic.

WE ARE BUT LOWLY WORMS

Myrddin and his partner Toni have recently attended two or three services at their local Anglican church. They plan to get married there in the summer and some sort of sporadic attendance at services is expected. Like all our children Myrddin (for our sins) has not been baptised, let alone confirmed. And there is more to being a Christian than going to church. Eternal life is not such a simple matter. Myrddin does not himself hold many of the tenets of the Church of England. I'm not sure he knows what they are. But is it necessary nowadays to hold tenets in order to avail oneself of the services of the Anglican Church? There can be no doubt that attending his local church services has led Myrddin to take much more seriously the claims of Christianity. He is a wise and sensitive seeker. So perhaps the Anglican Church is right in its openness, and right to welcome all to its life-cycle rituals, even though they are at the moment often more social customs than a spiritual commitment.

Myrddin tells me that he rather enjoys the Anglican Eucharist. He particularly enjoys the communal aspects, where he can enthusiastically greet others (bless him!) with the sign of peace. But he constantly returns to his thorough dislike of the bit about being lowly worms: 'We are not worthy so much as to gather up the crumbs under your table.' I suspect that many young people nowadays find this self-abasement difficult. They often *do* experience themselves relatively powerless in the face of market forces and social and financial expectations and demands. But they aim for the self-image of supermen (and women). They are also encouraged to aspire to the heights of gods. God has been dethroned, but we ourselves can be as gods.

Well – I am sure that actually we *cannot* be as gods, and history is littered with the victims of those who have tried. I am sure also that a large part of success lies in combining a realistic sensitivity to our potential with an awareness of our limitations. Wonderful as humans are, we are far from perfect. It is this very fact that the Christian refers to when he or she speaks of us as 'unworthy', that is, as sinners. This, I have come to think, is simply common sense. As Schleiermacher emphasised so strongly, we are all created by God and utterly, totally, dependent on Him for our very being. Realism about our potential lies in an awareness of just this – as the Buddhist would have it, 'seeing things the way they really are'. Compared with God we are infinitely less than little worms. If there is a God – and I have argued that there is and what sort of God He might be – then we can express our difference from Him not in our feeble words but in our behaviour. This behaviour is of worship, the worship that out of God's love the Church has established for us. One way or another (I have come to think) a person who is not engaged in properly orienting his or her life to God, that is, not engaged in worship, is living a life which is radically awry. One way or another that awry life is founded on placing some sort of creation on the throne of the Creator, of God. That is the collapse of all coherent foundation for morality. Truly, as we are, 'we are not worthy so much as to gather up the crumbs under your table'.

For the difference between ourselves and God is not one of degree. It is a difference of kind so profound we cannot even begin to encompass it in language or thought. Only God Himself can bridge that difference in the incarnation. The history of arrogance and dictatorship, of megalomania and torture, is a history of denial, of repression, of this fact. I suspect that those who object to thinking of themselves as lowly worms have not really taken on board who God truly is. There is nothing demeaning in seeing things the way they really are. This seeing is the very prerequisite of sanity. Happiness can lie only in orienting ourselves to God. Try it out and see (as Buddhists are always saying).

I have argued that real altruism – and true humility – spring from orienting ourselves to a God who is Wholly Other. Yet the Christian message is not just that we are lowly worms. The God that we worship, the God we partake of at the Eucharist that Myrddin has such difficulties with, is not just a Wholly Other God. He is also the God who loves us so much – more than any possible human love – that He became man. More than that.

His love was so great that He became a poor baby in a stable. And he died a horrible death, we are taught, in order to show us what is possible for us in love and obedience to God.

This, Myrddin, is what we celebrate at the Eucharist. Think what that means. Think what it is like to see the world that way. This is the magic, the mystery, of the Christian faith.

If we are lowly worms, our God is a God who is willing to crawl in the mud with us. We are all lowly worms. In love God is a lowly worm too. Such, I suppose, is my reply to Myrddin. A God who becomes man seems to me to make all the difference.

You should know this, Myrddin. Don't lovers in private make themselves ridiculous for the ones they love? The whole Church is the bride of Christ. The Church is the lover of God.

Perhaps you should be careful before peeping at what lovers get up to in private.

But Myrddin has just told me he plans to get baptised and confirmed as an Anglican this year. We have made a deal. If he comes to my reception into the Roman Catholic Church, I will go to his Anglican reception.

And that, dear readers, is what we did!

CONCLUSION

In conclusion I have not much to say really. The conclusion is not saying but doing. I have become a Roman Catholic.

Perhaps it was Buddhism that really brought home to me the urgency of religious awareness and practice, but it was Christianity that really, finally, forced upon me the significance of the *choice*. The Buddhist thinks in terms of infinite rebirths. Partly to offset any tendency to complacency that this might entail, in Buddhism one is also taught to value the human rebirth that we now have. A human rebirth offers almost unparalleled opportunities for spiritual growth and the attainment of enlightenment. A human rebirth is also extremely rare – 'as rare as stars seen in the daytime'. If we look around us at our fellows it is not often that we see the particular combination of virtue which we are told will, other things being equal, lead to a human rebirth next time round. The ever-present possibility of death is carefully meditated upon. At any moment we could lose our 'precious human rebirth'. Then where would we be? We should practise Buddhism now, with urgency, like there is no tomorrow. In Mahāyāna Buddhism one is also exhorted to take, at the appropriate time, the vows of a bodhisattva. In taking these vows one follows the path to Full Buddhahood – the very perfection of wisdom and compassion – for the benefit not just of oneself but of all sentient beings without exception. This path is very long. It is commonly said to take 'three incalculable aeons'. One vows to follow it to the end, throughout all one's future rebirths, out of compassion for others no matter what sufferings that may involve. In exhorting one to take the bodhisattva vows, once more we see how Buddhism reinforces a sense of the importance of this life and the choices we make.

For orthodox Christianity – I would argue, for any meaningful sense of 'Christianity' – there is no rebirth. There is effectively this life and eternity. I have urged that this should not be seen as in any sense 'unfair'. And it has the positive advantage of giving effectively infinite value to the person (and therefore other persons), i.e. the person one actually is. Every person has this life and eternity. Every person is the person he or she becomes. We are taught that what this also does is give infinite value to the choice one makes in this life. The fundamental existential question cannot be put to one side. 'Yes?' or 'No?' demands a response.

I have been immensely moved by the story of Cassie Bernall. She was a seventeen-year-old student at an American high school when a couple of her fellow students decided to go on the rampage with guns. Placing a gun to Cassie's head a killer asked her if she believed in God. Cassie said 'Yes'. Her brains were blown out. At her funeral her body was in no state to be viewed by the other mourners.

There is a prototype for Cassie and those like her. Or perhaps an archetype. I wonder if her friends from the Protestant Bible belt in the USA realise it. The archetype is that of the Blessed Virgin Mary. She it was who originally said 'Yes': 'You see before you the Lord's servant, let it happen to me as you have said' (Luke 1:38). The very idea of a Son of God would have been most peculiar to Jews. Yet Mary said 'Yes'. Should she have said 'Yes' or 'No'? Christians revere the Blessed Virgin Mary as a human being who said 'Yes' to the request of God. Nothing more. Mary is the Mother of God because she said 'Yes'. All else flows out of that. If Cassie is worthy of respect – and she is – then so much more is the Blessed Virgin Mary worthy of respect. If Cassie is a model for us – and she is – then so much more is the Blessed Virgin Mary a model for us. The Blessed Virgin Mary is a model for Cassie.

We have just returned from a visit to some cathedrals and pilgrimage sites of Eastern England. In becoming a Catholic I find myself surrounded by holy places of my religion. Catholicism is the true Old Religion of the British Isles, not the pseudo-Celtic and other pagan religions of this country's New Age movement. Everywhere I look I see reminders of ancient Catholicism. And reminders of the destruction wrought at the Reformation. Particularly in Eastern England, which was both a rich source of medieval holiness and also later a centre of Protestantism and an original home for the Pilgrim Fathers. In the wonderful cathedral of Ely there is the largest medieval Lady Chapel – dedicated to the Blessed Virgin Mary – in the country. In bay after bay we find statues smashed, with their heads knocked off by the reforming enthusiasts. Nearly all its stained glass was destroyed. A chapel that would have been the rival of the famous Sainte Chapelle in Paris was torn apart in the name of 'pure, reformed Christianity'. It was a chapel to the one who said 'Yes'. 'Yes' is the very archetype of our human response. The Blessed Virgin Mary is that archetype in human form, the archetype of 'Yes'.

At Walsingham, in Eastern England, we find a restored pilgrimage centre for the cult of the Blessed Virgin Mary. Nowadays even Protestants go there. Here, in the Middle Ages, a replica of the Holy House of Nazareth was built, as a result, it is said, of a vision of the Blessed Virgin who asked that a replica of the house in which she said 'Yes' should be built in England. Consequently Walsingham became after Canterbury the most important pilgrimage spot in the British Isles, and England became so devoted to the Blessed Virgin Mary that in the later Middle Ages the whole country was known as 'Mary's Dowry'. The very blood of the English is devoted to Mary. All was destroyed at the Henrician Reformation, and the original statue of Our Lady of Walsingham was burnt at Smithfield in London. Now pilgrims have returned to Walsingham, to the new Catholic, Orthodox and Anglican shrines, and also to reflect in and on the ruins of the original monastery and shrines, memorials to the original girl who said 'Yes'.

According to one version her murderer asked Cassie 'Why?' before killing her. He did not wait for an answer. 'Do you believe in God?' and 'Why?' are primordial questions. Cassie answered 'Yes' to the first. That was her salvation. Her killer did not wait for the answer to the second. There he lost (save by the mercy of God) his chance of joining her. But we can still ask the question, the very same question. And we are fortunate. We can still listen to the answer and its reasons. If we will.

We do not know whether he would still have killed Cassie if she had said 'No'. Probably she would nevertheless have died. But perhaps not. Still, she said 'Yes', and in the actual context of her saying it her gut feeling must have been that she was being offered a choice of life or death. I have no doubt that Cassie is a martyr. She died a witness for the truth, if not directly of Christianity, at least of theism. What particularly moves me is the starkness of the choice that she was given.

There was no room for philosophical subtleties. It was either 'Yes' or 'No'. At least one of the options was irrevocable. 'Today, I call heaven and earth to witness against you: I am offering you life or death, blessing or curse. Choose life ...' (Deuteronomy 30:19–20). In dying, Cassie chose life.

What went through Cassie's mind in the split second before her murderer pressed the trigger? Did she hope he would not kill her? Surely she hoped that. Did she consider whether he was asking about her psychological state at the time – 'Do you *believe* in God?' What is belief? Is it a psychological state? Is it a disposition? She could believe in God without God actually existing. But did Cassie perhaps think that the killer was asking not whether she believed in God, but whether God actually exists or not? Did she rehearse the *reasons* for her belief? Or did she simply think that if she said 'No' she would have to live with having said that for the rest of her life? Actually, if she had said 'No' she could have been taken as saying either that she did not believe in God, or that He does not exist. But here they both amount to the same thing.

However, she could have lied. No one would have blamed her, would they?

I suspect none of these thoughts actually happened. She had to say either 'Yes' or 'No'. She said 'Yes'. Because it was true. She *did* believe in God, and believing in God meant that she believed that God actually existed. As far as Cassie was concerned God existed. Forced to make a choice even at the cost of her life she could not lie, she could not betray her identity, her very being. 'But what is truth?', as Pilate would have said.

I would have lied, a real lie, for I hold to the possibility of the objectivity of truth. I know I would have lied. I am a coward. *I* could not have done anything else. Yet I might actually have uttered 'Yes'. How can I tell? Whatever comes out of the mouth under those circumstances is unpremeditated. It flows directly from what one is. And I am a coward. But I do not know what God's grace might have made of me, under the circumstances.

For it is God that makes martyrs.

What are we to say of Cassie's killers? I don't know. One of the things that strikes me about the account of their murderous rampage[32] is that they seem to have considered it all a game. They laughed and cheered as they killed. Were they mad? I am not so sure. Were they possessed by Satan? I rather doubt it. They were kids. Keen on Hitler, but still kids. Is being unable to distinguish between reality and a computer game madness or Satanic possession? For I suspect it was something like that which possessed them. The same, I suspect, possesses modern pilots in war.

Their 'madness' or 'possession' looks to me like a breakdown of reality. Computers are well on the way to creating all the sensations associated with what we are still pleased to call the 'real' world.[33] If reality *is* sensations, experiences, then we can look forward to the time when computers will generate reality for us. Is that what they call 'virtual reality'? It seems that where experiences are all there is, the virtual will soon become actual. So long as we base ourselves on the primacy of sensations – 'the world is but the play of consciousness', 'all exists in dependence upon the imputing mind' – how can we distinguish between experiences and reality itself? Perhaps Cassie's killers were solipsists. How could they be expected to distinguish between the computer-generated sensations associated with killing, and killing itself? How could we, so long as we give priority to sensations, to experiences, as the arbiters of reality?

Perhaps eventually computers will give us all the sensations associated with enlightenment. But, as Cassie's killers found, we still die. As Sir Walter Raleigh put it in a poem written just before his execution, 'Onely we dye in earnest, that's no Jest'.

For non-theists Cassie might have been very brave, but her life was an unmitigated tragedy and its end in the last analysis was futile. She should have lied. She was foolish to die for a belief which is unimportant nowadays, and that anyway is actually false. One might admire Cassie for her adherence to the truth. She *did* believe in God. But that truth is actually based on confusion and is surely not worth dying for. One who is not a theist, I think, *has* to say Cassie made the wrong choice. Even some modern theists (maybe some liberal Anglicans?) might think that Cassie should have adopted the pragmatic option, the option that would appeal to most people in the contemporary world and that would enable her to grow and continue to help others (perhaps through becoming a Christian therapist).

Really, only for the Christian who holds to the absolute and non-negotiable objectivity of truth was Cassie's witness right and her death also a triumph. Only if God actually, factually, objectively exists is Cassie's witness finally vindicated.

Cassie was no saint, in the conventional sense of the word 'saint'. She had a darker side to her, as do all teenagers who are normal. Cassie was an ordinary normal teenager. But the Church does not consider Saints necessarily to be saints. It is a modern notion that Saints have somehow to be paragons of virtue. Many Saints actually have been rather unpleasant. What those who are recognised by the Church as Saints do is show forth to a heroic degree qualities that are hoped for to some degree in all those who follow Christ. They thus serve as examples to the rest of us. Whether Cassie was a saint or not, she was a martyr, a witness for the truth, an example to all of us that the objectivity of truth is important enough to be worth dying for (postmodernists take note). And that truth is God, absolute Objectivity beyond the play of consciousness.

How are we to see Cassie's life and death? Is it a tragedy? Certainly it's a tragedy if someone so young, with all her life ahead of her, dies under such circumstances. But is Cassie's life also a triumph?

Tragic as it was, I think Cassie's death was a triumph. All martyrdom is tragic triumph. Or a triumphant tragedy.

I have come to think that we are all given that stark choice, even if the immediate consequences are not so dramatic and perhaps few of us realise it until it is too late. To that extent Cassie was lucky in that she saw the truth so immediately. There is finally no middle between 'Yes' or 'No' in this most fundamental of existential questions. We need to decide *as if* a gun is at our head. This is one reason why Christianity has always had such difficulty with the idea of reincarnation. Reincarnation denies that urgency. And if we say 'Yes' to God, then perhaps in the last analysis it will have to be on no more grounds than Cassie had. We have looked at the arguments. We have analysed and pondered. Pondered and analysed. We have no proof. But we have to make a choice. The choice will have to be made with no further evidence. Under the circumstances it will have to be a risk, unpremeditated in the sense that it cannot flow directly out of previous considerations. And like Cassie we shall have to live (or die) with that choice. We reach the point where we shall have to say 'Yes' or 'No', and if we say 'Yes' there is no point in going back over it all over again. In saying 'Yes' there is only action, demonstrating the choice one has irrevocably made.

Given that we all have the choice, the Christian has to see Cassie's life and death as a triumph too.

In a letter to a friend written less than a year before her death, Cassie wrote:[34]

> I wonder what God is going to do with my life. Like my purpose. ... What does God have in store for me? ... I'm confident that I'll know someday. Maybe I'll look back at my life and think 'Oh, so that was it!'

I thank God for the witness of Cassie, a true twentieth-century martyr. One of the many. May she rest in blessed perfection and peace.

Since writing the above on the death of Cassie Bernall a month or so ago, I have been sent a newspaper article (*Daily Telegraph*, 30 September 1999) which suggests that in fact it may not have been Cassie who was the girl who said 'Yes'. The girl may have been a certain Valeen Schnurr, who actually survived the shooting although with savage shotgun wounds. How sad. I feel so sorry for Cassie's parents. If the new version is true (and it looks to me as if it might well be), they are deprived not only of their daughter but also of a vision of her as a martyr that must have been of some comfort to them. Yet the book that Cassie's mother wrote[35] shows well the construction of a modern evangelical protestant hagiography, a story of a Saint. Throughout history hagiographies have always been valued for the spiritual lesson they teach and for their role in moulding the faith community rather than for their literal truth. In the last analysis we shall never know if it was Cassie who said 'Yes'. We shall never know what went through her mind in the split second before the trigger was pulled. Cassie's parents, in their uncertainty, must also share in the martyrdom. But God knows. And if Cassie Bernall was not the girl who said 'Yes', let her nevertheless stand for those many, many martyrs who throughout history have said 'Yes' and have had no one to sing their praises. Perhaps in doing that Cassie herself will find her purpose, will find what God had in store for her – 'Oh, so that was it!'

I have heard it said that the twentieth century has seen more Christian martyrs than any other century. I doubt it. I suspect we simply have more information on our recent martyrs. But history has seen many martyrs who had no witnesses. Let Cassie be the name of the girl who said 'Yes' when given the choice between faith and denial, and who paid the penalty of death for it. *Whoever* that girl may be, *whenever* it occurred.

And my point still stands. From the newspaper article Valeen Schnurr impresses me as a nice and modest girl who is not attempting to gain anything by telling her story. It has come out as part of the police investigation into the shootings. According to the new version, Valeen herself was asked 'Why?' by one of the gunmen. She simply replied that 'my parents believed and that was the way I was brought up'. She escaped while the killers reloaded.

Valeen's story has the ring of truth. If true, she still said 'Yes'. She could have been killed at that point. Then Valeen would have been Cassie.

During the time of my instruction in the Catholic faith and the writing of these reflections we have passed New Year's Eve, the end of a ghastly century and the beginning of a new millennium. This year I shall be 50. Time, therefore, to make decisions in the light of eternity. For some years I have recognised that if I were told I would die tomorrow the first thing I would do (after panicking) is to be received into the Catholic Church. Why wait (as did Charles II) until the death-bed? Why deprive oneself of the joys of communion with the Church as soon as possible?

Of course (as Pascal said so famously) becoming a Christian is a gamble. It is a wager for which one has to take complete responsibility. It seems to me there is no less of a gamble in choosing Buddhism either, or indeed in choosing agnosticism or atheism.

I have a dear friend whom I much admire for his wisdom, intelligence and love. He wishes me the very best in my decision to be received into the Roman Catholic Church. But he confesses that he finds my choice 'incomprehensible'. I hope he can now begin to comprehend why I had to make the decision I did, astonishing though it may have seemed to him. It saddens me that it should be incomprehensible. Who knows? It may turn out to be quite wrong. But not, I hope, incomprehensible.

I have suggested at numerous points in this book that the orthodox Christian position, at least as represented by the Catholic tradition, and that of the Buddhist are exact opposites on many fundamental issues. The Christian orients him- or herself towards God, the absolutely Other. This orientation is essentially dualistic. The Buddhist does not hold to the existence of such a God. In response to this orientation, the Christian sees everything in terms of God and the grace of God. The Christian is acutely aware of his or her own spiritual incapacity. Everything flows from God, a God who is quite Other than His creation even if He is a God who has in Christ entered into creation and become part of it. All initiative comes from without. Christianity is all and entirely about God. As such it is not about personal experiences at all. The Buddhist thinks in terms of mental transformation, a transformation of the mind from greed, hatred and delusion to their opposites. Thus the orientation of the Buddhist is towards the primacy of certain types of experience, and key experiences are frequently expressed in terms of nonconceptuality and nondualism. Buddhism is all about the mind. With the exception of someone like Shinran, in the last analysis the Buddhist brings about his or her own mental transformation. 'Buddhas but point the way.'

These (and other) differences between orthodox Catholic Christianity and Buddhism are differences of whole orientation. They are frequently missed in concentrating on details and superficial similarities. Frequently nowadays one suspects a degree of embarrassment (at least on the side of some Christians) at these differences and what follows from them.[36] But in choosing they are essential and absolutely crucial. For one cannot be half a Christian. Christianity demands that one make a choice, a wholehearted commitment. I could not avoid that choice. It is either 'Yes' or 'No'. Realising this choice, realising the *urgency* of this choice – facing it and making it once and for all, even if that involves a gamble – realising with the Buddhist that the ever-present possibility of death makes the choice imperative *now*, I (the person I am, for the reasons I have given) could not say 'No'. Consequently I had to say 'Yes'.

I suppose in the last analysis it was as simple as that.

APPENDIX ONE: ON REBIRTH

The Buddhist position on rebirth is always stated to be that the rebirth is neither the same as, nor different from, the one who died. The Buddhist sees our present life as a causal continuum. We are constantly changing, with each moment of our life arising in causal dependence upon a preceding moment that has since ceased, and acting to cause the next moment in the continuum. It is a bit like the flow of a river. This flow that we are is made of five 'strands': physical matter, sensations, determinate perceptions, additional factors like volition (intentions), and consciousness. These are called the 'five aggregates' (Sanskrit: *skandha*). They are each a flow, each constantly changing. Upon this fivefold flow we superimpose for everyday practical purposes a singular identity, called by a name like 'Archibald', or 'Fiona'. Thus we are in fact a bundle, or a bundle of bundles. But because of beginningless ignorance we have a tendency to overrate this practical everyday unity and to think that there is some sort of unchanging essence constantly present. The presupposed unchanging essence, the stable referent for the use of 'I', we think of as our 'Self' (Sanskrit: *ātman*). This Self as such is a fiction. We attach to this fiction, with cravings associated with 'I' and 'mine'. These cravings based on delusion power our egoity, our endless series of rebirths, and ultimately all our misery. In letting-go of this fiction of Self (that is, of a self as anything more than just a practical way of giving an identity to the flow) we let go of the forces that power rebirth. In finally bringing about this letting-go at the deepest possible level of our being, all rebirth ceases. Thence ceases all misery, all suffering. That is *nirvāṇa*, liberation or enlightenment.

Just as we are actually a fivefold flow in this life, the Buddhist wants to say, at death all that happens is that there is a particular sort of break caused in the *physical* flow. Powered by forces resulting from egoity (in other words, powered by *karman*) the flow, the continuum, continues and is reconfigured into another everyday identity. Thus, in everyday language, we speak of the death of Archibald, and 'his' rebirth as Fiona. But really Archibald is no longer there. He is dead. The flow that was explained for practical purposes as 'Archibald' has been reconfigured into 'Fiona', but of course Fiona as such is a further stage in the flow. Archibald ceases; the flow continues, Fiona begins; the flow continues. This flow is literally beginningless. There is no first beginning. It ends only in *nirvāṇa*.

Now, using my example of Archibald and 'his rebirth' Fiona, what is the relationship between Archibald and Fiona? The answer, the Buddhist wants to say, is that they are clearly not the same. Archibald is dead. This is Fiona. Thus it follows that the rebirth is not the same as the one who died. In fact (and this is important to my argument) the rebirth is not at all the same person as the one who died. But also, the Buddhist wants to say, the rebirth is not different from the one who died either. What does the Buddhist mean by this? What is meant is that the rebirth is a practical everyday construct superimposed upon a later phase of a single causal flow. Thus the rebirth exists in causal dependence upon the one who died. In this respect the relationship between Fiona and Archibald is not the same as the relationship between Fiona and her friend Dougal, who is himself a rebirth of Archibald's great partner Morag. Fiona is a later 'stage' in the same causal flow as Archibald. Dougal is a later stage in the same causal flow as Morag. But the relationship between Fiona and Dougal is merely lust, not one of a causal continuum and rebirth. Thus we can say that Fiona and Archibald are not 'different' in the same way that Fiona and Dougal are different. Hence, the Buddhist wants to say, the relationship between the one who dies and the rebirth is one of 'neither the same nor different'.

This is the common Buddhist position. But it seems to me we should note the following.

The rebirth is not the same person as the one who died. Indeed there are Buddhist traditions (such as the dGe lugs pa in Tibet) that would have no problem in affirming that the rebirth is a different person (Sanskrit: *pudgala*; Tibetan: *gang zag*) from the one who died. I treated this in my article 'Altruism and rebirth'.[37] It is a textual point.

Philosophically, I am certain that on Buddhist premises they are right in saying the rebirth has to be a different person from the one that died. Consider the following: Imagine that I die and am reborn (as I might be) as a cockroach in South America. For our present purposes let us understand by 'person' (as does the Buddhist) any conscious subject of experience. Thus the cockroach is a 'person' in this context. Now, it is clear that the cockroach in South America is not the same person as me, Williams, professor in England. But I can also make absolutely no sense of any claim that, nevertheless, the cockroach is also not a *different* person from Williams. Clearly the cockroach is indeed a different person. What follows from this is that the person that Williams is has actually ceased to exist. There is now a cockroach called Pablo. In terms of what it is to be me, the ongoing lived life that it is to be me, this has come to an end. A cockroach is now having an ongoing lived life that is indeed a cockroach life, the life of Pablo the cockroach. It seems to me that it is sheer confusion to think that somehow Williams continues in, or within, or underlying, Pablo. It makes no sense for me to look forward to my life as Pablo. It also makes no sense for me to carry out actions aimed at benefiting my future life as Pablo. If this story is not one of Williams ceasing to exist, I do not know what would be.

I say all this notwithstanding the fact that the Buddhist position is said to be that the rebirth is also not different from the one who died. By 'not different' here, what is meant is that the rebirth is not different in the sense that it is not a different causal continuum. It is actually causally dependent upon the one that died, and thus both the dead being and the rebirth form one causal continuum. Pablo is the reincarnation of Williams in the sense that there is a particular type of causal connection between Williams and Pablo. But it seems to me that in terms of personal survival, being causally dependent upon the one that died is irrelevant. The Buddhist claim of 'not different' rests on an idiosyncratic sense of 'difference', i.e. as 'not causally related'. But for my purposes, what counts is whether or not Pablo is a different *person* from Williams. It seems clear that he is, and various Buddhist philosophers admit this fact.

Thus, notwithstanding the Buddhist position on rebirth, I want to claim that in fact, given the Buddhist premises when I die *I* simply cease. The fact that there will be a cockroach then existing which bears a causal relationship to me is, in terms of personal survival and thus in terms of specifically *my* interests, irrelevant. If I were told I was to be shot at dawn I would be terrified. If I were told not to worry because after I had been shot there would be born a cockroach in South America bearing a particular (even close) causal relationship to me, I think I should still be terrified. And I would be terrified, not because I do not want to be a cockroach, but because whether or not there is a cockroach there would not be *me* at all. What is that cockroach to me? If I am told I am to be shot at dawn I should plead for survival, not a lesson in entomology.

I have used the examples of Williams and a cockroach because it seems so obvious here that Williams would have ceased. But supposing I am reborn as a baby in my very own family, looking exactly like I do now. Still, Williams (the person I am) will have ceased, just as much as in the case of a cockroach. If rebirth as a cockroach involves cessation of the person I am, then any other rebirth based on the same principles would involve cessation of the person I am. Thus, in the terms used above, in this case too it makes no sense for me to carry out actions aimed at benefiting my future life as the Williams lookalike. It is still a story of Williams ceasing to exist.

Thus, even though the Buddhist position is that the rebirth is neither the same nor different from the one that died, I want to claim that the Buddhist (or at least some important Buddhist thinkers) maintains that the rebirth is a different person from the one that died. Moreover, it seems to me that this must be correct. Therefore as far as I am concerned the Buddhist position entails that at death the person I am shall cease. Someone else may exist in causal dependence upon me, but what is that to *me*?

It seems to me that on any Buddhist understanding of rebirth this is likely in most if not all cases to be the way it is. None of this in itself means that the Buddhist position is wrong. But what it does mean is that, if the Buddhist position is correct, then unless we attain a state (such as *nirvāṇa*) where in some way or another our rebirth will not matter, our death in this life is actually, really, the death of us. Death will be the end for *us*. Traditionally, at least on the day-to-day level, Buddhists tend to obscure this fact in their choice of language by referring to '*my* rebirth', and 'concern for *one's* future lives'. But actually any rebirth (say, as a cockroach in South America) would not be oneself, and there is a serious question therefore as to why one should care at all about 'one's' future rebirths. Of course, one Buddhist response would be to say that it is an example of the very egoism one is trying to escape to be concerned whether the rebirth will be oneself or not. But I am not sure that helps much. We tend to forget that the original direction of Buddhism was towards the overriding urgency of the need to *escape* from the cycle of rebirth. Rebirth, in Buddhism and other early Indian systems of liberation, was seen as horrific. To point out that 'my' rebirth involves among other things the destruction of everything that counts as *me* would have been seen simply as emphasising how horrible rebirth is, and the need to escape from it through spiritual liberation, *nirvāṇa*.

In the last section of my book *Altruism and Reality*[38] I also engaged in a much more extensive critical study of problems which, it seemed to me, emerge in the Buddhist conception of persons (and other things) as actually nothing more than conventional constructs. Part of my concern here and elsewhere has been to provoke scholars working in Buddhist Studies to a far greater critical sensitivity. Christian philosophers have spent many years defending their positions against philosophical criticism. In the last twenty years this has borne fruit in some immensely sophisticated defences and sometimes modifications of traditional Christian positions. I can see only gain in engaging in the same constructive criticisms and defence of Buddhist philosophy. In my essay I range over a number of key Buddhist presuppositions that seem to me to be questionable. Thus I criticise the idea that the whole is simply a mental super-imposition upon the parts. I attack the idea that the world of everyday life is a mental construct, and I argue that persons are not bundles, not constructs out of a series of evanescent mental and physical 'parts', but are rather prior to analysis into parts and presupposed in it. I criticise the idea of data such as pains as conceptually prior to the person who possesses the pains, on the basis that pains necessarily involve subjects ('persons', in the sense in which I use the term, which would include animals) and make no sense as free-floating. The broad direction of my critique is in favour of what might be called some form of 'commonsense realism', and towards minimalising the role of subjectivity (our minds) in the construction of our world. I see the problem of solipsism (the world is no more than the product of my consciousness) as endemic in all of Buddhist thought. I also see the move towards subjectivity, reflected in a tendency towards privileging individual mental states such as sense data and feelings over 'everyday objects', as ethically and religiously problematic. I tend to favour some form of ethical objectivism. I argue that the Buddhist tendency to reduce persons to other impersonal data claimed to be more fundamental, far from making Buddhism more coherent as an ethical base, actually removes what I am now inclined to think of as a mainstay of coherent ethics. That mainstay is the primacy and irreducible uniqueness of the person.

Anyone familiar with Buddhist thought is able to see that in all of this I am attacking central presuppositions of the very direction Buddhism takes. Anyone familiar with Christian thought might also see here why I found Christianity intellectually tempting.

APPENDIX TWO: HOW TO BECOME A CATHOLIC

This is for those who might be interested in finding out more from the Church itself, or are interested in actually becoming Catholics. It is intended to offer a little help based on my own experiences. It is *not* for my Buddhist friends. Please could they look away now.

I am easily embarrassed, and about things that really affect the heart I tend to be rather shy. I used to haunt Catholic bookshops and churches with the feeling of embarrassment and anxiety that (I would imagine!) people sometimes visit sex shops. I felt I was exposing myself. I dearly hoped I would not meet anyone I knew. I looked at others there as if they were denizens of a different world, with a mixture of envy and fear in case they thought I might be a Catholic and say something to me. I sometimes awkwardly and self-consciously did Catholicky things, like dipping my fingers in the blessed water, crossing myself and genuflecting. I looked at wedding-cake Baroque ornateness and the syrupy naïve Catholic art with a degree of repulsion. I lit candles and prayed. My prayers were always prayers of yearning and prayers for forgiveness. Forgive me that I am not now a Christian. Forgive my inability to believe. And – in more recent years – help me to become a Catholic. Give me the courage. Smooth the way. How long, O Lord, how long? If one prays for faith does one have faith or not?

I hid my Catholic books, or pretended I was reading them 'for comparative purposes'.

I dearly wanted a book on what one actually *did* in order to become a Catholic. There might well be such a book, but if so it did not come my way. I had to find out from my own researches.

As we have seen, Christianity is a communal religion of public performance. It is not about private experiences and things going on inside one's own head. Christianity is not a religion intended for an elite of hermits. One cannot be a

Christian and not in some way a member of the Church. One cannot be a Catholic entirely by oneself. Having decided to become a Catholic this was my first obstacle to overcome. All my 'Catholicism' had been a form of romantic 'mood-making' inside my head. It was quite another thing actually to confess to other Catholics that I wanted to become a Catholic, to attend instruction and go through ceremonies. But faith involves making public assertions, an act of will. And I have argued that central to what Christianity is all about as a series of transformative strategies is openness to grace through participation in such things as the sacraments. Thus one cannot really be a Christian and not take part with others.

Therefore, along with reading and prayer, eventually one has to pluck up courage and approach the Catholic community in some way. If you have Catholic friends whom you can speak to, then all well and good. They will no doubt put you in touch with the next stage, if you wish. Alternatively (or as well) you can go and see a priest. In my own case actually having a brief word with a wise and sensitive priest was a major stage in finally making my intention to become a Catholic real for myself, although it was well over a year later before I did anything very definite about it. I was at Clifton Cathedral, the Catholic cathedral in Bristol. I offered a candle to the Blessed Virgin Mary and prayed that she would help me in my wish to become a Catholic. I was also interested to find details of a series of classes I had heard about on Catholicism. I did not want to meet any Catholics there and then, though! Someone in the cathedral asked me if I needed any help. I'm not sure what I said, but he asked me (it seemed with some surprise) if I wished to become a Catholic. 'You had better see a priest.' Even then I was unsure whether to go, but eventually I did. I was very nervous. But I am very glad I did. In bringing my wishes out of my head and embodying them in actions and speech, I was forced to face the question of whether they had any extra-mental reality.

I discovered that if you meet a priest, while you may be embarrassed and awkward, he will not be frightening. Catholic priests are used to acting as counsellors and are quite familiar with people approaching them for information on Catholicism. You will not have to tell him about yourself if you do not wish to. You can say just as much or as little as you like. You will not be made to confess all your sins. And – and this is important – contrary to what many people believe you will not be grabbed and forcibly turned into a Catholic against your will. You can explain exactly what your interests are. If you simply wish to know more, without commitment, say so. In my experience the Church nowadays is very emphatic that conversion should be an act of free choice, made without duress. Thus, if anything, you will be *discouraged* from becoming a Catholic until you are quite sure you are willing to make that commitment. One is constantly being told there is no hurry. On the other hand, if you do decide to go through with it you will find immense joy and support. The biblical paradigm is always, of course, the return of the prodigal son.

Even if you are very keen to become a Catholic you are unlikely to be received into the Church there and then. Receptions occur in a special ceremony normally conducted by the Bishop after an appropriate period of instruction. The classes that I had heard about at the cathedral were the RCIA classes. RCIA stands for 'Rite of Christian Initiation of Adults'. This is the normal way nowadays for teaching enquirers about the Catholic faith. If at all possible you should find out about RCIA classes in your neighbourhood. If my experience is anything to go by, they start in mid-September and continue with a Christmas break until Easter.

As a Buddhist academic, I had to swallow my pride and be willing to be seen talking seriously about my own beliefs with Catholics and – God forbid! – attending services. I had to admit I had previously been wrong. I did not know everything. I had to learn new behaviour, new responses and be willing to get things muddled. One of my first difficulties after so many years as a Buddhist was simply getting used to using 'God-language' again with those for whom it was second nature. But as I became more and more confident of the rightness of my choice, speaking of God – and to God – began to flow with relative ease. Eventually I had to work out how to tell friends, family, other Buddhists about my interests, and – slowly, slowly – my intentions.

The RCIA classes met one evening a week for about two hours. They consisted of prayer, music, sometimes singing, readings, talks by priests and others, and discussion in small groups. There were also books available for purchase, and a small library. In case that all sounds too forbidding, the classes were informal and informative, with tea, coffee, biscuits, and even wine at Christmas. Most important, one got used to the idea of attending the cathedral and *being* a Catholic. To repeat again, Catholicism even at a big cathedral is very much a communal affair. One is received into a *community*, just as the Kingdom of Heaven will be a community. That is why it is called a 'kingdom'.

So this was the first stage. The classes were run by the RCIA team, consisting entirely of laity. Many were women. Many were themselves converts and could speak of their own experiences of conversion. Of those attending the RCIA classes, about half were lapsed Catholics wishing to return to the faith. The rest were completely new, from a variety of backgrounds, mainly Christian. The lapsed Catholics had separate talks and discussions.

At the regular Solemn Mass one Sunday near the end of November those enquirers who were seriously interested in becoming Catholics at some time in the future formally declared their intention. In a very nice ceremony (the Rite of Acceptance) we were accepted and offered support by the community. We were each given a Bible as well, although I do not know how frequent that is. The commonly used Catholic Bible is the *New Jerusalem Bible*, which has the so-called Apocrypha integrated into it. The Catholic Church does not consider the 'Apocrypha' to be apocryphal.

From then on I decided to attend Mass regularly and to do all the things I would be required to do when I was finally received into the Catholic Church. I felt the Solemn Mass to be like heaven on earth. I absolutely cannot understand those who are Catholics and yet do not want to go to Mass, or find it a burden. Clifton Cathedral has one of the very best choirs in the country. It has recorded many CDs and toured abroad. I threatened to bring my sleeping bag and live at the cathedral. The one thing I could not yet do, of course, was actually partake of the body and blood of Christ in the communion. Although I could go up to the front with the others and receive a blessing from the priest, over the months in which I attended

Mass unable actually to partake in the meal I felt it more and more as a sort of purgatory. It was a necessary purification to render me, through the grace of God, fit for the body and blood of Christ. I felt so impure, and yet I so wanted to partake fully in the Feast.

Those who have already been baptised into another Christian tradition are not required to be baptised again. Baptism is once and for always. Thus, in my own case, since I had been baptised, I was now known as a 'candidate' (that is, a candidate eventually for full communion with the Catholic Church). Had I not been baptised already, I would have been known as a 'catechumen'.

On the first Sunday of Lent the Rite of Election takes place in the presence of the Bishop. During Lent one undergoes preparation for full acceptance by the Church. The final acceptance, Initiation into the Church, takes place at the Easter Vigil in the cathedral after sunset on the eve before Easter Day.

In spite of all that I have said, perhaps there are still those who think in terms of the primacy of religious experience, and Buddhism as (probably) the best way to bring about those experiences. Well, nothing prepared me for the overwhelming experience of Holy Week – the entry into Jerusalem, the washing of the feet, the institution of the Last Supper, the happy yet dreadful fault of Jesus' betrayal, arrest, travesty of a trial and horrible, horrible execution. The early prayers, the late vigils, the fasting and my first confession. 'Forgive me Father, for I have sinned. It has been forty-nine years – no, it has been an eternity – since my last confession.' Confession – I felt as if I was picked up, turned inside out, shaken and returned to purged, transformed, transfigured normality. Forgiveness, forgiveness. I was – I am – so *grateful*. In the light of that gratitude everything changes, everything is repolarised around Christ's redemptive sacrifice and His ever present forgiveness. This sounds like the language of theology. It is not – or it is more than that. It is the stammering (if you like) of religious experience. Experiences beyond my wildest dreams and my wildest hopes.

Acceptance into the Church at the Easter Vigil is an astonishingly powerful and moving event. It is associated with the wonderful story of resurrection and life. Those who are to be baptised are first baptised and then confirmed. Those who have been baptised before are simply confirmed. Confirmation is through anointing with chrism, blessed oil. After confirmation the new members of the Church take their first full communion. Walking home after Mass on Easter morning, with Christ Himself incorporated into my body as I was now fully incorporated into His, the sun shining and flowers and birds singing of spring, all the world seemed radiantly transformed. Everything – trees, leaves, stones, buildings, even the rubbish on the roadside – appeared to me crisply crystal clear, shining forth with its own individuality in a way that I had never seen previously. I noticed features of the landscape and buildings that I had never observed, no matter how much I had walked through the Victorian graveyard and along those roads before. Things were radiant in their own particularity and yet, it seemed to me, were also expressing, singing, their interdependence and deep-rooted unity. This was no absurd pantheism. Everywhere I looked ordinary objects were singing, singing of their dependence on God, their Source. Like us, things are most themselves when they sing of God. And all are trying to sing of Him. The signature, the fingerprint, of God is on *everything*. Only the human beings I passed on the road sometimes seemed to be trying to tear themselves away from their dependence and interdependence, vainly trying thereby to be *individuals*. I wanted to cry out to them, to tell them, to help them, to live and enjoy what I was enjoying.

The joy of this vision, for me a whole and wholly new vision of the world, is with me still. All in the mind? Of course. Experiences (as such) have a tendency to be all in the mind! If they go, if they fade, so what? I am in love. And lovers are foolish. These things are only experiences. But truth in such things is not a matter of experiences. It is not a case of 'true for me'. It is true, whether I experience it or not. Period. That, I think, is a comfort. It is a comfort to believe that whether one can meditate, whether one can pray, whether one sins or not, whether one has a headache or is dying, the teachings of the Catholic Church are actually true and their truth is fully present and available here and now. They are wonderful too. Love and forgiveness, and all else, are true. How wonderful that Wonderful Things are also true!

But Pete has now abandoned all hope that I might discover truth on his behalf. I started as an Anglican, became a Buddhist and now I am a Catholic. It is no use relying on me. There is nothing for it, Pete says. He will have to discover the truth for himself.

That, it seems to me, is progress.

SELECTIVE BIBLIOGRAPHY

This bibliography includes all the works referred to in the text, as well as a short list of books of which I have personal knowledge, that I have enjoyed, and that have in various ways been influential on me in my journey. They are included because they might be a good place to start for those with no knowledge of the main subjects covered in this book.

The books I have asterisked would be my own 'it makes you think' (or do-it-yourself conversion) kit. For a graded course on Catholic doctrine from absolutely elementary to advanced, try Henesy and Gallagher, Triglio and Brighenti, Pasco and Redford, the *Catechism*, and Kreeft (in that order). Afterwards try Aquinas (1991). If you are coming to Catholicism from an evangelical Protestant background, try the Longenecker and Martin. Before beginning the 'graded course' you might want to become aware of some of the prejudices against Catholicism in the modern (and not so modern) world by reading the book by Jenkins (who is not himself a Catholic).

All quotations from the Bible have been taken from *The New Jerusalem Bible*, Reader's Edition, Darton, Longman and Todd, 1990.

Basic books on Catholicism

*Henesy, M., and Gallagher, R. (1997) *How to Survive Being Married to a Catholic*, Liguori, MI: Liguori Publications. More than its title would suggest, this is the most basic book imaginable on Catholicism. It is very entertaining, with absolutely no intention of preaching or converting, and makes liberal use of amusing cartoons. Another excellent book by M. Henesy (1989), also with cartoons, is *Len Chimbley's Dream: Questions and Answers About God*, Liguori, MI: Liguori Publications. Although it does not say so, this is the simplest possible introduction to Aquinas on God.

Holy See (1994) *Catechism of the Catholic Church*, London: Geoffrey Chapman. There is a further edition since this one, with revisions.

211

*Finnegan, S. (ed.) (1997) *The Essential Catholic Handbook: A Summary of Beliefs, Practices, and Prayers*, Norwich: Canterbury Press.

Johnson, K. O. (1994) *Why Do Catholics Do That? A Guide to the Teachings and Practices of the Catholic Church*, New York: Ballantine Books.

Knox, R. (1952) *The Hidden Stream*, London: Burns Oates. A book not easy to get hold of, and pre-Vatican II. But in some ways it is one of my favourite introductions to Catholicism. Knox was a friend of Chesterton and Waugh.

McCabe, H. (1985) *The Teaching of the Catholic Church: A New Catechism of Christian Doctrine*, London: Catholic Truth Society. A summary in question and answer form by an important contemporary Dominican philosopher.

*Pasco, R., and Redford, J. (1994) *Faith Alive: An Introduction to the Catholic Faith*, New Catechism Edition, London, Sydney, Auckland: Hodder and Stoughton.

*Redford, J. (1997) *Catholicism: Hard Questions*, London: Geoffrey Chapman. An excellent response to many of the issues which those new to Catholicism find so difficult. Very good for coming to appreciate the Catholic orientation.

*Trigilio, J., and Brighenti, K. (2003) *Catholicism for Dummies*, New York: Wiley Publishing.
Quite comprehensive, with a North American orientation. Easily available and written in an engaging and amusing style.

Works on Buddhism, including Shinran

Bloom, A. (1965) *Shinran's Gospel of Pure Grace*, Tucson, AZ: The University of Arizona Press sixth printing 1985. A classic. Very influential. Perhaps a bit Christianised, but still well worth reading.

Gethin, R. (1998) *The Foundations of Buddhism*, Oxford and New York: Oxford University Press. The best basic introduction to mainstream Buddhism.

Tenzin Gyatso, Dalai Lama XIV (1980) *Universal Responsibility and the Good Heart*, Dharamsala: Library of Tibetan Works and Archives.

Ueda, Y., and Hirota, D. (1989) *Shinran: An Introduction to His Thought*, Kyoto: Hongwanji International Center. The best available introduction to Shinran, with extensive selections from his writings.

Williams, P. (1989) *Mahāyāna Buddhism: The Doctrinal Foundations*, London and New York: Routledge. For a short introduction to Shinran see the last chapter.

(1998) *Altruism and Reality: Studies in the Philosophy of the Bodhicaryāvatāra*, Richmond: Curzon.

Williams, P., with Tribe, A. (2000) *Buddhist Thought: A Complete Introduction to the Indian Tradition*, London and New York: Routledge.

The resurrection

Davis, S. T. (1993) *Risen Indeed: Making Sense of the Resurrection*, London: SPCK. A philosopher on the resurrection.

Davis, S., Kendall, D., O'Collins, G. (eds) (1997) *The Resurrection*, Oxford: Oxford University Press. A collection of scholarly papers from a 1996 symposium. Very up-to-date and authoritative.

*Grieve, V. (1996) *Your Verdict on the Empty Tomb*, 3rd edn, Carlisle: OM Publishing. By a lawyer. A good summary of the material and arguments. Very easy to read. Recommended.

O' Collins, G. (1983) *Interpreting Jesus*, London: Geoffrey Chapman. A reliable, scholarly yet readable book. A further book – this time specifically on the resurrection – by the indefatigable and always worth-reading O'Collins is *Easter Faith: Believing in the Risen Jesus*, London: Darton, Longman and Todd, 2003.

Swinburne, R (2003) *The Resurrection of God Incarnate*, Oxford: The Clarendon Press.

A sophisticated essay by a leading contemporary philosopher of religion. Swinburne argues among other things that if there is a God, resurrection is just the sort of thing we might find Him doing.

Walker, P. (1999) *The Weekend that Changed the World: The Mystery of Jerusalem's Empty Tomb*, London: Marshall Pickering.

See also Groothuis, under 'Others' below. And watch also Mel Gibson's riveting film *The Passion of the Christ*. The (rather Protestant) obsession of critics with precise historical accuracy and faithfulness to the Biblical accounts is less important than precise *spiritual* accuracy. Watching Gibson's film can be an act of devotion rather like seeing deeply into the great medieval paintings of the crucifixion, such as Matthias Grünwald's Isenheim altarpiece.

On Aquinas

Aquinas, St Thomas (1991) *Summa Theologiae: A Concise Translation*, edited by Timothy McDermott, London: Methuen. A way of coming to grips with Aquinas's *magnum opus* without the enormous length of the original. Very useful.

*Chesterton, G. K. (1933) *St Thomas Aquinas*, London: Hodder and Stoughton. Recently reprinted. Concentrates mainly on the historical context, particularly opposition to the world-negation of the Cathars. A masterpiece, still very much admired.

Davies, B. (1992) *The Thought of Thomas Aquinas*, Oxford: Clarendon Press. Davies is a trained philosopher who is also a Dominican. In my experience by far the best single-volume introduction to Aquinas's philosophy and theology. A more accessible book by Brian Davies is *Aquinas*, Outstanding Christian Thinkers Series, London and New York: Continuum, 2002.

Williams, P. (2004) 'Aquinas meets the Buddhists: Prolegomenon to an authentically Tomas-ist basis for dialogue', in Jim Fodor and Frederick Christian Bauerschmidt ed., *Aquinas in Dialogue: Thomas for the Twenty-First Century*, Oxford, Malden, MA, and Carlton, Victoria: Blackwell Publishing: 87–117.

A discussion of what Aquinas would have made of Buddhist arguments against the existence of God.

See also under 'Henesy' above.

Medieval heresies (including Cathars)

Lambert, M. (1992) *Medieval Heresy: Popular Movements from the Gregorian Reform to the Reformation*, 3rd edn, Oxford, UK and Cambridge, USA: Blackwell.

Wakefield, W. L., and Evans, A. P. (trans.) (1991) *Heresies of the High Middle Ages*, New York: Columbia University Press.

A number of medieval heretical movements, including the Cathars, had views a bit like Buddhism. In looking at how the Church responded to these movements (intellectually, not through burning!) one can get interesting insight into the differences between the Buddhist and Christian orientations.

The religious history of the late Middle Ages and Reformation in Britain

Ackroyd, P. (1999) *The Life of Thomas More*, London: Vintage.

Duffy, E. (1992) *The Stripping of the Altars: Traditional Religion in England 1400–1580*, New Haven and London: Yale University Press.

Waugh, E. (1953) *Edmund Campion*, Melbourne, London and Baltimore: Penguin Books. First published 1935.

Each of these books is thoroughly enjoyable to read and shows the vitality of the late medieval and early reformation Catholic Church. They are important counter-balances to the view that the Church was decadent and needed reforming, still widespread in lands influenced by Protestantism. Duffy's book in particular has been widely praised and is becoming very influential.

G. K. Chesterton and others

Before we come to Chesterton, anyone considering becoming a Catholic will eventually want to read something by John Henry Newman. His own spiritual autobiography, *Apologia Pro Vita Sua*, is interesting, but I have found in many ways his best apologetic piece – at least for those new to Catholicism and particularly if you come from an Anglican background – is *Discourses Addressed to Mixed Congregations*, recently reprinted in James Tolhurst DD (ed.), *The Works of Cardinal John Henry Newman*, Birmingham Oratory Millennium Edition Volume VI, Leominster and Notre Dame: Gracewing and University of Notre Dame Press, 2002.

Chesterton, G. K. (1908) *Orthodoxy*, London: John Lane.

(1925) *The Everlasting Man*, London: Hodder and Stoughton.

(1937) *Autobiography*, London: Hutchinson.

Pearce, J. (1997) *Wisdom and Innocence: A Life of G. K. Chesterton*, London, Sydney, Auckland: Hodder and Stoughton.

*Sparkes, R. (ed.) (1997) *Prophet of Orthodoxy: The Wisdom of G. K. Chesterton*, London: Collins Fount.

See also above, under 'Aquinas'. The Sparkes book is a good selection. Chesterton wrote a great deal, much of it in short essays. I find anything by him entertaining and thoroughly recommendable.

Chesterton was a major influence on the conversion of C. S. Lewis. Lewis also wrote a great deal on Christianity. Of his apologetics I have enjoyed most:

Lewis, C. S. (1977) *The Great Divorce*, London: Fount. First published 1946. On heaven and hell. Great fun.

(1997) *Mere Christianity*, London: Fount. First published 1952.

(1977) *Surprised by Joy: The Shape of my Early Life*, London: Fount. First published 1952.

But I find his theological writings relatively dour and harsh compared with the bubbling humour of Chesterton. Perhaps this reflects Lewis's upbringing as a Protestant in Northern Ireland. He was never really at ease with 'Papists'. Much better, and an excellent introduction for those new to Christianity providing one reads it as Christian allegory, is Lewis's fiction. This means particularly his Narnia series of books for children, especially *The Magician's Nephew*, *The Lion, the Witch, and the Wardrobe* and *The Last Battle* (basic Christianity in the most readable and moving manner). One should also mention Lewis's astonishing science fiction trilogy for adults, *Out of the Silent Planet*, *Perelandra* and *That Hideous Strength*. The trilogy is highly recommended for the insight it gives into the Christian perspective.

The other novelist I have found very interesting in this context is Charles Williams. Williams was a friend of C. S. Lewis and a major influence on him. Together with Lewis he formed a triumvirate at Oxford with J. R. R. Tolkien (a traditional Catholic). Charles Williams's novels have been called 'spiritual shockers'. As a means of expressing Christian ideas they can be quite weird and very stimulating. His *Descent into Hell* and *All Hallows Eve* have been important in my own reflections on the dangers of complete subjectivity, self-obsession, and the difficulties of overcoming it, as well as the dangers of guru-worship.

For a study of Lewis, Tolkien, Williams and friends see:

Carpenter, H. (1978) *The Inklings*, London, Boston and Sydney: George Allen and Unwin.

Catholicism in the contemporary world

Luciani, A., Pope John Paul I (1979) *Illustrissimi: The Letters of Pope John Paul I*, London: Fount.

Stourton, E. (1999) *Absolute Truth: The Catholic Church Today*, Harmondsworth: Penguin Books.

Stanford, P. (1999) *Cardinal Hume and the Changing Face of English Catholicism*, London: Geoffrey Chapman. First published 1993.

Both these latter books are by authors sympathetic to a liberal approach to Catholicism, particularly to issues like contraception. For the church's own view see Redford below. Stanford's book gives a much-warranted, sympathetic and warm portrayal of the late Cardinal Hume.

Wilkins, J. (ed.) (1994) *Understanding* Veritatis Splendor: *The Encyclical Letter of Pope John Paul II on the Church's Moral Teaching*, London: SPCK. A debate on the Church's teachings as expressed in Pope John Paul II's encyclical.

Redford, J. (2000) *Sex: What the Catholic Church Teaches – The alternative to moral anarchy*, London: St Paul's Press.

A clear and much needed statement of the actual teachings of the Church.

Contemporary Christian theology

Milbank, J., Pickstock, C., and Ward, G. (eds) (1999) *Radical Orthodoxy: A New Theology*, London and New York: Routledge.

In spite of a rather turgid style at times, this book is very important. It argues for a radically different way of looking at the world from the dominant presuppositions and perspectives of secularism, a different way that involves the reappropriation of what is in fact orthodox Christianity. Orthodox Christianity, it is argued, provides a radical alternative approach to issues such as knowledge, revelation, aesthetics, erotics, the city, bodies and music from the approach of secularism, which also avoids problems of postmodern relativism in truth and morals. This alternative is more adequate to both the material itself and to current needs. A Catholic response to this book is:

Hemming, Laurence Paul (ed.) (2000) *Radical Orthodoxy? A Catholic Enquiry*, Aldershot, Burlington USA, Singapore, Sydney: Ashgate.

Philosophy of religion

Copan, P., and Moser, P. (eds.) (2003) *The Rationality of Theism*, London: Routledge.

Davies, B. (ed.) (1998) *Philosophy of Religion: A Guide to the Subject*, London: Cassell. Mainly Catholic contributors.

John Paul II, Pope (1998) *Faith and Reason: Encyclical Letter Fides et Ratio*, London: Catholic Truth Society. The Pope is himself a professional academic philosopher. This is his latest statement on what the nature and role of philosophy should be.

McCabe, H. (2000) *God Matters*, London and New York: Mowbray. Originally 1987, Geoffrey Chapman. A very stimulating collection by an important Catholic Dominican philosopher. McCabe has been influential on the work of Brian Davies and Denys Turner, for example. Partly on philosophy, partly theology. A further collection of McCabe's essays is Brian Davies OP (ed.) *God Still Matters*, London and New York: Continuum, 2002.

McGhee, M. (ed.) (1992) *Philosophy, Religion and the Spiritual Life*, Cambridge: Cambridge University Press.

Morris, T. V. (ed.) (1994) *God and the Philosophers: The Reconciliation of Faith and Reason*, New York and Oxford: Oxford University Press. A number of well-known contemporary American Christian philosophers tell how they became and/or remain Christians, and how they reconcile their religion with their professional activity as philosophers. Only one Catholic contributor, I think.

*Murray, M. J. (ed.) (1999) *Reason for the Hope Within*, Grand Rapids, MI, and Cambridge: Eerdmans. A very useful collection in which philosophers try to express for the layman the perspectives and resources for Christian apologetics of contemporary discussions in the philosophy of religion. Most main topics of Christian philosophy are treated, including 'other religions', with handy and stimulating attempts to defend Christian orthodoxy rationally and with clarity and simplicity.

Turner, D. (1995) *The Darkness of God: Negativity in Christian Mysticism*, Cambridge, New York and Melbourne: Cambridge University Press. A brilliant book on philosophy and 'negative mysticism'. Beautifully written, it throws into very clear form the way in which the stress on weird paranormal experiences as being what mysticism is all about is a relatively modern development that would not have been at all appreciated in e.g. the Middle Ages. Very influential on my own appreciation of the Catholic orientation on these issues in relationship to Buddhism.

Yandell, K. E. (1998) *Philosophy of Religion: A Contemporary Introduction*, London and New York: Routledge. One of the best introductions to contemporary philosophy of religion, including a critical treatment of some Hindu and Buddhist views.

Others

*Augustine, St (2001) the *Confessions*, trans. Maria Boulding, Hyde Park, New York: New York City Press. After the account of St Paul, still the original and the best Christian conversion story. Essential reading. This is a super recent translation that supersedes the Penguin translation by Pine-Coffin used in this book.

Bede (1968) *A History of the English Church and People*, trans. Leo Sherley-Price, Harmondsworth: Penguin Books. Revised edition.

Bernall, M. (1999) *She Said Yes: The Unlikely Martyrdom of Cassie Bernall*, Farmington: The Plough Publishing House. An interesting example of evangelical hagiography (construction of a Saint's or other ideological 'biographies') at work, written by Cassie's mother very soon after the tragic events themselves and as such no doubt part of the grieving and healing process. From my own distance I have some doubts about some of the analysis and implications of this deeply disturbing work, particularly as regards Cassie's earlier 'satanic' phase three years before her death. But the starkness of the choice at the end, Cassie's purported response, the raw anguish of the story and their implications still stand (even if as a matter of fact it were to turn out that Cassie was not the one who said 'Yes').

Duffy, E. (2004) *Faith of Our Fathers*, London and New York: Continuum. The distinguished historian of the late Middle Ages and Reformation reflects on his traditional Irish Catholic upbringing, and his view of the place of the Catholic Church in the modern world.

Farmer, D. H. (1992) *Saint Hugh of Lincoln*, Lincoln: Honywood Press. First published by Darton, Longman and Todd, 1985. A scholarly and readable account of a saintly Saint.

Groothuis, D. (1996) *Jesus in an Age of Controversy*, Eugene, OR: Harvest House. A reply to modern attacks such as those of 'The Jesus Seminar' on what we can know of Jesus and His teaching, and the reliability of the beliefs of the mainstream Christian Churches.

Guibert of Nogent (1996) *A Monk's Confession: The Memoirs of Guibert of Nogent*, trans. Paul J. Archambault, University Park, PA: Pennsylvania State University Press. A wonderfully candid insight into the mind and world of a twelfth-century monk.

James, O. (1998) *Britain on the Couch: Treating a Low Serotonin Society*, London: Arrow.

*Longenecker, D. (ed.) (1999) *The Path to Rome: Modern Journeys to the Catholic Church*, Leominster: Gracewing. Short accounts of modern, mainly British, conversions. Very interesting, although almost all cases are of conversion from Anglicanism, often of conservative Anglo-Catholics incensed by the decision of the Anglican Church to ordain women.

Montefiore, H. (1995) *Reaffirming the Church of England: Why It Is, What It Is, and How It Is*, London: SPCK Triangle.

Paxman, J. (1999) *The English: A Portrait of a People*, Harmondsworth: Penguin Books.

Slouka, M. (1996) *War of the Worlds: Cyberspace and the High-tech Assault on Reality*, London: Abacus.

Staniforth, M. (trans.) (1968) *Early Christian Writings: The Apostolic Fathers*, Harmondsworth: Penguin Classics.

Thompson, F. (1996) *The Hound of Heaven*, London: Phoenix.

Thekla, Mother (1997) *Eternity Now: An Introduction to Orthodox Spirituality*, Norwich: Canterbury Press.

Waugh, E. (1981) *Helena*, Harmondsworth: Penguin. First published in 1950.

*Wilson, I. (1999) *The Blood and the Shroud: New Light on the Turin Shroud Mystery*, London: Orion. A fascinating read, and it seems to me quite fair and reliable. Particularly recommended for its detailed treatment of crucifixion and what the crucifixion of Christ might have involved. Note the suggestion that someone being crucified may have *faced* the wooden posts, and the picture on p. 61 of what this could have looked like. If correct then crucifixion, with its writhing bodies in this sort of position, must have been much, much more horrific than the rather 'tame' versions we have become used to (but cf. Gibsons *The Passion of the Christ* film, that goes a long way towards correcting the 'tame' version). No wonder Classical writers viewed it with so much horror that we have no descriptions to go on.

Young, J. (1996) *Christianity*, London: Teach Yourself Books. A basic survey for absolute beginners. Rather uninspired, but a reasonable summary of arguments for the authenticity of the resurrection. It is interesting that in *Teach Yourself Christianity* the author's brief is taken to include advocating the *truth* of Christianity, whereas we would not expect to find the same (nor do we) in, say, *Teach Yourself Islam*, or *Teach Yourself Buddhism*.

NOTES

INTRODUCTION

1 I just happened to catch a television programme from the USA in which a woman was explaining to an audience that since she stopped losing her temper and shouting at others for no apparent reason, her relationships had improved. Her company had also made an extra million dollars last year. She broke down and cried while explaining how much better her life had now become. The audience seemed to consider the tears a particularly Good Thing. An expert nodded sagely and noted how we can all empower ourselves and make improvements in our lives. I think he had written a book about it. Another expert, this time in conflict resolution, recommended regular mindfulness meditation, in origin a Buddhist practice.

Imagine a shopkeeper who said that since he had stopped murdering his customers his relationship with his customers had improved, and his company now made a good deal more money.

What no one quite wants to say is that murdering people – or shouting at people for no apparent reason – is actually *wrong*. And one should not do things that are wrong. I suppose to mention morality might be thought of as intolerant, or 'getting on the moral high-horse'. So one has to encourage people to do good by appealing to self-interest.

2 Quoted in D. Groothuis, *Jesus in an Age of Controversy* (Eugene, OR: Harvest House, 1996), pp. 13–14.

3 G. K. Chesterton, *The Everlasting Man* (London: Hodder & Stoughton, 1925), p. 3.

4 *Confessions* 1:1 (translated R. S. Pine-Coffin; Harmondsworth: Penguin, 1961).

5 Pope John Paul I (A. Luciani), *Illustrissimi: The Letters of Pope John Paul I* (London: Collins Fount, 1979), p. 31.

6 Paul Williams, 'Non-conceptuality, critical reasoning and religious experience: Some Tibetan Buddhist discussions', in

M. McGhee (ed.), *Philosophy, Religion and the Spiritual Life* (Cambridge: Cambridge University Press, 1992).

7 Quoted in Pope John Paul II, *Faith and Reason: Encyclical Letter Fides et Ratio* (London: Catholic Truth Society, 1998), p. 116.

GOD, BUDDHISM AND MORALITY

1 Robert Collins, 'A scientific argument for the existence of God: The fine-tuning design argument', in M. J. Murray (ed.), *Reason for the Hope Within* (Grand Rapids, MI: Eerdmans, 1999), pp. 48–50.

2 See Brian Davies' article 'The problem of evil', in B. Davies (ed.), *Philosophy of Religion: A Guide to the Subject* (London: Cassell, 1998).

3 See Davies again (above, n. 2) and H. McCabe, *God Matters* (London and New York: Mowbray, 2000).

4 *God Matters*, ch. 3.

5 Quoted in P. Stanford, *Cardinal Hume and the Changing Face of English Catholicism* (London: Geoffrey Chapman, 2nd edn, 1999), p. 196.

6 Gavin D'Costa, like the good scholar he is, has asked me for the source of this quote. I got it from my friend George Chryssides. I've no idea from where he got it. Anon. (or should that be 'a nun'?) perhaps.

7 A. Nichols, *The Splendour of Doctrine: The Catechism of the Catholic Church on Christian Believing* (Edinburgh: T&T Clark, 1995), p. 157.

8 See in M. McGhee (ed.), *Philosophy, Religion and the Spiritual Life*. Paul Williams, 'Non-conceptuality, critical reasoning and religious experience: Some Tibetan Buddhist discussions', (Cambridge: Cambridge University Press, 1992).

9 R. Pasco, and J. Redford, *Faith Alive: An Introduction to the Catholic Faith* (New Catechism Edition, London, Sydney, Auckland: Hodder & Stoughton, 1994), p. 79.

10 R. Strange, *The Catholic Faith* (Oxford: Oxford University Press, 1986, repr. 1996), p. 163.

11 Pope John Paul II, *Faith and Reason* (1998), para. 90.
12 See, for example, Tenzin Gyatso, Dalai Lama XIV, *Universal Responsibility and the Good Heart* (Dharamsala: Library of Tibetan Works and Archives, 1980), p. 35; cf. p. 40.
13 Suppose that someone accepted that God exists, but still questioned our duty to worship and obey God. Sadly there are plenty like that – those who say they accept the existence of God but do nothing about it. If they do not think – I am tempted to say 'feel' – that they have a duty towards a God to whom they owe *everything*, how could I persuade them? For me, this is overwhelmingly a moral matter. It is a matter of gratitude for that which by its very nature is totally unmerited, gratitude so deep that one's very being becomes gratitude, so deep that one can only say over and over again with devotion and tears of love, 'Thank you – it's so wonderful, marvellous – thank you!' If someone accepts God and yet does not have gratitude, what can one say? Perhaps they do not really understand who or what God is. Or perhaps they are just simply ungrateful. Can I *persuade* someone to be grateful?
14 Who was it who said that mysticism begins in mist, is centred on I, and ends in schism?
15 Tenzin Gyatso, *Universal Responsibility*, pp. 8–11.
16 Ibid., p. 2. I have just seen in a bookshop a new book by Deepak Chopra. Chopra is a medical doctor based in the United States who has gained a great reputation as a New Age self-help advisor. His books sell widely. This new work is on the stages of coming to experience God. I am not sure how being a medical doctor qualifies one as an expert in this, or whether Chopra himself claims to have experienced God. But the book is endorsed by many authorities, with pride of place given to the Dalai Lama and the Buddhist R. A. F. Thurman, who both seem to think that this book will be of great benefit to others. But what puzzles me is that as a Buddhist the Dalai Lama does not believe in God. What is he thinking of, then, when he endorses a book on coming to experience God? Surely the answer is that whatever Chopra means by 'God' is perfectly compatible with the atheism of the Dalai Lama. I suspect that Chopra

(in common with many in the Indian traditions) in fact means by 'God' the 'True Self', the final, ultimate, innermost nature of conscious beings, or something like that. The issue of a True Self is of course also problematic for Buddhists, but as far as the Dalai Lama is concerned that is a matter of ontological dispute at a level far too rarified for ordinary people. If we take the 'True Self' as the subtlest level of the mind, what the Dalai Lama would accept and call the 'Clear Light', the fundamental level of consciousness, then it may be permissible for ecumenical reasons to call that the 'True Self'. I strongly suspect that Chopra's book is actually about one's own experiences, experiencing levels of one's mind, oneself, or (if you like) one's Self. Like the Dalai Lama, Chopra's concern is with happiness, bringing about happy feelings. Metaphysical subtleties – differences – can come later.

What has all this to do with God? The only God here is one's Self – oneself. Thus the 'God-theory' becomes a matter of the practicalities of description: which description is best suited to bring about the agreed goal of happiness.

17 W. M. Abbott (ed.), *The Documents of Vatican II* (London and Dublin: Geoffrey Chapman, 1966), p. 29.

18 Ibid., p. 66.

19 Ibid., pp. 70–1.

20 Holy See, *Catechism of the Catholic Church* (London: Geoffrey Chapman, 1994), p. 438.

21 E.g. Hebrew: *tam*, used of Job at Job 1:8, or *tamiym*.

22 R. E. Brown, J. A. Fitzmyer and R. E. Murphy (eds), *The New Jerome Biblical Commentary* (London: Geoffrey Chapman, 1989), p. 644.

23 Quoted in D. W. Bercot (ed.), *A Dictionary of Early Christian Beliefs* (Peabody, MA: Hendrickson, 1998), pp. 507–8.

24 St Thomas Aquinas, *Summa Theologiae: A Concise Translation*, edited by Timothy McDermott (London: Methuen, 1991), pp. 454–5.

25 Quoted in R. McBrien, *Catholicism* (London: Geoffrey Chapman, 1994), p. 216.

26 P. Stanford, *Cardinal Hume*, p. 196.

27 My wife Sharon has commented that the Christian doctrine

of the resurrection of the body and the life everlasting is 'the ultimate survival of the person'. I think she intends her comment a little disparagingly. Still, on the resurrection of the body and the survival of the person Sharon is undoubtedly right. Aquinas argues for the resurrection of the body precisely because the person we are is intimately bound up with our embodiment. Survival of the soul (whatever that is) would finally not be enough. I am inclined to think Aquinas is right here. If our lives are to be more than an insignificant flash in infinite time, if we have value as such, if this value entails – as it must – survival of death, then that survival must be of the persons we will have become. This must finally be understood in some sense in bodily terms. Christianity is the religion of the infinite value of the person. The person we are, or can become, is not accidental to us and is not unimportant. Each person is an individual creation of God and as such infinitely loved and valued by God. On this is based the whole of Christian morality, from the value of the family to the altruism and self-denial of the Saints. Because we are infinitely valuable to God, Jesus died to save each one of us. He did not die to save chains of reincarnations, or reincarnating Selves who (as the Hindu *Bhagavad Gītā* has it) put on new bodies like new garments. He died to save *us*. And we are the persons we are. Contrary to the myth of the Christian hatred of the physical and the body, Christianity is actually the religion of embodiment and the essential goodness of all physical creation.

28 Of course, people will object that historically Christians have by no means been paragons of moral behaviour. That is true, but it misses the point. We are here discussing ideas, not their application. The fact that someone cannot live up to his or her theory does not falsify the theory. The fact that others with a different ideology live better lives does not in itself make the other ideology true. The actual behaviour of Christians is irrelevant to my argument. Historically Christians have been all too aware of their failure to live up to their ideals. That is why they go on about sinfulness so much. Paradoxically, critics of Christianity tend to condemn Christians both for their awareness of sin and for their moral failings, their sinfulness!

29 Yesterday I heard on the news that a nineteen-year old boy had been given three months in a detention centre for microwaving his kitten. This crime seems to me unimaginably horrific, partly because kittens are so vulnerable. We can just imagine certain nineteen year-old boys nowadays doing that sort of thing. I seem to recall a science fiction comedy by Spielberg aimed at just this age level which has an alien 'gremlin' or something like that microwaved. The viewers, I gather, find it quite amusing.

30 Greek *psuche* at e.g. Luke 12:19, or Hebrews 10:39, in this usage an equivalent for the Hebrew *nephesh*, 'the life or the self, the centre of desire, emotions and loyalty' – *New Jerusalem Bible*, p. 1448.

31 Cf. Genesis 2:7, where God created man 'a living being'; here 'being' = Hebrew *nephesh*.

32 M. Henesy and R. Gallagher, *How to Survive Being Married to a Catholic* (Liguori, MI: Liguori Publications, 1997), p. 186.

33 Perhaps those who attack Christians who say that animals will not exist in heaven have a rather childish view of what heaven is supposed to be. Perhaps they think of it as a sunny field where everyone will wear white and we will want to play with Wensleydale (I wonder if her black fur would become white?) for all eternity. Such a heaven would, I fear, become hell long before eternity is out.

34 Gavin D'Costa has raised with me the issue of what happens, under these circumstances, to humans who lack the requisite capacities, such as those who are born with severe brain damage. I have no idea. Presumably for those who are so brain damaged at some time after birth the situation as regards following Christ would be similar to that of those who die at the same point. So for those brain damaged from the very beginning I would imagine the situation is a bit like those who are still-born. What happens to those who die in infancy (a still-birth is still an infant) is left in the hands of a wholly merciful God, who loves those infants so much more than any human can. The same must be the case, presumably, for those who through no fault of their own are unable to actualise their human capacities. What about the following hypothetical scenario?

After death, all humans so chosen through God's grace are able to grow to the stage where they attain the perfection that God intended for them. But necessary to this (although not sufficient, of course) is that they are human. It occurs through qualities intrinsic to their being human. Someone born brain damaged will still, in that state, be human, now with all the functioning faculties of a human. It was not their fault that they were born brain damaged. God intended that they should be human, with a human potential. Thus he or she can grow to perfection. An animal, however, will never have those faculties, at least *qua* animal. Thus Wensleydale still could not be saved. I don't know if it is anything like this. But for all I know, it could be. Anyway, there is no inconsistency in leaving it all in the hands of God, who is perfectly merciful and just.

35 D. H. Farmer, *Saint Hugh of Lincoln* (Lincoln: Honywood Press, 1992), p. 25.

36 It does not follow, incidentally, that a good which ceases is *ipso facto* bad. Hitler was a good, as created by God. But Hitler's ceasing would scarcely be bad.

37 We cannot complain to *God* – we could certainly complain of unjust social and political systems. But that is a different issue. And God might support us in that complaint.

38 I should add that Tārā is completely unconvinced by my arguments. She says that for all I know Wensleydale may well have all of the capacities that are necessary for heaven, and be acting on them. This looks to me like sentimentality. But if so, then perhaps Wensleydale *will* be saved. It would be totally presumptuous of me to claim to know for certain that she will not. Tārā also points out that some animals (such as some chimpanzees) have been shown to have characteristics of rationality and so on, at least as much as a two-year-old child. I am not so sure about the accuracy of the data and its interpretation, here. But putting to one side specific details of disagreement, her general point is a good one. The boundaries between humans and animals may be much less clear than Aristotle and perhaps Christian tradition would have us believe. Still, given what (it seems to me) heaven must be, at least inasmuch as it relates to souls, and the purpose and nature of Christ's salvific

activity, it is nevertheless difficult to imagine that animals *as animals* could attain heaven. But I am content to leave all this in the hands of God. I don't think these issues involve anything definitive of Christian adherence and affiliation. Since I hold on the basis of other arguments that God exists, and since I hold also that God is good, I am sure that a good God has done and will do what a good God does.

39 Isn't it unfair that in Christianity hell is permanent? After all, hell must be the result of finite wicked deeds. How can God condemn beings to hell time without limit on the basis of limited wickedness? Doesn't it make God unjust? The presuppositions here are not those of Aquinas. Hell is not as such a proportionate direct punishment for sins committed. Rather, if I understand Aquinas correctly, in (mortal) sinning we voluntarily turn away from God, rejecting His friendship. In so doing we turn away from an eternal (in the sense of timeless) Good. But in turning from the Good we turn towards the absence of Good. The absence of Good, absence of God, is hell. Thus in voluntarily turning from an eternal Good we voluntarily turn ourselves to an absence of Good, hell. And when death takes place our will is finally set. After death we are not in a situation where we can choose again for or against God. That is not the *post mortem* circumstances we shall find ourselves in. (How many opportunities do you want? And under what circumstances?) Thus we have finally turned away from an eternal Good. But no change can occur in the Good from which we have turned. And no change can occur in our will. Thus the hell of freely chosen absence of God must be for ever.

40 J. Redford, *Catholicism: Hard Questions* (London: Geoffrey Chapman, 1997), p. 43.

41 Tenzin Gyatso, *Universal Responsibility*, p. 11.

42 Paradoxically, perhaps, the tendency in Protestant theology is to emphasise both this self-reliance and direct experience, and at the same time salvation through faith alone rather than through any works that we sinners can perform. This Protestant emphasis on religion through individual experience may well have fed into the New Age concern with subjectivity, the priority of positive sensations

(sensations of pleasure, relaxation, calmness, harmony, self-empowerment, and so on) rather than, say, an objective God 'out there', or 'conventional (objective) morality'. It may again go some way towards explaining the growing popularity of a particular way of seeing, presenting and practising Buddhism in the contemporary world, especially in countries influenced by Protestant ideology.

43 Interestingly, John's Gospel (19:34–37) is the only one to mention the detail of the lance thrust in the side. This is a prominent feature of the Shroud image. John's Gospel is the latest of the Gospels, and it also connects the lance thrust with the fulfilment of a prophecy. *If* the Shroud were genuine, then, it would show a detail of the crucifixion preserved by John that, notwithstanding its relatively late date, is not in the Synoptic Gospels. John's Gospel itself claims to base this detail on an eyewitness account. This is quite credible, as it is only John's Gospel that mentions nails being used in Jesus' crucifixion (20:25), as well as the breaking of the legs of crucifixion victims (19:31–33). We know from archaeological sources that nails and, almost certainly, breaking the legs did occur in crucifixions. John's fuller and apparently trustworthy description suggests an interest in the details of Jesus' death that relies on an eyewitness account, rather than subsequent imaginary elaboration. If the Shroud were authentic it would also show in the lance thrust an event in fulfilment of a prophecy, not simply made up for early Christian polemical reasons. Thus not all the New Testament claims that something in the life of Jesus fulfilled an ancient prophecy would entail (as some modern scholars are inclined to think) that the event did not actually occur, but was constructed by the early Church for sectarian reasons.

44 S. Davis, D. Kendall and G. O'Collins (eds), *The Resurrection* (Oxford: Oxford University Press, 1997), p. 2.

45 Currently two million people a year are dying of Aids in Africa. Twelve million children have been made orphans by Aids, and most of those are now dead. At the recent Aids conference in Durban a Buddhist speaker declared that 'Aids is the destination of those who fail in the teaching of religion' (*The Tablet*, 22 July 2000, p. 981). It is not clear

to me whether this means that Aids occurs when religious teaching fails, or that each case of the occurrence of Aids is the result of someone failing to heed the teaching of religion. The first is debatable and probably unhelpful. The second must be false, at least as it applies to the particular person (say, a week-old baby) who is found to have Aids. Individual persons are here passed over in the interests of general religious principles or 'laws'. The *Tablet* columnist comments that 'If that is the sound we are making in the faith communities, it is no wonder it is heard against a background of deafening silence.' I have observed elsewhere (in Chapter 5 of *Altruism and Reality*) that, because of its metaphysical base, Buddhist ethics has (perhaps paradoxically) a tendency to move away from the uniqueness of each individual person and prefers to deal in abstract principles. 'Compassion for all sentient beings' can easily end up ignoring each *individual* sentient being. This has long worried me, but would require more extended treatment than is possible here.

46 Quoted in A. Greely, *The Catholic Imagination* (Berkeley and Los Angeles: University of California Press, 2000), p. 47.

ON THE RESURRECTION

1 Quoted in Mother Thekla, *Eternity Now: An Introduction to Orthodox Spirituality* (Norwich: Canterbury Press, 1997), p. 28.

2 See Davis, Kendall and O'Collins (eds), *The Resurrection*, ch. 2.

3 M. Staniforth (trans.), *Early Christian Writings: The Apostolic Fathers* (Harmondsworth: Penguin, 1968), p. 147.

4 Ibid., p. 119.

5 Ibid., p. 162.

6 Illustrated in I. Wilson, *The Blood and the Shroud: New Light on the Turin Shroud Mystery* (London: Orion, 1999), p. 57.

CATHOLICISM

1 Translated by Leo Sherley-Price (Harmondsworth: Penguin, revised edn., 1968), p. 127.
2 See E. Stourton, *Absolute Truth: The Catholic Church Today* (Harmondsworth: Penguin, 1999).
3 I should add that I include in 'Protestant' here the Anglican denomination, while aware that there are Anglicans who would claim not to be Protestant as such but themselves perfectly Catholic, albeit out of communion with the Bishop of Rome.
4 As is asserted in H. Montefiore, *Reaffirming the Church of England: Why It Is, What It Is, and How It Is* (London: SPCK Triangle, 1995), p. 5.
5 See E. Duffy, *The Stripping of the Altars: Traditional Religion in England 1400–1580* (New Haven: Yale University Press, 1992).
6 Perhaps, out of deference to the faith and sensitivities of their builders, some of those cathedrals and churches should now be given to the Roman Catholic Church!
7 J. Paxman, *The English: A Portrait of a People* (Harmondsworth: Penguin, 1999), p. 95.
8 True to his age he means by 'civilisation', of course, *Western* – in fact Graeco-Roman – civilisation.
9 I, for one, would not tolerate those who would destroy democracy and set up a dictatorship. The nascent Nazi party in Germany should have been destroyed in the 1920s. Modern neo-Nazi parties should be banned (if that would effectively bring about their demise). I do not see any of this as inconsistent. Its *apparent* inconsistency has always been the Achilles heel of liberalism. In terms of logic, the consistency of intolerance of intolerance can be treated using a strategy developed for apparent paradoxes concerning truth by the logician Alfred Tarski. Call 'first order statements concerning tolerance and intolerance' statements that refer to actual acts (including statements etc.) of tolerance and intolerance (such as racist slogans, or beating up a member of another religion). 'Second order statements concerning tolerance and intolerance' take as their referents first order statements (such as 'One should not utter racist slogans').

That is, they are metastatements. Logical inconsistency occurs only between statements of the same order. Thus we have a logical inconsistency if we at the same time and in the same way say that person X 'is a nigger bastard', and 'is not a nigger bastard' (first order inconsistency concerning intolerance) or that we should, and should not, tolerate racist abuse (second order inconsistency concerning tolerance). But the statement 'One should not tolerate intolerance' is a second order statement about first order statements. It is thus not in any way logically inconsistent or contradictory.

10 Staniforth, *Early Christian Writings*, pp. 77–8.
11 Ibid., p. 121.
12 Ibid., p. 119.
13 Ibid., p. 82; cf. Romans 1:3.
14 Ibid., p. 89.
15 Pope John Paul II, *Faith and Reason*, para. 84.
16 Ibid., para. 80.
17 Ibid., para. 82.
18 Stanford, *Cardinal Hume*, p. 203.
19 It should be clear here that I hold to the objectivity of aesthetic judgements, as well as those of ethics. It seems to me that is explicit in Neoplatonism, and implicit in the idea of God as Perfect Beauty.
20 Just as excellence in a range of things is to be discovered by what 'nine out of ten people said' – or what was 'voted the best pub in Shropshire'. But they might all be deranged, or have impaired taste-buds!
21 The need to explain it to the faithful is one reason why for hundreds of years it was thought better not to have the Bible in the vernacular. The proliferation of subjective interpretations (not to mention religious wars) when the Bible did become available to all and sundry might suggest the wisdom of these restrictions.
22 'I believe in order that I may understand.' See St Anselm's *Proslogion* (*Anselm of Canterbury: The Major Works*, Oxford University Press, Oxford World's Classics, 1998, p. 87). It is interesting to reflect that if one adopts (with certain Buddhist approaches) a holistic perspective, and sees everything as interconnected, then presumably it should

follow that in order to understand any one thing fully one would also have to understand everything else. If there is a God, it would seem that without knowing or at least believing in God one could not understand fully (or perhaps even properly) any other thing. At least, *if* there is a God, I could not even begin to understand a stone, or a cat, or the structure of matter fully without believing that there is a God. It would follow from this that it is not possible to separate out (and marginalise) the faith perspective from 'doing science' or whatever. There is a faith perspective that (if there is a God) is more true, or closer to truth, on each and every thing.

23 Augustine, *Confessions*, pp. 116–17.

24 Actually, as we have seen, we read in one of the Psalms that there is no place without God. But hell, I suppose, is where there is no God for those who are there. For a wonderful fictional account of how it might be that hell-dwellers voluntarily choose hell for themselves, see C. S. Lewis's *The Great Divorce*. Hell, without God, is an endlessly boring, rainy, grey, suburban city. There are even bishops there (Liberal, of course), with Theology Societies. Once a year hell dwellers are allowed to take a coach trip to heaven. They can stay if they want. No one makes them return to hell. But (in most cases) heaven somehow doesn't come up to their expectations. It doesn't have what they want. You know where you are in hell. They like hell. They choose it.

25 The issue of abortion is different. It seems to me that this is not a matter of sexual ethics. It is one of life and death, and therefore morally comes under 'killing'. For a traditional Catholic it is an issue of the sanctity of life. Buddhists too hold that in (almost) all cases abortion is completely wrong. My position has not changed on this since ceasing to be a Buddhist. As with all issues of morality, one can think of counter-examples where we might be forced to countenance abortion as the lesser of two evils. But that is not the point. It should be clear from the discussion above that a Catholic cannot approach the issue of abortion in terms of the woman's right to choose, or to do what she likes with her own body. This individualism is quite contrary to the traditional Catholic approach to ethical issues (but for

alternative – and, it seems to me, confused – views in modern North American Catholicism see M. Dillon, *Catholic Identity: Balancing Reasons, Faith, and Power*, Oxford: Oxford University Press, 1999). Rather, we should ask what life is for, and thus what the life of the foetus, the new human being, is for. This life is not a neutral thing. It exists for a purpose, a divine purpose. It is also innocent of any crime of unforgivable interference in the well-being of society (that might be taken as justifying the death penalty for, say, a mass-murderer). Thus it cannot be right to terminate the life of the foetus. This has nothing to do with any 'right to choose'. Moreover, on the basis of what I have argued earlier, there can be no rights without duties. If a woman has a right to choose, or a right to do what she likes with her own body, it can surely only be at the expense of a duty not to interfere in the divine purpose, or not to kill the innocent. A great deal of misunderstanding of the Catholic position on abortion, it seems to me, stems from failing to grasp the inherent *teleological* direction of Catholic ethical teaching.

26 Quoted by John Paul II in his encyclical *Veritatis Splendor*; text in J. Wilkins (ed.), *Understanding Veritatis Splendor: The Encyclical Letter of Pope John Paul II on the Church's Moral Teaching* (London: SPCK, 1994), p. 129.

27 Ibid., p. 136.

28 In *Veritatis Splendor*; ibid., p. 133.

29 Greely, *The Catholic Imagination*, p. 78.

30 G. K. Chesterton, *Autobiography* (London: Hutchinson, 1937), p. 329; italics original.

31 Guibert of Nogent, *A Monks' Confession: The Memoirs of Guibert of Nogent*, translated by Paul J. Archambault (University Park, PA: Pennsylvania State University Press, 1996), p. 4.

32 M. Bernall, *She Said Yes: The Unlikely Martyrdom of Cassie Bernall* (Farmington: The Plough Publishing House, 1999).

33 See M. Slouka, *War of the Worlds: Cyberspace and the High-tech Assault on Reality* (London: Abacus, 1996).

34 Bernall, *She Said Yes*, p. 100.

35 Ibid.

36 And perhaps a certain triumphalism on the part of Buddhists.
37 P. Williams, 'Altruism and rebirth', in *Altruism and Reality: Studies in the Philosophy of the Bodhicaryāvatāra* (Richmond: Curzon, 1998).
38 Williams, *Altruism and Reality*, ch. 5.

Index of Names

The Unexpected Way